EMBRACING THE SEASON OF YOUR SINGLENESS

THE BEAUTY AND PURPOSE

Grace Mamigo

Embracing the Season of Your Singleness

Author: Grace D. Mamigo

Copyright © 2024 by Grace D. Mamigo

ISBN: 978-621-419-530-5

Published by: Book of Life Publication

Printed in Philippines

For information about special discounts for bulk purchases, please contact 09994271188 or zaimamigo25@gmailcom.

Contents

Chapter 1 : Singleness Unlocked: Embracing Your Journey in Christ

Chapter 6 : Anchored in Trust: Navigating Doubt with God's Promises

Chapter 7 Strengthening Faith: Scriptures for the Journey to Your Kingdom Spouse

Chapter 8 Guarding Your Heart: Identifying Counterfeits and Embracing True Love

PREFACE

In a world that often glorifies romantic relationships and partnerships, the season of singleness can sometimes feel overlooked or undervalued. Yet, this time in your life is rich with opportunities for self-discovery, growth, and empowerment. "Embracing Your Season of Singleness" is an invitation to celebrate this unique chapter, to explore the depths of who you are, and to cultivate a fulfilling and meaningful life beyond societal expectations.

This book is for anyone navigating the complexities of being single whether by choice or circumstance. It aims to shift the narrative from one of loneliness or lack to one of abundance and possibility. Throughout these pages, you will find insights, reflections, and practical guidance that encourage you to embrace your individuality, pursue your passions, and build a strong foundation for your future.

As you embark on this journey of self-exploration, remember that this season is not a waiting room for love; it is a vibrant and essential part of your life story. Let us celebrate the freedom, self-awareness, and joy that come from truly embracing this time. Welcome to your season of singleness may it be a time of profound growth and discovery.

The Author

Chapter 1 : Singleness Unlocked: Embracing Your Journey in Christ

Understanding Singleness in a Christian Context

The Biblical Perspective on Singleness

The Biblical perspective on singleness offers a profound understanding of this life stage, emphasizing its unique value and potential. In scripture, singleness is often portrayed not as a deficiency but as a purposeful season for growth and service. Paul, in his letter to the Corinthians, in the book of 1 Corinthians 7: 7-8, highlights that unmarried individuals can focus on the interests of the Lord without the distractions that come with marriage. This underscores the idea that singleness provides a unique opportunity for deepening one's relationship with God, allowing for greater devotion and spiritual exploration.

Throughout the Bible, several figures exemplify the blessings of singleness. Jesus Himself lived a single life, showcasing how one can fullfill their purpose without the need for marital companionship. His ministry was marked by profound love, compassion, and dedication to others, illustrating that one can lead a rich, impactful life while being single. Likewise, the prophet Jeremiah (Jeremiah 16:2 Do not get married and have children in this place), and the Apostle Paul (1 Corinthians 7: 7-8) serve as reminders that God calls individuals to serve Him in various capacities, regardless of their marital status. Their stories encourage single Christians to embrace their current season, recognizing that it can be a time of significant contribution and personal growth.

Embracing singleness can lead to a deeper understanding of oneself and one's calling. It provides an opportunity for self-discovery, allowing individuals to explore their passions, develop skills, and engage in hobbies that might otherwise be sidelined. This period can also be pivotal for building healthy friendships and creating a supportive community. By investing in relationships with other singles, individuals can cultivate meaningful connections that enrich their lives and foster a sense of belonging, which is vital for mental health and well-being.

Furthermore, the Bible encourages believers to view their singleness as a chance to serve others and engage in community efforts. Volunteering and participating in church activities can be fulfilling ways to channel energy and resources into meaningful projects that benefit others. This service not only enriches the lives of those being helped but also cultivates a sense of purpose and fulfillment within the individual. By actively contributing to the community, singles can grow in their faith and expand their social networks, leading to new friendships and experiences.

Ultimately, the biblical perspective on singleness invites individuals to focus on their spiritual journey while embracing their current life stage. This season should be viewed as an opportunity for personal development, allowing for the exploration of interests, career ambitions, and financial independence. By investing in oneself and nurturing a close relationship with God, singles can prepare for the future—whether that includes marriage or a continued commitment to a single life devoted to service and spiritual growth.

The Purpose of Your Season of Singleness

Understanding the purpose of your season of singleness is essential for Christian single men and women seeking to embrace this unique phase of life. Singleness is often viewed through a lens of longing for companionship, but it can also be a time rich with opportunities for personal growth and self-discovery. This period allows individuals to delve deep into their identities, values, and aspirations, fostering a stronger sense of self that can enhance future relationships. By focusing on spiritual development and understanding one's worth in Christ, singles can lay a strong foundation for their future, whether it involves marriage or a fulfilling single life.

During this season, building healthy friendships can serve as a vital aspect of personal development. Engaging with a diverse group of friends allows for the exchange of ideas, experiences, and support. These friendships can provide the emotional and social nourishment necessary for well-being, enabling singles to cultivate a sense of belonging and community. Furthermore, investing time in these relationships can teach valuable lessons about communication, conflict resolution, and empathy, all of which are crucial in any future romantic partnership.

Exploring hobbies and passions is another fundamental purpose of singleness. This is an ideal time to pursue interests that ignite joy and creativity, whether that involves art, music, sports, or travel. By engaging in activities that resonate personally, individuals can discover their talents and preferences, which contributes to a fulfilling life. Moreover, pursuing passions not only enhances self-esteem but also creates opportunities for meeting like-minded individuals, potentially leading to meaningful connections. Embracing this time to explore one's interests can transform the perception of singleness from a waiting period into an exciting adventure.

Financial independence and budgeting are critical skills that often receive less attention during this period. Being single allows individuals to establish their financial footing without the complexities that come with shared finances. This time can be used to learn about budgeting, saving, and investing, which are essential for a secure future. By developing financial literacy and independence, singles can create a stable environment for themselves and prepare for any future partnership, ensuring that they enter relationships with a healthy financial mindset.

Finally, focusing on mental health and well-being during this season is paramount. Singleness can sometimes lead to feelings of loneliness or inadequacy, but it is essential to prioritize self- care practices and spiritual reflection. Engaging in activities that promote mental wellness, such as prayer and worship, meditation, exercise, or volunteering, fosters resilience and a positive outlook. By understanding oneself better and nurturing mental health, individuals can approach the future with confidence and clarity, recognizing that their worth is not defined by relationship status but by their identity in Christ, His love for them and their journey of self-discovery.

Common Misconceptions About Being Single

Common misconceptions about being single often cloud the perception of this life stage, particularly among Christian singles. One prevalent belief is that being single equates to being lonely. Many people assume that without a romantic partner, individuals must be missing out on deep emotional connections. However, this overlooks the rich tapestry of relationships that can flourish outside of romantic involvement. Friendships, family bonds, and spiritual connections can provide profound fulfillment. Emphasizing these relationships can help singles recognize that loneliness is a state of mind rather than a condition dictated by relationship status.

Another common misconception is that being single means one is incomplete or less valuable. This notion can be particularly damaging in Christian circles, where the emphasis on marriage can inadvertently suggest that fulfillment is found only in partnership. In reality, being single offers a unique opportunity for personal growth and self-discovery. It allows individuals to explore their identities, passions, and goals without the distractions or compromises that often accompany romantic relationships. Singles can embrace their whole selves and contribute meaningfully to their communities, reaffirming their worth and purpose beyond marital status.

Furthermore, there is a belief that being single is a time of stagnation, where individuals wait for their lives to begin until they find a partner. This perspective can lead to a passive approach to life, filled with unfulfilled potential. In truth, this period can be one of active engagement and exploration. Singles have the freedom to pursue hobbies, travel, and embark on adventures that enrich their lives. This proactive mindset fosters a spirit of adventure and personal development, encouraging singles to cultivate their interests and passions, ultimately leading to a more fulfilling life.

Additionally, many people assume that being single means an absence of intimacy and emotional depth. While romantic relationships often provide a specific type of intimacy, single individuals can cultivate emotional connections in various ways. Building healthy friendships and engaging in open, honest communication can create deep, meaningful relationships that satisfy the human need for connection. Volunteering and engaging with the community can also foster a sense of belonging and purpose, proving that intimacy isn't limited to romantic partnerships.

Finally, some may believe that being single is synonymous with being uninterested in dating or relationships. This misconception can create pressure for singles to conform to societal expectations of dating or to rush into relationships before they are ready. In reality, many singles approach their status with a mindset of self-care and intentionality. They prioritize personal development and spiritual growth, creating a strong foundation for future relationships. By focusing on their mental health, financial independence, and career ambitions, singles can navigate their journey with confidence, preparing themselves for healthy future partnerships when the time is right.

Embracing Your Season of Singleness Finding Joy in Your Current Situation

Finding joy in your current situation requires a shift in perspective, especially for Christian singles navigating their unique season. Embracing the idea that this time of singleness is not merely a waiting period but a valuable phase for personal growth can lead to profound transformation. This journey of self-discovery enables you to deepen your relationship with God, allowing Him to work within you as you explore your interests, passions, and purpose. Through prayer and reflection, you can uncover the beauty and potential that lie within this chapter of your life.

Building healthy friendships is another essential aspect of finding joy in your current situation. Surrounding yourself with supportive people who share your values can foster an environment of encouragement and growth. Engage in community activities, church groups, or hobby clubs where you can establish meaningful connections. These relationships not only provide companionship but also enrich your life by offering diverse perspectives and experiences. Investing in friendships during your singleness can lead to a deeper understanding of yourself and your place in the world, helping you to cultivate a sense of belonging and joy.

Exploring hobbies and passions is a vital avenue for personal fulfillment. This is the perfect time to delve into activities that you've always wanted to try or to rediscover old interests. Whether it's painting, hiking, or learning a new language, engaging in hobbies can bring a sense of accomplishment and joy. As you dedicate time to these pursuits, you may find new talents and interests that enrich your life and deepen your relationship with God. Allowing yourself to enjoy these activities not only enhances your well-being but also helps you grow into the person God designed you to be.

Travel and adventure can also play a significant role in finding joy during your season of singleness. Exploring new places and cultures can broaden your horizons and provide fresh experiences that invigorate your spirit. Whether it's a weekend getaway or a more extended journey, travel can offer a sense of freedom and excitement that rejuvenates your perspective on life. Embrace the opportunity to discover God's creation in different environments, and allow these adventures to strengthen your faith and appreciation for the life He has given you.

Lastly, focusing on financial independence and budgeting can contribute significantly to your sense of security and joy. By taking control of your finances, you empower yourself to make choices that align with your values and goals. This independence fosters a sense of responsibility and achievement, allowing you to pursue your passions without unnecessary stress. Additionally, consider volunteering and engaging with your community as a way to give back, which can further enhance your sense of purpose and fulfillment. In striving for personal growth and joy in your current situation, you'll find that this season of singleness can be a time of incredible blessing, growth, and connection with both God and others.

The Importance of Acceptance

Acceptance plays a crucial role in the journey of single Christians, serving as a foundational pillar for personal growth and spiritual development. Embracing your season of singleness is not merely about navigating loneliness or societal expectations; it is an opportunity to cultivate a deeper understanding of oneself and one's relationship with God. Acceptance enables individuals to recognize their current status not as a limitation but as a unique phase that can lead to significant self-discovery and emotional maturity. By accepting their singlehood, men and women can shift their focus from what is lacking to what can be developed, allowing them to engage fully in their lives.

As single Christians, cultivating healthy friendships becomes paramount. Acceptance fosters the ability to connect authentically with others, creating an environment where meaningful relationships can thrive. When individuals acknowledge their singleness without shame, they open themselves up to deeper connections with friends and family. These relationships can provide support, encouragement, and companionship, essential for mental health and well- being. By accepting where they are, singles can invest time and energy into building networks that uplift and inspire, rather than feeling isolated or pressured by societal norms.

Moreover, acceptance encourages exploration of hobbies and passions that may have been previously overlooked. Singleness provides an invaluable opportunity to invest in personal interests, whether that be travel, artistic pursuits, or volunteer work. By embracing their current season, individuals can explore new avenues that align with their values and interests, enriching their lives. This exploration not only enhances personal joy and fulfillment but also leads to greater self-awareness and confidence. When singles accept their status, they can prioritize experiences that contribute to their growth, making their journey more vibrant and purposeful.

Financial independence and career development also greatly benefit from acceptance. When single individuals embrace their current circumstances, they can focus on setting financial goals and pursuing career ambitions without the distractions or compromises that often come with romantic relationships. Acceptance allows them to take calculated risks, invest in their future, and build a stable foundation for themselves. By acknowledging their independence, singles can cultivate a sense of responsibility and empowerment, enabling them to achieve their aspirations while preparing for any future commitments.

Lastly, acceptance is integral to spiritual growth and self-reflection. By recognizing and embracing their season of singleness, individuals can deepen their relationship with God, focusing on prayer, meditation, and service to others. This period can be a time of profound spiritual awakening, where one learns to and fulfillment in God rather than in relationships. Volunteering and engaging with the community can also stem from this acceptance, allowing individuals to make meaningful contributions while finding purpose in their lives. Ultimately, acceptance transforms the narrative of singleness from one of lack to one of abundance, encouraging a life filled with growth, adventure, and an unwavering faith.

Learning to Be Content

Learning to be content is an essential aspect of embracing your season of singleness. For many Christian single men and women, the pressure to pursue romantic relationships can overshadow the importance of personal growth and self-discovery. Contentment does not mean complacency; rather, it involves finding joy and fulfillment in the present moment while cultivating a rich relationship with God. By learning to appreciate your current circumstances, you can foster an attitude of gratitude that enhances your overall well-being and allows for deeper connections with others.

One of the key elements of contentment is recognizing the value of building healthy friendships. During your single season, investing time in nurturing friendships can provide emotional support and enrich your life. These relationships often serve as a mirror, reflecting your strengths and areas for growth. Engaging with a diverse group of friends can also expose you to new hobbies and passions, allowing you to explore interests that may not have previously crossed your mind. This exploration not only expands your horizons but also contributes to a more fulfilling and adventurous life.

Travel and adventure offer unique opportunities for personal growth and self-discovery. As a single individual, you have the freedom to embark on spontaneous trips or plan elaborate adventures without the constraints that come with a romantic relationship. Traveling can challenge your comfort zone and expose you to different cultures, perspectives, and experiences that foster personal development. Each journey can deepen your understanding of yourself and your place in the world, helping to cultivate a sense of contentment and appreciation for the life you are living.

Financial independence and budgeting play a critical role in your ability to feel content in your singleness. By taking charge of your finances and establishing a solid budget, you can reduce stress and create opportunities for experiences that align with your values. This financial freedom allows you to invest in your passions, whether through travel, hobbies, or community engagement. When you are secure in your financial situation, you are better equipped to focus on personal growth, mental health, and well-being, all of which are foundational to a life of fulfillment.

Finally, embracing self-care practices, such as dating yourself, is vital for developing a sense of contentment. Taking the time to invest in yourself through activities that bring joy and relaxation can enhance your mental and spiritual well-being. Whether it's spending a weekend alone in nature, trying a new restaurant, or simply enjoying a quiet evening at home, these moments of self-reflection and care strengthen your relationship with yourself and with God. By becoming comfortable in your own company, you pave the way for healthy relationships in the future, rooted in mutual respect and understanding.

Personal Growth and Self-Discovery Identifying Personal Values and Beliefs

Identifying personal values and beliefs is a fundamental step in the journey of self-discovery, particularly for Christian singles seeking to embrace their season of singleness. Personal values are the principles and standards that guide our decisions, actions, and interactions with others. For many, these values are rooted in their faith, shaped by biblical teachings and the example set by Christ. Understanding what truly matters to you can empower you to navigate life's challenges with confidence, make informed choices that align with your beliefs, and build relationships that reflect your core values.

To begin identifying your personal values, it is essential to engage in self-reflection. Take time to consider the experiences that have shaped you—both positive and negative. Reflect on moments when you felt fulfilled or proud, as well as times when you felt disappointed or frustrated. What was at stake in those moments? What principles were being honored or violated? Journaling can be a powerful tool to help you articulate your thoughts and feelings, allowing you to uncover the values that resonate most deeply within you.

In addition to personal experiences, consider the teachings of Scripture. The Bible provides a wealth of wisdom regarding values such as love, integrity, humility, and service. As you read through passages, think about how these values align with your own beliefs and how they can guide your actions in daily life. You might find it helpful to create a list of values that inspire you, prioritizing them according to what feels most important. This exercise not only clarifies your identity but also serves as a foundation for making choices that lead to personal growth and fulfillment.

As you uncover your values, it's equally important to recognize how they influence your relationships, including friendships and potential romantic interests. Building healthy friendships requires a mutual understanding of values, and knowing your own can help you connect with others who share similar beliefs. When it comes to dating, having a clear understanding of your values allows you to establish boundaries and seek partnerships that reflect your commitment to your faith. This clarity can also serve as a protective measure against compromising situations that may arise during your journey.

Finally, embracing your values opens doors to exploring hobbies, passions, and opportunities for community engagement. When your actions align with your beliefs, you find a deeper sense of purpose and joy in your pursuits. Whether it's volunteering for a cause that resonates with your values, traveling to experience God's creation, or engaging in self-care practices that nurture your mental and spiritual well-being, the alignment of your values with your actions will enhance your overall quality of life. As you continue to navigate your singleness, remember that identifying and living out your values is a lifelong journey, one that will enrich your relationships and your relationship with God.

Setting Goals for Yourself

Setting goals for yourself is a vital step in embracing your season of singleness and cultivating a fulfilling life. In this unique phase, you have the opportunity to focus on personal growth and self-discovery without the distractions that often come with romantic relationships. Establishing clear, attainable goals will not only give you direction but also help you understand your passions, strengths, and areas for improvement. Whether it's exploring new hobbies, enhancing your career, or developing spiritual practices, goal-setting can shape your journey in Christ and lead to a more enriched life.

When setting goals, it is essential to consider various aspects of your life, including your spiritual health, mental well-being, and personal interests. Start by reflecting on what matters most to you. Are there areas in your spiritual life that you want to deepen, such as prayer, study, or community service? Perhaps you feel called to explore new hobbies or travel to places that inspire you. By identifying these key areas, you can create specific goals that align with your values and aspirations, making your journey more meaningful and fulfilling.

In addition to personal interests, building healthy friendships is crucial during this season. As you set goals, think about how you can cultivate deeper connections with those around you. This might involve scheduling regular meet-ups with friends, joining a community group, or volunteering together. Investing in these relationships will not only enhance your social life but also provide you with a support system that encourages your personal and spiritual growth. Remember, as you work towards your goals, the people you surround yourself with can significantly impact your journey.

Financial independence and budgeting are also important goals to consider. Being single often means managing your finances independently, which can be both empowering and challenging. Setting financial goals, such as creating a budget, saving for travel adventures, or investing in personal development courses, will help you build a solid foundation for your future. This financial stability allows you the freedom to explore opportunities without the burden of financial stress, enabling you to focus on personal growth and self-care practices that enrich your life.

Lastly, don't overlook the importance of self-reflection and mental health in your goal-setting process. Regularly assess your mental well-being and consider incorporating practices such as journaling, meditation, or counseling into your routine. These practices not only promote self- care but also encourage you to align your goals with your inner desires and Christ's purpose for your life. By taking the time to set thoughtful, well-rounded goals, you can navigate your season of singleness with confidence and joy, ultimately unlocking the potential that lies within you.

The Role of Reflection in Personal Growth

Reflection serves as a powerful tool for personal growth, especially during the unique season of singleness. For Christian single men and women, taking time to reflect can foster a deeper understanding of oneself and the purpose God has ordained for their lives. This process encourages individuals to pause amidst the busyness of life and consider their experiences, values, and aspirations. By engaging in regular reflection, one can identify patterns in behavior, clarify thoughts and feelings, and develop a clearer vision of personal and spiritual goals.

Incorporating reflection into daily life allows individuals to explore their faith and how it intertwines with their journey of self-discovery. This practice can involve journaling, prayer, or meditative thought, providing a space to consider how one's relationship with God influences personal growth. By assessing moments of joy, struggle, and learning, individuals can recognize the hand of God in their lives, leading to increased faith and reliance on His guidance. Embracing this connection nurtures, a profound sense of purpose and direction during a season that can often feel uncertain.

Moreover, reflection plays a vital role in building healthy friendships. As single individuals engage in self-reflection, they become more aware of their values and boundaries, which is essential for establishing meaningful connections. Understanding one's own needs and desires enables better communication and fosters mutual respect in relationships. This awareness can also help individuals discern which friendships align with their spiritual journey, allowing them to surround themselves with uplifting influences that encourage growth rather than hinder it.

Exploring hobbies and passions is another area where reflection can ignite personal development. Taking the time to consider what activities bring joy and fulfillment can lead to discovering new interests that enrich one's life. Whether it's traveling, engaging in community service, or pursuing career ambitions, reflecting on past experiences can provide insights into what truly resonates with the heart. This newfound understanding can motivate individuals to step outside their comfort zones, try new things, and ultimately, grow in confidence and creativity.

Finally, reflection is crucial for maintaining mental health and well-being during singleness. Individuals often face societal pressures and expectations regarding relationships, which can lead to feelings of isolation or inadequacy. By reflecting on their unique journeys and recognizing the value of their experiences, they can cultivate a positive self-image and practice self-care. This process encourages individuals to appreciate their worth and the contribution they make to the world, reinforcing the idea that their season of singleness is not a limitation but a time for growth, exploration, and preparation for future relationships, including a potential romantic partner.

Building Healthy Friendships, The Importance of Community

The importance of community in the lives of Christian single men and women cannot be overstated. It serves as a vital support system that nurtures growth, fosters connections, and provides a foundation for self-discovery. For those navigating the often-complex journey of singleness, engaging with a community of like-minded individuals can enhance personal development and encourage spiritual growth. In a world where isolation can be prevalent, community acts as a lifeline, reminding individuals that they are not alone in their experiences or struggles.

Building healthy friendships within a community allows singles to share their joys and challenges, creating a space for authentic relationships. These friendships can offer encouragement during difficult times and celebrate victories, no matter how small. Engaging in meaningful conversations with others who are on a similar journey can inspire self-reflection and personal growth. Through shared experiences and mutual support, individuals can gain new perspectives and insights, which are essential for navigating the complexities of life and faith.

Exploring hobbies and passions is another aspect enriched by community involvement. When singles connect with others who share similar interests, they can discover new activities and experiences that enhance their lives. Whether it's joining a book club, participating in volunteer work, or exploring outdoor adventures, these shared pursuits can lead to lasting friendships and unforgettable memories. The encouragement and motivation found within a community can push individuals to step outside their comfort zones, fostering a spirit of adventure and curiosity.

Community engagement also plays a crucial role in mental health and well-being. The act of participating in group activities, whether through church events, social gatherings, or service projects, can combat feelings of loneliness and isolation. Positive social interactions are essential for emotional health, offering a sense of belonging and purpose. Additionally, being part of a community allows singles to witness the diversity of experiences and struggles, which can normalize their feelings and promote resilience in facing personal challenges.

Finally, the spiritual dimension of community cannot be overlooked. Gathering with fellow believers for worship, prayer, and Bible study strengthens faith and deepens understanding of God's word. It provides a platform for singles to explore their spirituality in a supportive environment, encouraging them to seek God's will for their lives. Through shared faith journeys, individuals can discover their unique gifts and callings, empowering them to serve others and contribute positively to their communities. Embracing the importance of community ultimately enriches the journey of singleness, transforming it into an opportunity for growth, connection, and deeper faith.

Nurturing Meaningful Connections

Nurturing meaningful connections is an essential aspect of embracing your season of singleness, allowing you to cultivate relationships that enrich your life and deepen your faith. As Christian singles, it can be easy to feel isolated or disconnected during this period, but it is crucial to shift your focus from searching for romantic partnerships to fostering friendships and engaging with your community. Building a support network of like-minded individuals can create a sense of belonging and provide opportunities for personal growth and self-discovery.

One of the most effective ways to nurture connections is through intentional outreach. Consider joining small groups at your church, participating in community events, or engaging in volunteer work. These experiences not only allow you to meet new people but also encourage you to explore your passions and interests alongside others who share your values. By actively seeking out opportunities to connect, you create a space for authentic relationships to flourish, paving the way for deeper conversations about faith, purpose, and life goals.

In addition to community involvement, investing time in your hobbies can lead to meaningful interactions. Whether you enjoy painting, hiking, or cooking, sharing these interests with others can spark connections that go beyond surface-level interactions. Look for local classes or groups that align with your passions, as they provide a natural environment for building friendships. Engaging in activities you love while meeting new people not only enhances your happiness but also fosters a sense of camaraderie that can contribute to your mental health and overall well-being.

Travel and adventure also play a significant role in forming lasting connections. As a single individual, you have the freedom to explore new places and experiences without the constraints of a partner's schedule or preferences. Organize group trips with fellow singles from your church or community, or join travel clubs that focus on shared interests. These adventures not only create unforgettable memories but also give you the chance to meet diverse individuals, broadening your perspective and enriching your spiritual journey.

Lastly, remember that nurturing meaningful connections begins with self-care and self-reflection. Taking the time to understand who you are and what you value will enable you to engage more deeply with others. Practice self-care routines that promote mental health and well-being, and reflect on your experiences and relationships regularly. As you cultivate a strong sense of self, you will find it easier to establish and maintain connections that are fulfilling and aligned with your faith. Embracing this season of singleness with an open heart and a commitment to meaningful relationships can lead to transformative experiences that enrich your life in unexpected ways.

Setting Boundaries in Friendships

Setting boundaries in friendships is essential for maintaining healthy relationships, particularly during the season of singleness. As Christian singles, it is vital to recognize that friendships can significantly impact our personal growth and self-discovery. Establishing clear boundaries allows you to foster connections that are both meaningful and supportive while also protecting your emotional well-being. Boundaries help you communicate your needs and expectations, ensuring that your friendships nurture your spiritual and personal journey.

One key aspect of setting boundaries is understanding your own limits. Reflecting on your priorities and values can help you identify what you are comfortable with in friendships. For instance, if you find that certain social activities drain your energy or distract you from your personal goals, it is essential to communicate this to your friends. By articulating your needs, you not only safeguard your mental health but also encourage your friends to respect your individuality. This self-awareness fosters deeper connections, as it allows others to understand your perspective and engage with you more authentically.

Additionally, establishing boundaries can enhance your ability to explore hobbies and passions. When you create space for your interests, you allow yourself the freedom to grow and develop outside of your friendships. Engaging in activities that resonate with your spirit not only enriches your life but also helps you attract friends who share similar passions. By setting limits on how much time and energy you invest in friendships, you can prioritize personal growth and adventure, enabling you to lead a more fulfilling life.

Financial independence and budgeting also play a role in setting boundaries in friendships. With the pressure to participate in social outings or group activities, it's easy to overextend yourself financially. Establishing a budget and communicating your financial limits to your friends can help prevent feelings of guilt or obligation. This approach not only protects your financial well-being but also encourages more meaningful interactions. Friends who understand your financial boundaries are likely to respect them, leading to healthier, more supportive relationships.

Ultimately, setting boundaries in friendships is an exercise in self-care and spiritual growth. It empowers you to cultivate connections that align with your values and aspirations. By making intentional choices about the friendships you nurture, you create a community that uplifts you and supports your journey in Christ. Embracing your season of singleness means taking the time to reflect on what you truly want in your friendships, ensuring that they contribute positively to your life and spiritual walk.

Exploring Hobbies and Passions Discovering New Interests

Discovering new interests is a transformative aspect of embracing your season of singleness. This period in your life offers a unique opportunity to explore and cultivate passions that reflect your true self. By engaging in activities that resonate with your values and interests, you not only enrich your life but also develop a deeper understanding of your identity in Christ. Whether it's picking up a musical instrument, joining a book club, or learning a new language, each new interest can serve as a pathway to personal growth and self-discovery, helping you to feel more fulfilled and connected to your purpose.

Exploring various hobbies and passions is not just about filling free time; it's a vital component of building a well-rounded life. As Christian singles, you can use this time to dive into activities that inspire creativity and joy. Consider volunteering at local charities, which not only allows you to give back to your community but also introduces you to like-minded individuals who share your values. Engaging in these pursuits can lead to lasting friendships that enrich your life and provide a support system during your journey.

Travel and adventure also play a significant role in discovering new interests. Whether it's a weekend road trip or a mission trip abroad, stepping outside your comfort zone can open your eyes to new experiences and perspectives. Traveling allows you to meet diverse people and immerse yourself in different cultures, which can inspire you to try new activities and broaden your horizons. Each adventure can become a chapter in your story, equipping you with newfound skills and memories that contribute to your overall growth as a person.

Financial independence is crucial when it comes to exploring your interests. Learning to budget and manage your finances not only empowers you to invest in activities you love but also fosters a sense of responsibility and maturity. By creating a financial plan that accommodates your passions whether it's taking classes, traveling, or purchasing supplies for a new hobby you can freely pursue what excites you without the burden of financial stress. This balance between financial wisdom and personal exploration is essential for holistic growth during your season of singleness.

Finally, as you embark on this journey of discovering new interests, prioritize your mental health and well-being. Engaging in self-care practices, such as mindfulness, journaling, or prayer, can enhance your self-reflection and foster a deeper connection with God. This introspection allows you to identify the interests that truly resonate with you and align with your spiritual journey. By nurturing your mental and emotional health, you can approach new experiences with an open heart, ready to embrace all that God has instore for you during this season of life.

The Benefits of Pursuing Hobbies

Engaging in hobbies offers numerous benefits, especially for Christian singles seeking personal growth and self-discovery during their season of singleness. Hobbies provide a platform for individuals to explore their interests, talents, and passions, fostering a deeper understanding of themselves. This self-exploration is crucial as it allows individuals to align their pursuits with their values and spiritual beliefs, ultimately leading to a more fulfilling life. By dedicating time to activities that ignite their passion, single men and women can cultivate a sense of purpose and joy, which is essential for mental well-being.

Moreover, pursuing hobbies can enhance social connections and build healthy friendships. Engaging in group activities or classes allows singles to meet like-minded individuals who share similar interests. This not only expands their social circles but also creates opportunities for meaningful relationships. Building friendships through shared hobbies can lead to strong support systems, fostering an environment of encouragement and growth. In a world where loneliness can often feel overwhelming, these connections are invaluable, as they provide a sense of belonging and community.

Additionally, hobbies can serve as a powerful tool for personal development. Many hobbies require commitment, discipline, and time management, skills that are beneficial in various aspects of life, including career development. By setting goals and striving to improve in their chosen pursuits, individuals cultivate resilience and a growth mindset. This proactive approach to personal development not only enhances their skill set but also boosts self-esteem and confidence. As they achieve milestones in their hobbies, they become more equipped to tackle challenges in other areas of their lives, including their professional ambitions.

Hobbies also offer a unique avenue for self-care and mental health improvement. Engaging in enjoyable activities can be a form of relaxation and stress relief, allowing individuals to unwind and recharge. This is particularly important for singles who may navigate the complexities of life without a partner. By prioritizing hobbies, they create intentional time for self-reflection and rejuvenation, which contributes to overall mental well-being. Moreover, many hobbies, such as art, music, or writing, provide an expressive outlet for emotions, enabling individuals to process their feelings in a healthy way.

Finally, pursuing hobbies can enrich one's spiritual journey. Activities that resonate with an individual's faith can deepen their relationship with Christ and encourage spiritual growth. Whether it's volunteering, participating in a church choir, or engaging in nature through outdoor adventures, these pursuits can lead to a greater appreciation for God's creation and purpose. By integrating hobbies into their lives, Christian singles can experience a more holistic approach to their season of singleness, allowing them to thrive emotionally, socially, and spiritually as they cultivate their identities in Christ.

Balancing Hobbies with Other Responsibilities

Balancing hobbies with other responsibilities can be a challenging yet rewarding endeavor for Christian singles. In this season of life, it is essential to recognize that hobbies serve not only as a source of joy and fulfillment but also as a means of personal growth and self-discovery. Engaging in activities that resonate with your passions can help you develop new skills, foster creativity, and provide a sense of accomplishment. However, it is equally important to navigate these interests alongside the various responsibilities that come with work, relationships, and spiritual commitments. Finding this balance is key to leading a well-rounded life that honors both your aspirations and obligations.

To effectively manage your time, consider setting clear priorities. Start by identifying your responsibilities in different areas of your life, including your job, personal development, and social commitments. Once you have a comprehensive view of your obligations, allocate specific time slots for your hobbies. This could mean scheduling a weekly art class, a monthly hiking trip, or even dedicating a few hours each weekend to volunteer work. By treating your hobbies with the same importance as your other responsibilities, you create a structured environment that encourages growth and fulfillment without feeling overwhelmed.

Another important aspect of balancing hobbies with responsibilities is learning to say no. As singles, there may be a tendency to overcommit, whether it's to social engagements or additional work projects. While it's noble to help friends or colleagues, it's crucial to assess whether these commitments align with your passions and personal goals. Embracing the idea of selective engagement allows you to reserve time for the activities that truly inspire you. This not only enhances your hobbies but also ensures that your other responsibilities receive the attention they deserve without stretching yourself too thin.

Furthermore, incorporating your hobbies into your social life can enhance both your personal growth and your relationships. Invite friends to join you in activities you enjoy, whether that's a cooking class, a book club, or a weekend hike. This approach allows you to build healthy friendships while pursuing your passions. Sharing these experiences can deepen connections with others who share similar interests, fostering a community that supports your journey in Christ. Engaging in hobbies collectively also provides opportunities for accountability, encouraging you to remain committed to your personal growth while strengthening your social network.

Lastly, self-reflection plays a crucial role in maintaining this balance. Regularly assess how your hobbies are impacting your overall well-being and spiritual journey. Are they enriching your life and helping you grow in your faith? Or are they becoming distractions that hinder your responsibilities? Taking the time to evaluate your commitments ensures that your hobbies align with your values and purpose, allowing you to embrace your season of singleness fully. In this way, balancing hobbies with other responsibilities becomes not just a task but a transformative experience that enhances your journey in Christ.

Travel and Adventure for Singles the Value of Solo Travel

The value of solo travel is a profound aspect of embracing one's season of singleness, particularly for Christian single men and women. Traveling alone provides an opportunity for self-discovery and personal growth that is often difficult to achieve in the company of others. As you journey to new destinations, you will find not only diverse landscapes and cultures but also a clearer understanding of your own desires, strengths, and spiritual journey. This experience fosters a deeper connection with God as you take the time to reflect on your life, faith, and purpose, allowing for a unique opportunity to hear His voice amid the adventures.

Embarking on solo travel can significantly enhance your mental health and well-being. Stepping outside of your comfort zone and navigating unfamiliar environments can build resilience and boost self-esteem. As you manage travel logistics, interact with locals, and engage with new experiences, you cultivate essential life skills that promote independence. These moments of solitude also provide a chance for introspection, allowing you to process your thoughts and feelings. Engaging with nature and spending time in prayer or meditation can further deepen your relationship with God, leading to a more profound understanding of His plan for your life.

Traveling alone also opens the door to building healthy friendships and connections. While it may seem counterintuitive to travel solo, the experience often encourages interactions with fellow travelers and locals, fostering organic relationships that may not arise in a group setting. These connections can be meaningful and enriching, offering different perspectives and insights into life and faith. Additionally, solo travel can help you find your own interests and hobbies, leading to a renewed sense of passion and enthusiasm for life. Engaging with new cultures and activities can also guide you toward discovering new hobbies that align with your values and aspirations.

Financial independence and budgeting become crucial aspects of solo travel, teaching valuable lessons in resource management. As you plan your journey, you learn to prioritize spending and make informed decisions about accommodations, food, and activities. This experience encourages a sense of responsibility and accountability, which translates into other areas of life, including career development and ambition. The skills gained while traveling alone can enhance your professional capabilities, making you more adaptable and resourceful in the workplace.

Lastly, solo travel is a powerful form of self-care that emphasizes the importance of dating yourself. By investing time and resources into your own experiences, you affirm your worth and cultivate a sense of fulfillment that does not depend on a partner. This journey is a reminder that your identity is rooted in Christ, not in your relationship status. As you explore new places and engage in self-reflection, you deepen your understanding of what it means to love yourself as God loves you. Embracing solo travel as part of your singleness journey allows you to grow in faith, resilience, and joy, preparing you for the vibrant life God has in store for you.

Planning Adventures on a Budget

Planning adventures on a budget can be an enriching experience, especially for Christian singles looking to embrace their season of singleness. By being intentional about how you allocate your resources, you can create meaningful experiences that foster personal growth and self-discovery. Start by assessing what types of adventures excite you. Whether it's exploring nature, attending local events, or participating in community service, identifying your passions will help you prioritize activities that align with your values and interests.

One effective way to plan budget-friendly adventures is to explore local resources. Many communities offer free or low-cost events, such as concerts in the park, art walks, or church gatherings. Websites and social media platforms can be excellent tools for discovering these opportunities. Additionally, consider joining local meet-up groups centered around your hobbies or interests. This not only saves money but also helps you build healthy friendships with like-minded individuals, enriching your social circle while enjoying activities that you love.

Another key aspect of planning adventures is to utilize your existing skills and resources creatively. For example, if you enjoy cooking, host a potluck dinner with friends where everyone brings a dish. This allows for a fun social gathering without the expense of dining out. Outdoor activities such as hiking, biking, or picnicking in a park are also cost-effective ways to connect with others while enjoying God's creation. By thinking outside the box, you can find fulfillment in experiences that require little financial investment but yield significant joy and personal connection.

Traveling on a budget doesn't have to be a daunting task either. Consider planning a road trip to nearby destinations instead of more expensive flights. Look for deals on accommodations through platforms that cater to budget travelers or consider staying with friends or family. You can also volunteer for organizations that provide housing in exchange for your service. This not only saves money but also allows you to contribute positively to your community while experiencing new environments and meeting new people.

Ultimately, the key to successful budget adventures lies in prioritizing experiences over expenses. As you navigate your journey in Christ, remember that adventures do not have to be extravagant to be meaningful. They can be simple moments that lead to spiritual reflection and personal growth. By embracing this season of singleness with an adventurous spirit, you will uncover opportunities for self-care, mental well-being, and deeper connections with others, all while remaining financially responsible.

Building Confidence Through Exploration

Building confidence through exploration is a transformative journey that can profoundly impact your life as a single Christian. Embracing this season of singleness offers a unique opportunity to delve into personal growth and self-discovery. By stepping outside your comfort zone, you can explore new hobbies and passions that not only enrich your life but also help you uncover hidden talents and interests. Engaging in activities that excite you fosters a sense of accomplishment and boosts self-esteem, allowing you to see yourself as a capable individual created in God's image.

Travel and adventure are powerful tools for building confidence. When you embark on solo trips or group excursions, you confront new environments and challenges that push your boundaries. Each experience, whether it's navigating a foreign city or trying a new activity, teaches resilience and adaptability. As you conquer fears and embrace the unknown, you cultivate a deeper sense of self-assurance. This newfound confidence extends beyond travel; it seeps into various aspects of your life, influencing your relationships and career aspirations.

Financial independence and budgeting are also crucial elements of confidence-building. Understanding how to manage your finances empowers you to make informed decisions, whether it's planning a trip, investing in personal development, or simply enjoying a night out with friends. Mastering your financial situation leads to a sense of security and freedom, allowing you to focus on pursuing your passions and building healthy friendships without the stress of financial constraints. This independence fosters a strong sense of self-worth, reminding you that you are capable of creating a fulfilling life.

Taking care of your mental health and well-being is essential in this exploration phase. Engaging in self-reflection and spirituality allows you to connect with God on a deeper level, providing guidance and clarity as you navigate your journey. Incorporating practices such as journaling, prayer, or meditation can help you process your thoughts and emotions, leading to greater self-awareness. As you nurture your mental health, you equip yourself with the tools necessary to face challenges and embrace opportunities with confidence.

Lastly, volunteering and community engagement can serve as powerful avenues for building confidence. By giving back to others, you not only contribute to your community but also discover your strengths and passions. Whether you mentor a young person or participate in local outreach programs, these experiences enrich your life and deepen your understanding of your purpose. The connections you build through service can lead to lasting friendships and networks, reinforcing the idea that you are not alone in your journey. As you explore and engage with the world around you, you cultivate a confident and fulfilling life rooted in your identity as a beloved child of God.

Financial Independence and Budgeting

Understanding Financial Goals

Understanding financial goals is an essential aspect of personal growth and self-discovery, particularly for Christian singles who are navigating their unique journeys. Financial goals provide clarity and direction, helping individuals prioritize their resources in a way that aligns with their values and aspirations. Whether it's saving for a future home, investing in education, or building an emergency fund, establishing financial goals allows singles to take purposeful steps towards achieving financial independence. This process not only contributes to financial stability but also fosters a sense of accomplishment and confidence in one's ability to manage resources effectively.

For many Christian singles, the pursuit of financial goals can also be viewed through the lens of stewardship. The Bible emphasizes the importance of being responsible with the resources God has entrusted to us. By setting financial goals, singles can honor this principle by actively managing their finances and making informed decisions that reflect their faith. Whether it involves budgeting, saving, or giving, understanding the biblical context of financial stewardship can inspire individuals to approach their financial planning with a sense of purpose and responsibility.

In addition to fostering a sense of responsibility, understanding financial goals can enhance the journey of self-discovery. As individuals identify what they want to achieve financially, they may also uncover deeper insights about their values, priorities, and dreams. This reflection allows singles to align their financial aspirations with their personal and spiritual goals, creating a holistic approach to their lives. By exploring how their finances intersect with their faith and personal growth, individuals can cultivate a more meaningful and fulfilling experience during their season of singleness.

Moreover, financial independence is a vital component of building healthy friendships and exploring hobbies and passions. When singles develop a clear understanding of their financial goals, they can make more informed choices about their social engagements and leisure activities. This financial clarity enables them to engage in activities that enrich their lives, such as travel and adventure, without the burden of financial stress. By prioritizing their financial health, singles can create opportunities for enjoyable experiences that also foster growth and connection with others.

Lastly, the journey towards achieving financial goals is often accompanied by challenges that can impact mental health and well-being. Understanding and setting realistic financial goals can alleviate anxiety and uncertainty about the future. By creating a budget and tracking progress, individuals can gain a greater sense of control over their financial situations. This proactive approach not only promotes financial literacy but also encourages self-care practices that contribute to overall well-being. Ultimately, embracing financial goals as part of a broader journey of self-discovery empowers Christian singles to navigate their paths with confidence, purpose, and resilience.

Creating a Personal Budget

Creating a personal budget is an essential step for Christian singles who wish to embrace their season of singleness while also fostering personal growth and self-discovery. A budget not only helps in managing finances but also allows individuals to allocate resources towards experiences that enrich their lives, such as travel, hobbies, and community engagement. By understanding where your money goes, you can prioritize spending that aligns with your values and goals, leading to a more fulfilling and balanced life.

Begin by assessing your current financial situation. This involves gathering information about your income sources, such as salaries, freelance work, or any other revenue streams. Next, track your monthly expenses, categorizing them into fixed costs like rent, utilities, and insurance, and variable costs such as groceries, entertainment, and travel. This comprehensive overview will help you identify areas where you may be overspending or where you can cut back. Remember, this process is not just about restriction but about making intentional choices that reflect your priorities as a single person seeking to thrive.

Once you have a clear picture of your finances, set specific financial goals. These could include building an emergency fund, saving for a memorable trip, or investing in personal development opportunities like workshops or courses. Aligning your budget with your spiritual and personal aspirations can motivate you to stick to your plan. As you set these goals, consider incorporating elements of self-care and well-being, allowing you to allocate funds for activities that nurture your mental health, such as therapy or mindfulness retreats.

As you create your budget, it's crucial to remain flexible and adaptable. Life as a single person can be unpredictable, and your financial needs may change over time. Regularly review and adjust your budget to reflect new circumstances or priorities. This practice not only enhances financial literacy but also promotes resilience and resourcefulness, qualities that are beneficial in all areas of life, including relationships and career development. Moreover, being in control of your finances can lead to increased confidence and clarity in other aspects of your journey.

Lastly, consider sharing your budgeting journey with trusted friends or community members who can provide support and accountability. Building healthy friendships often includes sharing financial experiences and learning from one another. Engaging in discussions about budgeting can also lead to collaborative adventures, such as group travel or volunteer projects, which enrich your life and strengthen bonds with others. Embracing this season of singleness with a well-crafted personal budget can transform not just your financial health but also your overall well-being, allowing you to experience life to the fullest while deepening your journey in Christ.

Saving for the Future

Saving for the future is a crucial aspect of personal growth and self-discovery, especially for Christian singles navigating this unique season of life. Embracing your singleness offers a valuable opportunity to lay a strong financial foundation that can support your dreams and aspirations. By focusing on financial independence and budgeting, you can create a sense of security and freedom that allows you to explore your passions, travel, and even invest in your spiritual journey. This proactive approach not only enhances your well-being but also prepares you for future relationships, should they arise.

Setting financial goals is the first step in this journey. As a single individual, you have the flexibility to find your priorities and allocate resources according to your values and aspirations. Start by assessing your current financial situation, including income, expenses, and savings. Establish short-term and long-term financial goals that resonate with your life vision, whether that includes saving for a dream trip, investing in education, or building an emergency fund. This process encourages self-reflection, helping you to understand what truly matters in your life and how your financial decisions can align with your spiritual values.

Budgeting is not merely about limiting spending; it's a tool for empowerment. A well-structured budget allows you to track your spending habits and identify areas where you can save. This is an excellent opportunity to explore your hobbies and passions. Consider setting aside a portion of your budget specifically for activities that bring you joy or contribute to your personal development. Engaging in hobbies can enhance your mental health and well-being, providing a balanced approach to life that enriches your spiritual journey as well.

Investing in your future also means considering the importance of community engagement and volunteering. Allocating time and resources to help others not only cultivates a sense of purpose but can also lead to unexpected opportunities for personal growth and connection. As you build healthy friendships and engage with your community, you may discover new passions and interests that enrich your life further. This engagement can also provide valuable lessons in financial stewardship and the joy of giving, which are essential aspects of living a fulfilling Christian life.

Finally, remember that saving for the future is not solely about financial wealth; it's about cultivating a mindset of abundance and gratitude. As you save and plan, take the time to reflect on the blessings in your life and the ways God is leading you. This practice of self-reflection can foster a deeper relationship with Christ, helping you to see your journey of singleness as a gift rather than a waiting room. Embrace this season fully, knowing that your efforts in saving, budgeting, and personal development today will bear fruit in the future, both in your life and in the lives of those around you.

Mental Health and Well-Being Recognizing the Importance of Mental Health

Recognizing the importance of mental health is crucial for Christian singles as they navigate their journey of self-discovery and personal growth. Mental health influences every aspect of life, including relationships, career ambitions, and personal fulfillment. For those embracing their season of singleness, understanding and prioritizing mental well-being can lead to a deeper connection with oneself and a more meaningful relationship with God. It allows individuals to engage fully with their hobbies, passions, and friendships, ultimately enriching their experience during this unique phase of life.

Mental health issues can affect everyone, regardless of their spiritual beliefs or life circumstances. For Christian singles, acknowledging mental health struggles does not signify a lack of faith but rather an understanding of the human experience. The Bible encourages believers to care for their bodies and minds, as seen in verses that speak to the importance of peace and rest. By recognizing and addressing mental health, individuals are better equipped to serve others, engage with their communities, and volunteer effectively, all of which can bring immense joy and fulfillment.

Building healthy friendships is another vital aspect of fostering mental well-being. Authentic relationships provide support, accountability, and opportunities for growth. As singles interact with peers, they should prioritize friendships that encourage open dialogue about mental health. Sharing experiences and challenges can foster deeper connections and help reduce feelings of isolation. In a world where social media often portrays unrealistic expectations, cultivating genuine friendships can create a safe space for individuals to express their struggles and triumphs.

Exploring hobbies and passions is a powerful strategy for enhancing mental health. Engaging in activities that bring joy can serve as an effective form of self-care, allowing singles to invest time in their interests and talents. This exploration not only promotes personal growth but can also lead to new friendships and community involvement. Whether through travel, adventure, or creative pursuits, embracing these passions can provide an outlet for stress relief and a pathway to greater self-awareness and self-acceptance.

Lastly, integrating spirituality and self-reflection into the journey of mental health can lead to profound insights and healing. Christian singles can benefit from practices such as prayer, meditation, and journaling to process their thoughts and emotions. These practices encourage individuals to seek God's guidance, fostering a sense of peace and clarity in their lives. As they navigate the complexities of singleness, reflecting on their mental health in conjunction with their spiritual journey can ultimately lead to a more fulfilled and balanced life, paving the way for future relationships rooted in emotional and spiritual health.

Coping Strategies for Loneliness

Coping with loneliness is a significant aspect of the journey of singleness, particularly for Christian single men and women who seek to embrace this season of life. Understanding that loneliness is a common human experience can be the first step in addressing it. Acknowledging your feelings without judgment allows for a more profound self-reflection and the opportunity to turn these feelings into motivation for personal growth. Instead of viewing loneliness solely as a negative state, consider it a catalyst for spiritual and emotional development that can lead you closer to your true self and to God.

Building healthy friendships is a vital strategy to combat loneliness. Invest time in nurturing your existing relationships and seek out new connections within your church, community, or social groups. Engage in activities that interest you, such as joining a Bible study, participating in volunteer work, or attending community events. These interactions not only help to alleviate feelings of isolation but also promote a sense of belonging and support. Surrounding yourself with like-minded individuals can provide encouragement and companionship, reminding you that you are not alone in your journey.

Exploring hobbies and passions can also serve as a powerful coping mechanism. Use your singleness as an opportunity to discover activities that bring you joy and fulfillment. Whether it's painting, cooking, hiking, or learning a new instrument, immersing yourself in creative pursuits can enhance your mental well-being and provide a sense of accomplishment. These hobbies can become areas of reflection where you can connect with God's creation, allowing you to express yourself and grow in ways that enrich your spiritual life and personal identity.

Travel and adventure can be transformative experiences that help alleviate loneliness. Consider planning trips, whether short weekend getaways or longer adventures, to explore new places and cultures. Traveling alone can foster self-discovery, allowing you to learn more about yourself and your preferences. Moreover, consider joining travel groups or Christian retreats designed for singles, providing you with opportunities to meet others who share similar interests while broadening your horizons. These experiences can lead to lasting memories and new friendships that contribute positively to your life.

Lastly, incorporating self-care practices into your routine is crucial for mental health and well-being. Prioritize time for self-reflection through prayer, journaling, or meditation. Establishing a budget for personal development, such as attending workshops or pursuing further education, can also be beneficial. Volunteering within your community not only provides a sense of purpose but also connects you with others, creating a shared mission. By investing in yourself and your community, you foster resilience against loneliness, affirming that this season of singleness is not a time of lack but one of growth, exploration, and spiritual deepening.

Seeking Professional Help When Needed

Recognizing when to seek professional help is a crucial aspect of personal growth and self-discovery, especially during the season of singleness. Many Christian singles might feel a sense of pride in handling their struggles independently, but it is important to understand that seeking assistance is not a sign of weakness. Instead, it reflects a desire to grow and thrive in one's journey. Professional help can come in various forms, including counseling, therapy, or mentorship, and can provide valuable insights and tools to navigate life's challenges more effectively.

In the context of mental health and well-being, professional guidance can be particularly beneficial. Singleness can sometimes lead to feelings of loneliness, anxiety, or even depression. A mental health professional can help individuals explore these feelings in a safe and supportive environment, equipping them with coping strategies and resilience. This process not only fosters healing but also encourages self-reflection, enabling individuals to understand their emotional triggers and develop healthier responses to life's difficulties. Engaging in therapy can be a transformative step towards embracing one's season of singleness with confidence and joy.

Moreover, seeking professional help can significantly enhance one's relationships and social interactions. Building healthy friendships is essential during this time, and professionals can offer insights into effective communication and conflict resolution. By addressing personal barriers that may hinder the formation of meaningful connections, such as fear of vulnerability or past traumas, individuals can cultivate deeper, more fulfilling relationships. This not only enriches their social life but also prepares them for future romantic relationships by establishing a solid foundation of understanding and trust.

In addition to mental health support, professional help can also extend to career development and ambition. For many singles, this season is an opportunity to explore passions, acquire new skills, and advance in their careers. Career coaches and mentors can provide guidance on navigating professional landscapes, setting achievable goals, and maintaining a healthy work- life balance.

This support can empower individuals to pursue their ambitions confidently, ensuring that they are not only growing personally but also professionally during their time of singleness.

Finally, embracing the journey of self-care through professional help can be an enriching experience. Activities like volunteering and community engagement can significantly benefit from guidance in identifying personal strengths and interests. Professionals can assist individuals in discovering new hobbies and passions that align with their values and aspirations. This exploration fosters a sense of purpose and fulfillment, encouraging singles to actively engage with their communities and enhance their overall well-being. In seeking professional help, Christian singles can unlock a deeper understanding of themselves, ultimately leading to a more enriched and purposeful life during their season of singleness.

Spirituality and Self-Reflection

Deepening Your Relationship with God

Deepening your relationship with God is an essential aspect of navigating the journey of singleness. As you embrace this season, it's crucial to recognize that your relationship with the Lord can flourish in profound ways. Spending intentional time in prayer and meditation allows you to develop a deeper understanding of His character and His plans for you. Create a consistent routine that includes quiet time to reflect on scripture and listen for His guidance. This commitment not only strengthens your faith but also helps you cultivate a sense of peace and purpose in your life.

Engaging with a community of believers can significantly enhance your spiritual growth. Find a local church or small group where you can connect with others who share your faith. These relationships can provide support, encouragement, and accountability as you seek to deepen your walk with God. Participating in group studies or discussions on spirituality can introduce you to different perspectives and insights, allowing you to explore your faith more profoundly. Building healthy friendships centered around Christ can enrich your life and help you grow as an individual.

Incorporating spiritual practices into your daily routine is another effective way to deepen your relationship with God. Consider journaling your prayers, thoughts, and reflections as a means of self-discovery. This practice not only helps you articulate your feelings but also allows you to track your spiritual journey over time. Additionally, exploring hobbies that align with your faith such as art, music, or writing can be a creative outlet that fosters a deeper connection with God. These activities can serve as an expression of worship while providing opportunities for personal growth and self-exploration.

Travel and adventure can also play a vital role in deepening your relationship with God. Taking time to explore new places can open your heart and mind to the wonders of His creation. Whether it's a short trip to a nearby town or a mission trip abroad, experiencing different cultures and environments can enhance your appreciation for the diversity of God's handiwork. During these adventures, make it a point to seek out moments of prayer and reflection, allowing the beauty of your surroundings to inspire gratitude and worship.

Lastly, prioritize your mental health and well-being as you seek to deepen your relationship with God. Engaging in self-care practices that promote emotional and spiritual health is essential for personal growth. This may include setting boundaries, seeking professional help if needed, and practicing mindfulness. By nurturing your mental well-being, you create a healthier space for God to work in your life. Remember, this journey of deepening your relationship with God is ongoing; each step you take in faith leads to greater intimacy and understanding of His love for you.

Journaling as a Spiritual Practice

Journaling as a spiritual practice can be an enriching experience for Christian singles seeking deeper connections with themselves and God. This practice provides a safe space for reflection, allowing individuals to articulate their thoughts and feelings, explore their spiritual journeys, and cultivate a greater awareness of their relationship with Christ. By putting pen to paper, singles can process their experiences, assess their growth, and document moments of divine insight that often go unnoticed in the hustle of daily life.

Engaging in journaling encourages personal growth and self-discovery by prompting deeper contemplation of one's beliefs and values. It allows individuals to ask meaningful questions such as, "What does my relationship with God look like in this season of my life?" and "How can I embrace the unique blessings of my singleness?" Through this reflective practice, singles can identify patterns in their lives, recognize areas for improvement, and celebrate milestones in their spiritual journey. This self-awareness fosters a more profound understanding of one's identity and purpose, which is essential for personal development.

In addition to self-discovery, journaling can also serve as a tool for building healthy friendships and community engagement. By writing about their interactions and relationships, singles can reflect on their social dynamics and discern which friendships nurture their spiritual and emotional well-being. This practice also helps individuals articulate their needs and boundaries, leading to more meaningful connections with others. Sharing insights from one's journal can foster deeper conversations with friends and provide opportunities for accountability and support.

Travel and adventure can be integral to the journaling experience, allowing singles to document their journeys and the lessons learned along the way. Capturing the sights, sounds, and emotions of new experiences can deepen one's appreciation for God's creation and the beauty in life's adventures. Writing about these travels not only preserves memories but also encourages singles to reflect on what they have learned about themselves and their faith during these explorations. It becomes a way to witness God's hand in their lives, affirming that He is present in every season of their journey.

Finally, journaling can significantly enhance mental health and well-being by providing a therapeutic outlet for emotions and thoughts. For singles navigating the complexities of life, including career development and financial independence, this practice can alleviate stress and promote clarity. Writing about one's aspirations, fears, and triumphs creates a constructive dialogue with oneself, fostering resilience and hope. As individuals articulate their dreams and challenges on paper, they invite God's guidance into their lives, paving the way for a more fulfilling and spiritually grounded journey through singleness.

The Role of Prayer in Self-Reflection

The role of prayer in self-reflection is pivotal as it offers a structured approach to understanding oneself in the context of faith. For Christian singles, prayer serves as a powerful tool to delve into personal growth and self-discovery. It creates a sacred space where individuals can communicate openly with God about their thoughts, feelings, and aspirations. This dialogue not only fosters a deeper relationship with the divine but also encourages introspection, allowing one to explore the motivations behind their actions and decisions during this unique season of singleness.

Through prayer, singles can identify areas of their lives that may need attention or change. By seeking divine guidance, individuals can gain clarity on their personal goals, whether in terms of career development, financial independence, or cultivating healthy friendships. Prayer can illuminate the values and passions that resonate most deeply, helping to align daily activities with one's true calling. This alignment is crucial in a world filled with distractions and societal pressures, allowing singles to focus on what genuinely matters to them.

Incorporating prayer into one's daily routine can also enhance mental health and well-being. The practice of prayer encourages mindfulness and presence, which are essential for self- refection. As singles navigate their journeys, they may encounter feelings of loneliness or uncertainty. Engaging in prayer provides a means to process these emotions constructively, transforming moments of doubt into opportunities for growth. This practice fosters resilience, equipping individuals to handle life's challenges with a sense of peace and purpose.

Furthermore, prayer can inspire action beyond personal reflection. As singles reflect on their lives, they may feel called to engage in community service or volunteer work. This outward expression of faith can bolster one's sense of purpose and connection to others. By praying for guidance in these areas, individuals can discover new hobbies and passions that not only enrich their own lives but also positively impact those around them. The intertwining of prayer and action enhances the journey of self-discovery, allowing singles to contribute meaningfully to their communities.

Ultimately, the role of prayer in self-reflection is about building a holistic understanding of oneself through the lens of faith. For Christian singles, this practice fosters spiritual growth and personal development, guiding them in embracing their season of singleness. By actively engaging in prayer, individuals can navigate their journeys with intention, discovering who they are and who they are called to be. It is through this sacred practice that one can unlock the potential within, transforming singleness into a time of profound self-awareness and empowerment.

Dating Yourself: Self-Care Practices

Defining Self-Care

Defining self-care is essential for understanding how to nurture oneself during the season of singleness. Self-care encompasses a variety of practices that prioritize mental, emotional, and physical well-being. For Christian singles, self-care is not merely about indulging in personal pleasures; it is about honoring the body and spirit that God has gifted us. This holistic approach acknowledges that self-care is both a personal responsibility and a spiritual practice, aligning with the biblical principle of loving oneself as God loves us.

At its core, self-care involves recognizing one's needs and taking intentional steps to meet them. This may include establishing a balanced routine that promotes physical health through exercise, nutritious eating, and sufficient rest. Additionally, mental health practices, such as mindfulness and meditation, can be integrated to foster a peaceful mind. For singles, who may often navigate loneliness or societal pressures, engaging in self-care can serve as a powerful reminder of one's worth and purpose in Christ. By actively participating in self-care, individuals can cultivate resilience and a deeper understanding of their identity.

Emotional self-care is equally crucial, especially for those seeking personal growth and self-discovery. This involves cultivating healthy friendships and surrounding oneself with supportive communities that uplift and inspire. Building these relationships can also lead to enriching conversations about faith, life goals, and even challenges faced in the journey of singleness. By sharing experiences with like-minded individuals, Christian singles can create a network of encouragement that fosters both accountability and joy in their lives.

Exploring hobbies and passions is another vital aspect of self-care that encourages singles to pursue their interests. Whether it's traveling, engaging in creative arts, or volunteering within the community, these activities not only enhance personal fulfillment but also contribute to a well-rounded life. Engaging in new experiences can lead to self-discovery, revealing hidden talents and passions that enrich one's life. This exploration can be seen as a form of worship, expressing gratitude for the gifts and opportunities God has provided.

Lastly, self-care in the context of spirituality involves deepening one's relationship with God through self-reflection and prayer. This practice is essential for nurturing a strong spiritual foundation, allowing singles to seek guidance and purpose in their lives. By taking time for solitude and reflection, individuals can better understand their aspirations while aligning them with God's will. As they journey through their season of singleness, embracing self-care will empower them to grow, thrive, and prepare for the future God has in store for them while reinforcing the truth that their worth is inherent in their identity as beloved children of God.

Creating a Self-Care Routine

Creating a self-care routine is essential for Christian singles seeking to embrace their season of singleness. This journey is not merely about waiting for the right partner but rather about nurturing oneself in all aspects of life. A well-structured self-care routine can enhance personal growth, promote mental well-being, and deepen one's spiritual life. It allows individuals to reflect on their identity in Christ and to cultivate a fulfilling and purposeful life while single. As you embark on this journey, consider how each element of self-care contributes to your overall well-being.

To begin, it is important to incorporate physical self-care into your routine. Taking care of your body through regular exercise, a balanced diet, and adequate rest is crucial. Physical activity not only boosts your health but also elevates your mood and energy levels. This practice can include various forms, such as jogging, praying and worshipping your creator, or even group sports with friends. Additionally, nourishing your body with wholesome foods and ensuring you get enough sleep will help you feel more vibrant and ready to face the challenges of daily life. Remember, your body is a temple, and taking care of it honors God.

Mental health and emotional well-being are also vital components of a self-care routine. Engaging in activities that promote relaxation and mindfulness can significantly reduce stress. Consider incorporating practices such as meditation, journaling, or prayer into your daily life. These activities can help you reflect on your thoughts and feelings, allowing for greater self- discovery. Furthermore, surrounding yourself with healthy friendships offers support and accountability, creating an environment where you can thrive. Invest time in relationships that lift you up and encourage your growth in Christ.

Spiritual self-care should not be overlooked as you create your routine. Deepening your relationship with God is fundamental to embracing your singleness fully. Regularly engaging in Bible study, prayer, and attending church services can provide a solid foundation for your spiritual life. Additionally, consider setting aside time for solitude and reflection, where you can listen to God's voice and seek His guidance. This spiritual nourishment is essential for understanding your purpose and direction during this season of your life.

Lastly, explore hobbies and passions that ignite your creativity and joy. Engaging in activities that you love can provide a sense of fulfillment and adventure. Whether it's painting, hiking, or traveling, these experiences enrich your life and broaden your horizons. Volunteering for community service can also be rewarding, allowing you to give back while fostering connections with others. Financial independence and budgeting play a role here as well; learning to manage your resources wisely can enable you to pursue your interests without undue stress. By prioritizing self-care in these various dimensions, you can embrace your singleness as a time of growth, discovery, and joyful living in Christ.

Treating Yourself with Kindness

Treating yourself with kindness is an essential aspect of embracing your journey in singleness. As Christian single men and women, it is vital to recognize that kindness begins with you. This self-kindness is not about indulgence or selfishness; rather, it is a profound acknowledgment of your worth as a child of God. By treating yourself with kindness, you pave the way for personal growth and self-discovery, allowing you to fully understand your identity in Christ and the unique path He has set before you.

In moments of solitude, it is easy to fall into negative self-talk or feelings of inadequacy. However, practicing self-kindness involves challenging these thoughts and replacing them with affirmations of your value and purpose. Engaging in spiritual self-reflection can help you to see yourself through God's eyes. Spend time in prayer, asking for clarity and understanding of your strengths and the gifts He has bestowed upon you. This can foster a sense of peace and acceptance that is crucial for your mental health and well-being.

During this season, building healthy friendships can serve as a vital aspect of personal development. Engaging with a diverse group of friends allows for the exchange of ideas, experiences, and support. These friendships can provide the emotional and social nourishment necessary for well-being, enabling singles to cultivate a sense of belonging and community. Furthermore, investing time in these relationships can teach valuable lessons about communication, conflict resolution, and empathy, all of which are crucial in any future romantic partnership.

Exploring hobbies and passions is another fundamental purpose of singleness. This is an ideal time to pursue interests that ignite joy and creativity, whether that involves art, music, sports, or travel. By engaging in activities that resonate personally, individuals can discover their talents and preferences, which contributes to a fulfilling life. Moreover, pursuing passions not only enhances self-esteem but also creates opportunities for meeting like-minded individuals, potentially leading to meaningful connections. Embracing this time to explore one's interests can transform the perception of singleness from a waiting period into an exciting adventure.

Financial independence and budgeting are critical skills that often receive less attention during this period. Being single allows individuals to establish their financial footing without the complexities that come with shared finances. This time can be used to learn about budgeting, saving, and investing, which are essential for a secure future. By developing financial literacy and independence, singles can create a stable environment for themselves and prepare for any future partnership, ensuring that they enter relationships with a healthy financial mindset.

Finally, focusing on mental health and well-being during this season is paramount. Singleness can sometimes lead to feelings of loneliness or inadequacy, but it is essential to prioritize self- care practices and spiritual reflection. Engaging in activities that promote mental wellness, such as meditation, exercise, or volunteering, fosters resilience and a positive outlook. By understanding oneself better and nurturing mental health, individuals can approach the future with confidence and clarity, recognizing that their worth is not defined by relationship status but by their identity in Christ and their journey of self-discovery.

Begin by reflecting on your passions and skills. Engage in self-assessment to clarify what truly excites you and what talents you possess. This process can involve journaling, prayer, or seeking insights from trusted friends or mentors. Consider how these passions can be integrated into your career. For instance, if you have a love for helping others, think about how this could manifest in your professional life, whether through roles in healthcare, education, or community service. Understanding yourself is essential because it lays the foundation for setting realistic and fulfilling career goals.

Once you have gained clarity on your interests and strengths, it's time to set specific, measurable, attainable, relevant, and time-bound (SMART) goals. Instead of vague aspirations like "I want to be successful," break this down into actionable steps. Define what success looks like for you in your career, whether it's achieving a particular job title, obtaining a certification, or starting a business. Establish timelines for these goals, as deadlines create a sense of urgency and help you maintain focus. This structured approach not only enhances accountability but also allows you to celebrate small victories along the way.

Networking and building healthy friendships can play a significant role in achieving your career goals. As a single individual, you have the flexibility to invest time in forming connections with like-minded professionals. Attend industry events, engage in community groups, or seek mentorship opportunities. These relationships can provide valuable insights, open doors to new opportunities, and offer support as you navigate your career path. Remember that your career journey does not have to be a solitary endeavor; collaboration and community can lead to greater success.

Finally, as you pursue your career ambitions, it's essential to maintain a balance between your professional aspirations and your spiritual and personal well-being. Regularly engage in self-reflection and prayer to ensure that your goals align with your faith and values. Consider how your career can serve a greater purpose and contribute to the community. Volunteering or participating in service projects can enhance your sense of fulfillment and help you build a network of supportive relationships. By prioritizing both your career development and your spiritual growth, you can navigate this season of singleness with confidence and joy, fully embracing the journey that lies ahead.

Finding Fulfillment in Your Work

Finding fulfillment in your work is an essential aspect of embracing your season of singleness, particularly for Christian singles who seek to align their careers with their faith and personal values. In this phase of life, where self-discovery and personal growth are paramount, it is vital to view work not merely as a means of financial support but as an opportunity to serve God and others. By shifting your perspective on work, you can cultivate a deeper sense of purpose and satisfaction, transforming your daily tasks into acts of worship and service.

Engaging in activities that genuinely interest you is crucial to finding fulfillment in your career. As you explore your passions, consider how they can intersect with your professional life. Whether it's volunteering for a cause you care about, pursuing a hobby that brings you joy, or seeking a job that aligns with your values, each step can lead to greater personal satisfaction. This exploration of interests can also help you develop new skills and expand your network, enriching both your personal and professional life. By actively seeking roles that resonate with your passions, you create a work environment that promotes both growth and fulfillment.

Building healthy friendships within your workplace can also enhance your overall fulfillment. As a Christian single, fostering relationships that encourage accountability, support, and motivation is vital. Surrounding yourself with colleagues who share similar values and beliefs can create a positive atmosphere that uplifts and inspires. These connections can lead to collaborative opportunities, mentorship, and the sharing of resources, ultimately making your work experience more rewarding. Additionally, engaging in group activities, such as team-building exercises or community service projects, can strengthen these bonds and provide a sense of camaraderie.

Financial independence is another key aspect of finding fulfillment in your work. As you navigate your career, establishing a sound financial plan will empower you to focus on what you love without the burden of financial stress. Budgeting and managing your finances wisely can provide the freedom to pursue opportunities that align with your interests and values. This financial stability not only alleviates anxiety but also allows you to invest in experiences that contribute to your personal growth, such as travel and adventure. When you are financially secure, it becomes easier to seek out opportunities for development and fulfillment.

Lastly, embracing a mindset of self-refection is crucial to sustaining fulfillment in your work. Regularly assessing your goals, values, and the impact of your work on your life can lead to greater clarity and intentionality. Take time to pray and seek God's guidance in your professional pursuits, ensuring that your career aligns with His purpose for your life. Through this process, you can identify areas for improvement, set meaningful objectives, and celebrate your accomplishments. By viewing your work as a journey of growth and a platform for serving others, you can find profound fulfillment that transcends the daily grind, making your singleness a season rich in purpose and joy.

Networking and Building Professional Relationships

Networking and building professional relationships are essential components for Christian singles seeking to enrich their lives and careers during this season of singleness. This period can serve as a transformative time for personal growth and self-discovery, allowing you to cultivate connections that align with your values and aspirations. By engaging with like-minded individuals, you create opportunities for collaboration, mentorship, and friendship, which can significantly enhance both your personal and professional life.

Establishing a robust network begins with identifying your passions and interests. Whether you are exploring new hobbies or pursuing career development, connecting with others who share similar goals can provide valuable insights and support. Attend workshops, conferences, and community events that resonate with your passions, and don't hesitate to introduce yourself to new people. Building relationships with individuals in your field not only opens doors for career advancement but also fosters a sense of belonging that can be particularly fulfilling during your single years.

As you embark on this journey of networking, it's important to approach interactions with authenticity and a spirit of service. Genuine relationships are built on trust and mutual respect, so take the time to listen actively and offer assistance where possible. Volunteering for community projects or church initiatives can be an excellent way to meet others while contributing to a greater cause. These experiences not only enrich your spiritual life but also allow you to connect with individuals who share your commitment to serving others.

Incorporating travel and adventure into your networking efforts can also yield unexpected benefits. Exploring new places with fellow singles who share your interests can lead to deeper connections and lasting friendships. Whether it's a group retreat focused on spiritual growth or an adventure trip centered around a shared hobby, these experiences create lasting memories and strengthen bonds. Embrace opportunities to step outside your comfort zone and engage with others in settings that inspire both personal and professional growth.

Moreover, treating yourself with kindness means prioritizing self-care practices that nurture your body, mind, and spirit. This can manifest in various forms, from engaging in hobbies and passions that ignite joy to taking time for rest and relaxation. Consider exploring new interests or investing in activities that bring you fulfillment. Whether it's learning a new skill, volunteering in your community, or embarking on an adventure, these experiences can significantly enrich your life, building confidence and expanding your horizons.

Financial independence is another area where kindness towards yourself plays a critical role. Being mindful of your finances and budgeting wisely allows you to invest in experiences that matter to you. This could mean saving for a solo trip that nourishes your spirit or attending a workshop that advances your career development. By setting financial goals that align with your values, you reinforce a sense of agency and empowerment in your choices, reinforcing your worthiness of a fulfilling life.

Building healthy friendships is also an essential component of treating yourself with kindness. Surrounding yourself with supportive, uplifting individuals who encourage you in your journey can enhance your sense of belonging and connection. These relationships can provide opportunities for shared experiences and growth, as well as a network of support during challenging times. Remember, the kindness you offer to yourself can ripple outward, enriching not only your life but also the lives of others in your circle.

Career Development and Ambition Setting Career Goals

Setting career goals is a crucial step in navigating your journey as a single Christian individual. This phase of life often presents a unique opportunity for personal growth and self-discovery, allowing you to focus on your ambitions without the immediate distractions that come with romantic relationships. By intentionally defining your career aspirations, you can create a roadmap that not only leads to professional success but also aligns with your spiritual values and personal mission.

Finally, as you navigate your networking journey, remember the importance of self-care and mental well-being. Balancing your professional aspirations with your spiritual and emotional health is crucial. Take time for self-reflection, engage in activities that rejuvenate you, and seek guidance through prayer and meditation. Building professional relationships is a dynamic process that flourishes best when you are grounded in your own identity and purpose. By embracing your season of singleness and investing in meaningful connections, you can cultivate a supportive network that enhances your journey in Christ.

Volunteering and Community Engagement

The Importance of Giving Back

The act of giving back is a powerful expression of faith and community that resonates deeply within the Christian journey. For single men and women, this practice not only enriches the lives of others but also fosters personal growth and self-discovery. Engaging in acts of service provides an opportunity to step outside one's own circumstances and focus on the needs of others. This shift in perspective can lead to a profound understanding of one's purpose and calling, allowing individuals to cultivate a more grounded sense of identity. In this season of singleness, giving back becomes a pathway to discovering how one can contribute uniquely to the world around them.

Volunteering and community engagement can also enhance one's mental health and well- being. Many singles may experience feelings of isolation or uncertainty during this period of their lives. By connecting with others through service, individuals can build meaningful friendships and a sense of belonging. Sharing experiences and working toward a common goal with others not only alleviates loneliness but also brings joy and fulfillment. Such connections can be particularly impactful as they encourage the development of empathy and compassion, essential qualities for healthy relationships in any future dating scenario.

Moreover, the importance of giving back extends to exploring hobbies and passions. Engaging in community service can uncover latent interests or skills that individuals may not have fully realized. Whether it's helping at a local shelter, participating in community clean-up events, or offering tutoring to students in need, these activities can ignite a sense of adventure and purpose. This exploration can enrich one's life, leading to personal development that enhances both self-awareness and career prospects. As singles embrace their unique journeys, giving back can serve as a catalyst for discovering what truly excites and motivates them.

Financial independence and budgeting also play a crucial role in the ability to give back. When individuals are mindful of their finances, they can allocate resources to support causes they are passionate about. This practice not only demonstrates stewardship but also encourages responsible financial habits. By prioritizing giving within their budgets, singles can experience the joy of generosity without compromising their financial security. This thoughtful approach to money management reinforces the idea that giving back does not always require significant financial contributions; rather, time, talents, and resources can be shared in numerous ways.

In conclusion, the act of giving back is a vital component of the Christian singles' journey. It offers a means of personal growth, fosters mental health, and encourages the exploration of passions, all while cultivating healthy friendships and community connections. As individuals embrace their season of singleness, they are presented with a unique opportunity to invest in the lives of others, deepening their faith and understanding of service. Ultimately, giving back not only enriches the lives of those being served but also profoundly transforms the giver, making it an essential practice for anyone seeking to navigate their journey in Christ with purpose and intention.

Finding Opportunities to Serve

Finding opportunities to serve during your season of singleness can be a transformative experience that enriches both your personal growth and your spiritual journey. As a Christian single, engaging in service allows you to step beyond your own needs and desires, creating connections with others while developing a deeper understanding of your faith. Serving others not only fulfills a biblical mandate but also provides a platform for self-discovery. You may find that your skills, passions, and interests align with a particular need in your community, leading to a fulfilling experience that helps you grow as an individual.

One of the most rewarding ways to serve is through volunteering with local organizations or churches. This could involve anything from helping at a food bank to mentoring youth or participating in community clean-up efforts. By immersing yourself in these activities, you can build healthy friendships with like-minded individuals who share your values and interests. These connections can lead to a supportive network that encourages you to explore your own gifts and talents, ultimately fostering personal growth. The friendships formed in these environments often provide a sense of belonging and camaraderie that is especially valuable during your single years.

Another avenue for service is through the exploration of hobbies and passions that can benefit others. If you have a talent for art, music, or writing, consider leading workshops or offering your skills to those in need. For instance, teaching art classes at a local community center can not only help others discover their creativity but also enhance your own skills and confidence. Engaging in such activities allows you to share your passions while also serving your community, creating a fulfilling cycle of giving and receiving that can deeply enrich your life.

Travel and adventure can also present unique opportunities for service. Whether it's participating in a mission trip or volunteering at an international organization, these experiences can broaden your perspective and deepen your faith. Engaging in service while traveling helps you connect with diverse cultures and communities, allowing you to see the world through a different lens. Such experiences can lead to profound personal growth, expanding your understanding of God's work across the globe and how you into that larger narrative.

Ultimately, finding opportunities to serve is about recognizing that your season of singleness is not a time of waiting but a period of active engagement. Embracing this mindset encourages you to prioritize community involvement and personal development. Whether through local initiatives, shared hobbies, or global missions, the experiences you curate during this time can lay a strong foundation for your future relationships and career aspirations. By serving others, you not only contribute positively to your community but also cultivate a deeper sense of purpose and fulfillment in your own life.

Building Community Through Service

Building community through service is a vital aspect of the Christian journey, particularly for single men and women seeking to embrace their season of singleness. Engaging in service-oriented activities not only fosters connections with others but also enables individuals to discover their purpose and develop a deeper understanding of their faith. When singles dedicate time and energy to serving others, they cultivate a sense of belonging that transcends their individual circumstances, allowing them to build meaningful relationships and strengthen their communities.

Volunteering offers numerous opportunities for personal growth and self-discovery. It challenges individuals to step outside their comfort zones, develop new skills, and gain insights into their own strengths and weaknesses. Whether it's mentoring youth, participating in community clean-ups, or serving at local shelters, each experience provides a platform for singles to explore their passions and interests while contributing to a greater cause. This journey of self-exploration can reveal hidden talents and lead to new hobbies, enriching the lives of those involved.

Building healthy friendships is another benefit of community service. When singles come together with a shared purpose, they create bonds that are often deeper than those formed in more casual settings. Service projects encourage collaboration, communication, and teamwork, fostering an environment where individuals can support one another. These friendships can provide emotional support, accountability, and encouragement, all of which are essential for maintaining mental health and well-being during the often-challenging season of singleness.

Lastly, service can lead to financial independence and career development. Many organizations seek volunteers with specific skills, providing singles with opportunities to develop their professional abilities while contributing to a cause they care about. This dual benefit allows individuals to enhance their resumes and network with like-minded individuals, which can lead to potential job opportunities. By aligning their career ambitions with their passion for service, singles can create a fulfilling path that honors their journey while also making a positive impact in their communities.

Chapter 2

Fulfilled and Free: Finding Joy in the Everyday as a Christian Single

Understanding Your Purpose as a Christian Single

The Importance of Purpose in Everyday Life

The significance of purpose in everyday life cannot be overstated, especially for Christian singles navigating the complexities of their unique journeys. Purpose serves as a guiding light that shapes decisions, influences relationships, and fosters a sense of fulfillment. For those who find themselves single, the quest for purpose can be particularly profound, offering opportunities to explore and deepen one's faith while discovering personal passions and talents. Engaging with the idea of purpose encourages singles to view their lives through the lens of service, growth, and intentionality, allowing them to cultivate a rich and meaningful existence.

In the context of daily living, purpose acts as a catalyst for fulfillment. Christian singles are often confronted with societal pressures and expectations regarding relationships, which can lead to feelings of inadequacy or restlessness. However, by focusing on personal purpose, individuals can shift their perspectives. Rather than viewing their single status as a limitation, they can embrace it as a unique phase rich with opportunities for personal development, community building, and spiritual enrichment. This shift in mindset empowers singles to find joy in their current circumstances, reinforcing the belief that every moment has value and can contribute to a greater divine plan.

Building a community of purposeful Christian singles is essential for fostering a supportive environment where individuals can thrive. This community allows for shared experiences, encouragement, and accountability in pursuing fulfilling lives. As singles connect with one another, they can discuss their individual purposes, collaborate on service projects, and engage in meaningful conversations about faith. Such interactions not only strengthen relationships but also provide a platform for exploring spiritual gifts and discovering how these gifts can be used to serve others and enrich the community.

To live with purpose, developing spiritual disciplines becomes crucial. Practices such as prayer, meditation, and regular study of Scripture enable singles to cultivate a deeper relationship with God, which in turn clarifies their sense of purpose. Establishing a Christ-centered routine that includes time for reflection and self-assessment can help singles set meaningful goals aligned with their faith. These goals may include volunteering, participating in local church activities, or mentoring younger individuals, all of which contribute to building a purposeful life that glorifies God and impacts others positively.

Finally, embracing solitude as a means of spiritual growth allows Christian singles to reflect on their lives and deepen their understanding of their purpose. This time alone can be a powerful opportunity for introspection, prayer, and seeking God's guidance. By learning to navigate their singlehood with a purposeful mindset, individuals can engage fully with their lives, fostering an attitude of gratitude and openness. The journey towards fulfillment is not solely about finding companionship but rather about discovering joy in every moment and living out one's faith with intention, thereby creating a life that resonates with purpose and meaning.

Embracing Your Unique Journey

Embracing your unique journey as a Christian single involves recognizing the divine purpose woven into your life experiences. Each individual's path is distinct, shaped by personal history, spiritual gifts, and the specific calling God has placed on their heart. This journey is not merely about waiting for the next chapter, such as marriage, but about fully engaging in the present moment with joy and intention. Understanding that your worth is not defined by your relationship status is crucial to embracing this journey. Instead, view it as a time for personal growth, exploration of your faith, and deepening your relationship with God.

Finding fulfillment in daily life as a Christian single can be achieved by setting intentional goals that align with your values and beliefs. Consider what brings you joy and how you can incorporate those elements into your routine. Whether it's volunteering in your community, joining a Bible study group, or pursuing a hobby that ignites your passion, each activity can contribute to a sense of purpose. Embrace these opportunities as they allow you to develop your spiritual disciplines, such as prayer and meditation, which can enhance your daily experiences and help you cultivate a deeper relationship with Christ.

Building a community of purposeful Christian singles is essential for fostering a supportive environment where you can share your journey and experiences. Seek out groups that align with your faith and values, whether through your church or local organizations. These connections can lead to meaningful friendships and provide a safe space to discuss challenges and victories. Engaging with others who share similar goals can inspire you and offer a sense of belonging, reinforcing the idea that you are not alone in your pursuit of fulfillment and purpose.

As you embrace solitude and focus on spiritual growth, consider how your unique journey can be a source of strength. Solitude allows for reflection and deepening your understanding of your spiritual gifts. Take time to explore these gifts and how they can impact your life and the lives of others. Whether through teaching, encouragement, or service, recognizing and utilizing your spiritual gifts can bring a profound sense of fulfillment. Additionally, creating a Christ-centered routine can help you stay grounded and purposeful in your daily activities, ensuring that each day is lived with intention.

Finally, navigating dating with a purposeful Christian mindset can be an enriching experience if approached with clarity and intention. Rather than viewing dating as a mere means to an end, consider it an opportunity for growth and learning. Engage in meaningful conversations about faith and values with potential partners, ensuring that your pursuit aligns with your spiritual goals. This journey, when embraced, can lead to deeper connections and a greater understanding of what it means to live a fulfilled and free life as a Christian single.

Finding Fulfillment in Daily Life

Cultivating Gratitude

Cultivating gratitude is an essential practice for Christian singles seeking to find joy in their everyday lives. This discipline encourages us to focus on the blessings we have, rather than the things we lack. By intentionally recognizing and appreciating the goodness in our lives, we create a mindset that fosters joy and fulfillment. Gratitude can shift our perspective, enabling us to see our single journey not as a period of waiting, but as a unique opportunity for growth and connection with God and others.

One practical way to cultivate gratitude is through daily reflection. Setting aside time each day to consider the gifts we have received can deepen our appreciation for the present moment. This could take the form of a gratitude journal where we list things, we are thankful for, no matter how small. By regularly engaging in this practice, we train our minds to look for the positive aspects of our lives, which can enhance our overall well-being and encourage a more hopeful outlook. This exercise can also serve as a reminder of God's faithfulness and provision in our lives.

Building a community of like-minded Christian singles can further enrich our gratitude practice. When we gather with others who share our values, we can encourage each other to express appreciation and celebrate the blessings we often overlook. Whether through small group gatherings, church events, or volunteer opportunities, connecting with others allows us to share our experiences and cultivate a spirit of thankfulness together. This communal aspect of gratitude not only strengthens our bonds but also helps us recognize the diverse ways God works in our lives.

In addition to reflection and community, serving others is a powerful avenue for cultivating gratitude. When we engage in volunteer opportunities, we often gain perspective on our own circumstances. Helping those in need can remind us of our blessings and inspire gratitude for the resources, skills, and time we possess. Whether it's participating in a local outreach program or simply assisting a friend in need, serving others can ground us in purpose and highlight the interconnectedness of our lives within the body of Christ.

Ultimately, cultivating gratitude is a spiritual discipline that can significantly enhance our lives as Christian singles. It invites us to engage deeply with our faith, encouraging us to rejoice in our current season while looking forward to the future with hope. By practicing gratitude, building community, and serving others, we not only enrich our own lives but also contribute positively to the lives of those around us. In this way, we embrace our single journey with purpose and joy, fully experiencing the richness of life as God intended.

Discovering Joy in Routine Activities

Discovering joy in routine activities is a powerful practice for Christian singles seeking fulfillment in their everyday lives. While routines can often feel mundane or monotonous, they provide a structure that allows us to intentionally engage with our faith and the world around us. By embracing the ordinary aspects of daily life, we can uncover opportunities for spiritual growth and find joy in the tasks that often go unnoticed. This shift in perspective invites us to see our routines not merely as obligations but as avenues for experiencing God's presence and purpose.

A Christ-centered routine begins with the recognition that every moment of our day can be infused with meaning. Simple activities such as preparing meals, commuting to work, or even doing household chores can become acts of worship when viewed through the lens of gratitude. For instance, cooking can transform into a time of prayer, where each ingredient represents a blessing, reminding us of God's provision. By dedicating these moments to Him, we cultivate a heart of thankfulness, leading to a deeper sense of joy and fulfillment in our daily lives.

In addition to personal reflection, routine activities can serve as a foundation for building community among purposeful Christian singles. Engaging in shared activities, such as group workouts, Bible studies, or volunteering, fosters connections that enrich our lives. These communal routines not only provide accountability but also create spaces for meaningful conversations about faith and purpose. By involving ourselves in collective routines, we strengthen our bonds with others while also growing in our understanding of how God is moving within our community.

Exploring our spiritual gifts within the context of daily routines can also enhance our sense of fulfillment. Whether it's through encouraging a coworker, offering a listening ear to a friend, or volunteering in our neighborhoods, recognizing and utilizing our gifts allows us to serve others effectively. This service becomes a joyful expression of our faith, providing a sense of purpose that extends beyond ourselves. By incorporating acts of service into our routines, we not only bless those around us but also experience the joy that comes from living out our Christian values.

Ultimately, discovering joy in routine activities invites us to embrace solitude as an opportunity for spiritual growth. The quiet moments between our scheduled tasks can become sacred spaces where we reflect, pray, and listen for God's guidance. By intentionally setting aside time to connect with Him amidst our daily responsibilities, we cultivate a deeper relationship with our Creator. In this way, our routines become not just a series of actions but a rhythm of life that sustains our faith and deepens our joy, allowing us to navigate the complexities of single life with purpose and fulfillment.

Building a Community of Purposeful Christian Singles

The Value of Fellowship

The concept of fellowship holds profound significance in the life of a Christian single, serving as both a source of support and a catalyst for spiritual growth. In the Bible, believers are encouraged to come together, sharing not only their joys but also their struggles. For singles, this connection can be particularly vital, as it fosters a sense of belonging in a world that often emphasizes romantic relationships. Building a community of purposeful Christian singles allows individuals to experience mutual encouragement and accountability, helping them navigate the unique challenges of single life with faith and resilience.

Fellowship among Christian singles can take many forms, from small group gatherings to larger community events. These interactions offer opportunities for individuals to share their experiences, insights, and spiritual journeys. Engaging in meaningful conversations about faith can deepen one's understanding of Scripture and encourage personal growth. By discussing topics like purpose, fulfillment, and spiritual disciplines, singles can explore their paths in a supportive environment that nurtures both their faith and their friendships.

Moreover, fellowship can play a pivotal role in the development of spiritual disciplines. Regularly gathering with others for prayer, Bible study, or worship helps reinforce one's commitment to spiritual growth. Such practices not only enhance an individual's relationship with God but also cultivate a spirit of service and outreach. For Christian singles, finding volunteer opportunities within their community can be a fulfilling way to connect with others while making a positive impact. Serving alongside fellow believers fosters camaraderie and strengthens the bonds of friendship based on shared values and missions.

Navigating dating and relationships can be particularly challenging for singles seeking a purposeful mindset. Fellowship provides a safe space to discuss aspirations and concerns regarding dating, allowing individuals to share their thoughts on establishing healthy relationships grounded in faith. By participating in group activities, singles can meet potential partners within a community that shares their values, making dating a more enriching and intentional experience. This approach emphasizes the importance of building connections that align with one's spiritual goals rather than merely seeking companionship.

Ultimately, the value of fellowship for Christian singles extends beyond social interaction; it enriches their spiritual journey. Embracing solitude is essential, but it is equally important to balance that with meaningful connections. As singles engage in community life, they discover the joy of shared faith experiences, the support of like-minded individuals, and the strength that comes from collective worship. In this way, fellowship becomes a transformative element of living a fulfilled and purposeful life as a Christian single, reminding each individual that they are not alone on their journey.

Creating Supportive Relationships

Creating supportive relationships is essential for Christian singles seeking fulfillment and purpose in their daily lives. These connections not only enrich our experiences but also foster a sense of belonging within the Christian community. Engaging with others who share similar values and goals can provide encouragement and accountability as we navigate the unique journey of single life. By intentionally cultivating relationships, we can create a network of support that helps us grow spiritually and emotionally.

One key aspect of building supportive relationships is the importance of community. Surrounding ourselves with fellow believers allows us to share our struggles, joys, and aspirations. Participating in church activities, small groups, or volunteer opportunities provides a platform to form meaningful connections. These environments encourage open dialogue about faith and life's challenges, helping us to understand that we are not alone in our experiences as singles. As we interact with others, we can also discover diverse perspectives that enrich our own spiritual journey.

In addition to seeking community, we must also be proactive in nurturing these relationships. This involves investing time and effort into getting to know others on a deeper level. Regularly reaching out to friends, engaging in discussions about faith, and sharing personal experiences can strengthen bonds. By being present and attentive, we show others that they are valued, which fosters a supportive atmosphere. Moreover, these interactions can lead to collaborative efforts in serving our communities, as we join forces with like-minded individuals who share our mission of making a positive impact.

Developing spiritual disciplines within these relationships is another powerful way to enhance our connections. Praying together, studying the Bible, and participating in worship can deepen our understanding of faith and create a shared sense of purpose. These spiritual practices not only strengthen our individual walks with God but also unify us as a community. As we grow together in faith, we can encourage one another to pursue our spiritual gifts and actively seek ways to serve others, further aligning our actions with our beliefs.

Ultimately, creating supportive relationships as a Christian single is about embracing the journey with others who inspire and uplift us. By building a community grounded in faith and purpose, we can navigate the complexities of single life with confidence and joy. As we cultivate these connections, we not only enrich our own lives but also contribute to the spiritual growth of those around us, creating a vibrant and fulfilling environment that reflects the love of Christ.

Developing Spiritual Disciplines for Single Life

Establishing a Prayer Routine

Establishing a prayer routine is a vital practice for Christian singles seeking fulfillment in their everyday lives. A consistent prayer life not only deepens one's relationship with God but also provides clarity and purpose amid the unique challenges and opportunities of singlehood. To embark on this journey, it is essential to identify a specific time and place dedicated to prayer. This could be early in the morning before the day begins, during a lunch break, or in the evening as a way to reflect on the day. Choosing a quiet space free from distractions can create an inviting atmosphere for communion with God.

Incorporating various forms of prayer can enrich your routine and keep it engaging. Consider a mix of structured prayers, such as those found in the Psalms, alongside spontaneous prayers that arise from your heart. Journaling your prayers can also be beneficial, as it allows for reflection and can help track your spiritual growth over time. This practice enables you to look back on how your prayers have been answered and how your relationship with God has evolved. Additionally, using prayer prompts can guide your conversations with God, focusing on different aspects of your life, such as gratitude, guidance, intercession for others, and personal needs.

Building a community of like-minded individuals can enhance your prayer routine significantly. Engaging with fellow Christian singles through small groups or prayer circles fosters an environment of mutual support and accountability. Sharing prayer requests and participating in group prayers not only strengthens relationships but also helps in recognizing the collective struggles and joys of single life. This sense of community can serve as a reminder that you are not alone on your journey and that others are also seeking purpose and fulfillment in their Christian walk.

Embracing solitude as a time for prayer can be a transformative experience. Finding moments of silence in your day allows for deeper reflection and connection with God. Solitude provides space to listen for God's guidance and to discern His will for your life. In these quiet moments, you may find clarity about your purpose, goals, and the unique gifts God has bestowed upon you. This intentional solitude can lead to a more profound understanding of yourself and your relationship with God, ultimately enhancing your day-to-day fulfillment.

Lastly, integrating prayer into your daily routine can help you navigate the complexities of dating and relationships with a focused mindset. Setting aside time to pray about your dating life encourages you to seek God's wisdom and direction in your choices. Embracing a prayerful approach to dating fosters a sense of purpose, ensuring that your relationships align with your spiritual values. By prioritizing prayer in your daily life, you empower yourself to cultivate a deeper connection with God, enriching both your spiritual journey and the way you engage with the world around you.

Engaging in Scripture Study

Engaging in Scripture study is a vital practice for Christian singles seeking to deepen their faith and find fulfillment in everyday life. By immersing themselves in the Word of God, singles can gain clarity on their purpose, strengthen their spiritual disciplines, and cultivate a deeper relationship with Christ. This engagement not only enriches personal spiritual growth but also equips individuals to navigate the complexities of single life with a renewed perspective grounded in biblical truths.

To begin, establishing a consistent routine for Scripture study can provide structure and intentionality in daily life. Setting aside dedicated time each day to read and reflect on the Bible allows singles to create a rhythm that promotes spiritual growth. Whether it is early in the morning or during a quiet evening, finding a time that works best for each individual is key. Utilizing devotionals, study guides, or joining a Bible study group can enhance understanding and foster community among fellow believers, making the experience more enriching.

As singles explore Scripture, it is essential to approach the text with an open heart and a willingness to learn. Reflecting on how the passages relate to their current situations can lead to meaningful insights. Engaging in prayer before and after reading can invite the Holy Spirit to provide wisdom and guidance, transforming the study into a dynamic conversation with God. This practice not only deepens one's understanding of biblical teachings but also encourages singles to apply these lessons to their everyday lives.

Incorporating Scripture into various aspects of life can also enhance the sense of purpose among Christian singles. Memorizing key verses, meditating on them throughout the day, and sharing insights with others can create a deeper connection to the community of faith. Engaging in meaningful conversations about Scripture with friends or in small groups can foster a sense of belonging and support, allowing singles to grow together in their understanding of God's Word and its application to their lives.

Ultimately, engaging in Scripture study helps Christian singles to embrace their unique journey with confidence and joy. By grounding their identity and purpose in biblical truths, they can navigate dating, community involvement, and personal growth with a Christ-centered mindset. As they delve into the richness of Scripture, they will find not only fulfillment in their daily lives but also the tools needed to serve others, build lasting relationships, and live purposefully as they await the next chapter in their lives.

Serving Others: Volunteer Opportunities for Christian Singles

Identifying Your Passions

Identifying your passions is a foundational step for any Christian single seeking to find joy and fulfillment in everyday life. It is essential to recognize that God has uniquely designed each of us with specific interests, talents, and desires that can lead to a purposeful existence. By taking the time to explore what truly excites and motivates you, you can gain a deeper understanding of how to align your daily activities with God's calling in your life. This process often involves reflection, prayer, and a willingness to step outside of your comfort zone.

To begin identifying your passions, consider the activities that bring you joy and satisfaction. Reflection moments when you felt most alive—what were you doing, and who were you with? These experiences can offer valuable clues about what you are passionate about. Additionally, seek feedback from trusted friends or mentors who can provide insight into your strengths and interests. They may recognize talents in you that you might overlook. This collaborative approach can help illuminate your passions and guide you towards opportunities that align with your God-given purpose.

Engaging in spiritual disciplines can further aid in the discovery of your passions. Regular prayer, meditation, and study of Scripture create a space for God to speak into your life. Ask Him to reveal the desires of your heart and how they can be used for His glory. Many Christian singles find that journaling their thoughts and prayers can help clarify their passions over time. As you spend more time in communion with God, you may notice specific themes or interests emerging that resonate deeply with your spirit.

Once you have identified your passions, consider how they can be woven into your daily life and community. Look for opportunities to serve others using your unique gifts and interests. Volunteering at local organizations or participating in church activities can provide a fulfilling. outlet for your passions while allowing you to connect with like-minded individuals. Building a community of purposeful Christian singles not only enhances your journey but also fosters relationships that encourage growth and accountability in your pursuit of fulfillment.

In your pursuit of a purposeful life, remember that identifying your passions is an ongoing journey. As you grow and evolve, so too may your interests. Stay open to new experiences and remain adaptable in your approach. Embrace solitude at times, allowing for reflection and spiritual growth. By taking these steps, you can cultivate a life that is rich in purpose and fulfillment, rooted in your identity as a beloved child of God.

Finding Opportunities to Serve

Finding opportunities to serve as a Christian single can be a transformative experience that not only enriches your own life but also the lives of those around you. It's essential to recognize that service goes beyond traditional volunteer roles; it encompasses everyday actions that reflect Christ's love and purpose. Whether it's through community outreach, church involvement, or simple acts of kindness, each opportunity to serve can help you grow in your faith while fostering a sense of fulfillment in your daily life.

Start by exploring your local church and community organizations. Many churches offer programs specifically designed for singles, providing platforms for service that align with your passions and gifts. These can include outreach initiatives, mentoring programs, or organizing events that support local needs. Engaging with these opportunities allows you to connect with other like-minded individuals who share your faith and desire to make a difference, creating a community of purposeful Christian singles.

Another avenue to find service opportunities is through identifying your unique spiritual gifts. Take time to reflect on your strengths and how they can be utilized to serve others. Whether you have a talent for teaching, hospitality, or encouragement, there are countless ways to apply these gifts in service. This not only helps you find fulfillment but also deepens your understanding of how God has equipped you for His work. As you engage in service, you may discover new passions and insights about your purpose in the present.

In addition to church-related activities, consider how you can serve in your everyday environments. Simple actions, such as helping a neighbor, volunteering at a local shelter, or participating in community clean-up efforts, can have a significant impact. These moments of service not only contribute to the well-being of others but also allow you to experience the joy of giving. It's important to remember that serving doesn't always require a formal setting; often, the most meaningful acts occur in our daily interactions.

Lastly, embracing solitude and spiritual growth can enhance your ability to serve. Taking time for reflection, prayer, and seeking God's guidance can lead to a clearer understanding of where He wants you to make an impact. As you cultivate your relationship with God, you'll find that serving others becomes a natural extension of your faith. This intentional approach to service not only fulfills your purpose as a Christian single but also cultivates a life rich in joy, connection, and meaningful engagement with the world around you.

Navigating Dating with a Purposeful Christian Mindset

Understanding Healthy Relationships

Understanding healthy relationships is vital for Christian singles seeking fulfillment and joy in their everyday lives. Healthy relationships are characterized by mutual respect, open communication, and a shared commitment to growth, both individually and collectively. In the context of Christian singles, it is essential to approach relationships thoughtfully, ensuring that they align with one's faith and purpose. Understanding the foundational aspects of healthy relationships can help individuals navigate their interactions with others, whether they be friendships, family ties, or potential romantic interests.

At the core of any healthy relationship is a strong foundation built on trust and respect. Trust allows individuals to feel safe and secure, fostering an environment where they can express their thoughts and emotions without fear of judgment. Respect ensures that each person values the other's opinions and boundaries. For Christian singles, this means honoring not only their own boundaries but also those of others. By cultivating relationships grounded in these principles, singles can develop connections that encourage personal growth and spiritual development, aligning with their purpose in the present.

Effective communication is another pillar of healthy relationships. It involves not just speaking but also actively listening to others. For Christian singles, this means engaging in meaningful conversations about faith, values, and life experiences. Such discussions can deepen connections and provide opportunities for spiritual growth. By practicing open and honest communication, singles can navigate their relationships with clarity, addressing misunderstandings before they escalate and ensuring that they build a community of support and encouragement.

Healthy relationships also require a commitment to personal and mutual growth. This involves setting goals, both individually and as a part of a community. Christian singles are encouraged to explore their spiritual gifts and find ways to serve others, which not only enhances their own sense of purpose but also strengthens their connections with others. By engaging in volunteer opportunities together or participating in church activities, singles can form bonds that are rooted in shared mission and service, further enriching their lives and the lives of those around them.

Finally, embracing solitude and spiritual growth is crucial for understanding healthy relationships. While it may seem counterintuitive, taking time to reflect and nurture one's spiritual life can lead to healthier interactions with others. In solitude, singles can seek God's guidance and clarity about their relationships, ensuring that they are aligned with His will. This balance of solitude and community helps to create a holistic approach to relationships, allowing Christian singles to enjoy meaningful connections while remaining grounded in their faith and purpose.

Setting Boundaries and Expectations

Setting boundaries and expectations is essential for Christian singles seeking to live a fulfilled life rooted in faith. Boundaries act as protective measures that help maintain one's spiritual and emotional well-being while navigating the complexities of life. Establishing clear limits enables individuals to prioritize their values, ensuring they remain aligned with their purpose as they pursue fulfillment in their daily lives. This practice not only fosters personal integrity but also enhances relationships with others by creating a space where mutual respect and understanding can flourish.

In the context of dating, boundaries play a critical role in promoting healthy interactions. Setting expectations regarding physical intimacy, communication, and time spent together can prevent misunderstandings and misalignments in a relationship. As Christian singles, it is vital to approach dating with a mindset that reflects personal values and aligns with biblical teachings. This intentionality helps singles discern whether a relationship is genuinely nurturing their spiritual growth or detracting from it. By clearly communicating boundaries, individuals can cultivate connections that are both purposeful and enriching.

Moreover, establishing boundaries extends into the realm of community involvement. As Christian singles engage with others, whether through church activities or volunteer opportunities, it is important to recognize personal limits. Engaging in service work can be fulfilling, but overcommitting can lead to burnout and resentment. By setting realistic expectations about time and energy, singles can contribute meaningfully to their communities without compromising their well-being. This balance allows for deeper engagement and more impactful service, fostering a sense of fulfillment that aligns with their Christian values.

Another aspect of setting boundaries is the need for solitude and spiritual growth. In a world filled with distractions, creating intentional space for solitude can enhance one's relationship with God. Boundaries around social engagements and technology use can facilitate deeper prayer, reflection, and study of Scripture. This practice nurtures a robust spiritual discipline, allowing singles to explore their gifts and calling more fully. By prioritizing time alone with God, individuals can gain clarity on their purpose and cultivate a joy that transcends their circumstances.

Ultimately, setting boundaries and expectations helps Christian singles navigate their unique journeys with intention and grace. By creating a framework that supports spiritual growth, purposeful living, and meaningful relationships, individuals can embrace their single status as an opportunity for development rather than a deficiency. This perspective allows for the exploration of gifts and passions, fostering a vibrant community of like-minded individuals who encourage and uplift one another. In doing so, singles can find joy in the everyday and cultivate a life marked by fulfillment and freedom in Christ.

Embracing Solitude and Spiritual Growth

The Beauty of Solitude

The experience of solitude can often be misunderstood, especially in a world that champions constant connectivity and social interaction. For Christian singles, solitude is not merely the absence of companionship; it is an opportunity for profound personal growth and spiritual deepening. Embracing solitude allows individuals to cultivate a deeper relationship with God, providing a sacred space to reflect, pray, and listen for His guidance. This intentional time alone can lead to a greater understanding of one's purpose and calling, fostering fulfillment in the present moment.

In solitude, one can engage in self-reflection, which is vital for spiritual development. This process encourages singles to examine their thoughts, feelings, and motivations, aligning them with God's will. As they create a routine that incorporates time for prayer and meditation, they begin to discern their spiritual gifts and how these can be utilized in their daily lives. This practice of reflection and prayer not only enhances their connection to God but also refines their sense of identity and purpose as a Christian single.

Moreover, solitude provides the necessary space to serve others effectively. When individuals take time to recharge and reconnect with their inner selves, they are better equipped to engage in community service and volunteer opportunities. By understanding their gifts and passions, they can identify where they can make the most impact. This fulfillment derived from serving others contributes to a sense of belonging and purpose, reinforcing the belief that their single status does not limit their ability to contribute meaningfully to the lives of others.

Creating a community of like-minded Christian singles is also essential for growth during solitary moments. While solitude is a personal journey, it can be enriched by sharing experiences and insights with others on a similar path. Engaging in meaningful conversations about faith and purpose allows singles to inspire and uplift one another. Together, they can explore the depths of their spiritual journeys, fostering an environment where they can grow in their faith and celebrate the beauty of their individual paths.

Ultimately, the beauty of solitude lies in its potential to transform the lives of Christian singles. By embracing this time alone, they can cultivate a deeper relationship with God, serve others more effectively, and develop a supportive community. As they navigate their journeys with purpose and intentionality, solitude becomes a powerful ally in their quest for fulfillment and joy in everyday life. In this way, solitude is not a destination but a vibrant part of the journey toward a meaningful Christian life, rich with purpose and spiritual growth.

Using Alone Time for Reflection

Using alone time for reflection can be a powerful practice for Christian singles seeking to find fulfillment and purpose in their daily lives. In a society that often glorifies busyness and constant interaction, carving out time for solitude can feel countercultural, yet it is within this quiet space that we can engage deeply with our thoughts, emotions, and faith. Reflecting alone allows individuals to step back from the noise of everyday life and consider their personal relationship with God, their aspirations, and how they can live out their faith in practical ways. This intentional practice can lead to greater self-awareness and clarity regarding one's purpose.

Engaging in reflection offers an opportunity for spiritual growth, allowing singles to reconnect with their faith and explore how it informs their daily choices. As they spend time in solitude, individuals can meditate on scripture, pray, and listen for God's guidance. This practice can help clarify one's spiritual gifts and how they can be utilized in serving others, whether through volunteer opportunities or community engagement. By understanding their unique contributions, singles can cultivate a sense of belonging and purpose within a larger faith community.

Creating a routine that includes regular alone time can greatly enhance one's ability to re ect meaningfully. Setting aside specific moments each week to engage in solitude—whether through journaling, prayer walks, or quiet contemplation—can help establish a rhythm that prioritizes personal spiritual development. During these moments, individuals can examine their goals and aspirations, aligning them with their values as Christians. This alignment not only fosters a sense of fulfillment but also encourages singles to pursue their aspirations with a purpose-driven mindset.

Furthermore, reflection can illuminate areas for personal growth and development, which are crucial for navigating the complexities of dating and relationships. By understanding their own desires and boundaries through reflection, singles can approach dating with intention, seeking partnerships that align with their faith and values. This proactive mindset allows individuals to build relationships that are not only meaningful but also rooted in a shared commitment to growth and purpose.

Ultimately, using alone time for reflection empowers Christian singles to embrace their unique journeys with confidence. It creates space for individuals to explore their identity, deepen their faith, and foster connections within a community of like-minded believers. By prioritizing solitude and reflection, singles can cultivate a fulfilling life that honors their relationship with God while navigating the joys and challenges of singlehood with purpose and hope.

Purposeful Living: Setting Goals as a Christian Single

Defining Personal Goals

Defining personal goals is a crucial step for Christian singles seeking to find fulfillment and purpose in their lives. Setting specific, measurable, achievable, relevant, and time-bound (SMART) goals allows individuals to align their daily activities with their faith and values. This process begins with self-reflection, where one assesses their passions, interests, and the unique gifts God has bestowed upon them. By understanding personal strengths and weaknesses, singles can create goals that resonate with their identity in Christ, fostering a sense of direction and clarity in their lives.

In the context of Christian singles, personal goals can encompass various aspects of life, including spiritual growth, community engagement, and personal development. For instance, a single Christian may set a goal to deepen their relationship with God through daily scripture reading and prayer. This goal not only enhances their spiritual discipline but also encourages a more profound connection with their faith. Additionally, establishing goals related to community involvement, such as volunteering at a local church or participating in group activities, can create opportunities for meaningful relationships and a sense of belonging.

Moreover, the pursuit of personal goals should be rooted in the understanding of God's purpose for one's life. It is essential to seek divine guidance in goal-setting, ensuring that aspirations align with God's will. This can be achieved through prayer and meditation, allowing individuals to discern their path and identify goals that reflect their spiritual journey. When personal goals are established in this way, they serve as a roadmap for navigating life's challenges and opportunities, reinforcing a sense of hope and motivation.

Building a community of like-minded Christian singles can also enhance the goal-setting process. By connecting with others who share similar aspirations, individuals can encourage and support one another in their pursuits. Group discussions, accountability partnerships, and shared experiences can provide valuable insights and foster a sense of camaraderie. Engaging in meaningful conversations about faith and personal goals can spark inspiration and creativity, leading to a more fulfilling single life grounded in purpose.

Ultimately, defining personal goals is a dynamic and ongoing process that evolves as individuals grow in their faith and experiences. It requires a willingness to adapt and re ne aspirations based on new insights and circumstances. As singles navigate their journey, prioritizing flexibility and openness to change helps them remain aligned with God's purpose. By committing to this practice,

Christian singles can cultivate a life filled with joy, fulfillment, and a deeper understanding of their unique role in God's kingdom.

Aligning Goals with Faith

Aligning goals with faith is essential for Christian singles who seek to navigate their lives with purpose and fulfillment. As individuals striving to live a life that reflects their beliefs, it is crucial to ensure that personal aspirations resonate with the teachings of Christ. By connecting daily goals to spiritual values, singles can cultivate a sense of direction that not only enhances their personal growth but also deepens their relationship with God. This alignment encourages individuals to reflect on their motivations and the impact their choices have on their spiritual journey.

To begin this process, it is important to establish a clear understanding of what faith means in the context of personal aspirations. Christian singles should take time to pray, study scripture, and contemplate their values and priorities. This introspection helps clarify how goals can be shaped by biblical principles, allowing individuals to evaluate their desires against the backdrop of their faith. For example, aspirations related to career, relationships, and community involvement can all be examined through the lens of service, love, and stewardship, which are central tenets of Christianity.

As singles set their goals, they should consider the role of community support in this endeavor. Engaging with other purposeful Christian singles can provide encouragement and accountability. By sharing experiences, insights, and challenges, individuals can foster an environment where collective growth is prioritized. Participating in group activities such as Bible studies, volunteering, or social gatherings can help reinforce the idea that faith and goals are not solitary pursuits but are best cultivated in a community that reflects shared values.

Moreover, developing spiritual disciplines can greatly enhance the alignment of goals with faith. Establishing a routine that includes prayer, meditation, and scripture reading can provide a strong foundation for discerning God's will in personal aspirations. These practices encourage individuals to remain attentive to the Holy Spirit's guidance while pursuing their objectives. As spiritual disciplines become a regular part of daily life, it becomes easier to recognize how God may be leading one's goals toward fulfilling a greater purpose.

Finally, serving others is a powerful way to align personal ambitions with faith. By seeking opportunities to volunteer and support those in need, Christian singles can put their values into action. These acts of service not only contribute to the well-being of others but also create a sense of fulfillment and joy that comes from living out one's faith. Engaging in service can help singles discover their spiritual gifts and passions, further enhancing their clarity around goals and purpose. Through this journey of aligning goals with faith, singles can experience a richer, more meaningful life that reflects their commitment to Christ.

Exploring Spiritual Gifts and Their Impact on Single Life

Identifying Your Spiritual Gifts

Identifying your spiritual gifts is a crucial step in understanding your unique purpose as a Christian single. Each individual is endowed with specific talents and abilities designed to serve God and others in meaningful ways. To discern these gifts, begin by reflecting on your experiences and passions. Consider the activities that energize you and bring you joy. Are there particular tasks that you find yourself naturally inclined to? Often, our spiritual gifts align closely with what we love to do, providing clues to how we can contribute to our communities and the Body of Christ.

Engaging in self-assessment tools can also aid in identifying your spiritual gifts. Many churches and Christian organizations offer spiritual gift inventories that prompt you to consider your interests, skills, and experiences. These assessments are designed to highlight areas where you may excel and feel fulfilled. However, while these tools are helpful, they should not replace prayer and reflection. Seeking God's guidance through prayer can reveal insights about your gifts that may not be immediately apparent. Ask God to show you how He has uniquely equipped you to serve others and glorify Him.

Another important aspect of identifying your spiritual gifts is seeking feedback from others. Trusted friends, mentors, or leaders within your church can offer valuable perspectives on your strengths. They may have observed qualities in you that you might not recognize in yourself. Engaging in conversations about your experiences and asking for constructive feedback can illuminate your spiritual gifts further. This communal aspect of discovery is important, as it emphasizes the role of the Christian community in supporting one another in our spiritual journeys.

As you identify your gifts, consider how they can be integrated into your daily life. Living with purpose as a Christian single means finding opportunities to serve in your community, whether through volunteering, joining a ministry, or simply being available to help those around you. Your spiritual gifts may lead you to unexpected avenues of service that not only bless others but also provide you with fulfillment and joy. Embrace these opportunities as a way to express your faith and contribute to the world, all while deepening your relationship with God.

Ultimately, identifying your spiritual gifts is about more than personal fulfillment; it's about building a community of purposeful Christian singles who encourage and uplift one another. As you embrace your unique gifts, you create connections that foster spiritual growth and collective service. This journey can lead to meaningful friendships and deeper relationships grounded in shared faith and purpose. By actively engaging with your spiritual gifts, you not only fulfill your calling but also inspire those around you to discover and embrace their own.

Using Your Gifts in Everyday Life

Using your gifts in everyday life as a Christian single is an essential aspect of embracing fulfillment and joy. Each person is endowed with unique talents and abilities, often referred to as spiritual gifts. Recognizing and utilizing these gifts in daily interactions can transform not only your own life but also the lives of those around you. Whether it's the gift of encouragement, service, teaching, or hospitality, understanding how to apply these gifts allows for purposeful living that honors God and enriches community.

The first step in using your gifts is self-awareness. Take time to reflect on what you are passionate about and where your strengths lie. This can involve prayer, journaling, or seeking feedback from trusted friends or mentors. As you identify your spiritual gifts, consider how they align with your daily activities. For example, if you find joy in helping others, you might explore volunteer opportunities at local charities or churches. By actively engaging in service, you not only fulfill your calling but also build connections with other singles who share your passion for community.

Creating a routine that incorporates your gifts can lead to a more fulfilling daily life. Establishing a Christ-centered schedule allows you to prioritize time for service, prayer, and personal growth. Set specific goals that reflect your gifts and make a plan to pursue them regularly. Whether it's dedicating an hour each week to mentor someone or organizing a small group for prayer and discussion, these intentional actions can foster a sense of purpose and belonging. Engaging in meaningful activities deepens your faith and invites opportunities for divine encounters.

Moreover, building a community of like-minded Christians can amplify the impact of your gifts. Seek out groups or events where you can share your talents and collaborate with others on projects that serve the greater good. This could involve joining a church ministry, participating in a book club focused on spiritual growth, or attending workshops that enhance your skills. Through these interactions, you'll not only contribute to a shared mission but also cultivate friendships that encourage and uplift one another on your spiritual journeys.

Finally, embracing solitude is vital for spiritual growth and understanding how best to use your gifts. Taking time for reflection and connection with God helps clarify your purpose and enriches your ability to serve others. Through prayer and meditation, you can gain insights into how to navigate relationships and opportunities with a purposeful mindset. Ultimately, using your gifts in everyday life as a Christian single is not just about personal fulfillment; it's about creating a ripple effect of joy and purpose that touches lives far beyond your own.

Creating a Christ-centered Routine for Daily Purpose

Structuring Your Day with Intent

Structuring your day with intent is a vital practice for Christian singles seeking fulfillment and purpose in their daily lives. Creating a daily framework not only maximizes productivity but also aligns your activities with your spiritual goals. Begin by understanding that each day is a gift from God, offering opportunities for growth, connection, and service. By intentionally designing your day around your values and faith, you can cultivate a routine that reflects your commitment to living a purposeful life.

The first step in structuring your day is identifying your priorities. Reflect on what matters most to you as a Christian single. This could include spiritual disciplines such as prayer, Bible study, or meditation, as well as personal goals, community involvement, and relationships. Writing down these priorities helps to create a clear roadmap for your day. By establishing a hierarchy of tasks, you can ensure that you focus on what truly nurtures your spirit and supports your journey of faith.

Incorporating spiritual disciplines into your daily routine is essential for spiritual growth. Consider setting aside dedicated time each morning for prayer and scripture reading. This practice not only centers your thoughts but also sets a positive tone for the day ahead. Throughout the day, be mindful of incorporating brief moments of reflection or gratitude. These small acts can help you stay connected to your faith and remind you of your purpose, even amid a busy schedule.

Building a community of like-minded Christian singles is another critical aspect of structuring your day with intent. Make it a priority to engage with fellow believers through regular meetups, Bible studies, or volunteer opportunities. Surrounding yourself with others who share your values will provide encouragement and accountability. You might also consider integrating social activities into your routine that foster meaningful conversations about faith, allowing you to explore various perspectives and deepen your understanding of God's purpose in your life.

Finally, remember that serving others is a powerful way to find fulfillment. Look for volunteer opportunities within your community where you can contribute your time and talents. Whether it's mentoring younger singles, participating in church outreach programs, or helping at local shelters, these acts of service can enrich your life and provide a sense of belonging. As you structure your day around these intentional activities, you'll likely find a deeper joy and satisfaction that comes from living out your faith in practical and meaningful ways.

Incorporating Faith into Daily Activities

Incorporating faith into daily activities is a vital practice for Christian singles seeking to find joy and purpose in their everyday lives. This integration begins with the simple act of prayer. Taking a few moments each morning to connect with God through prayer allows individuals to set a spiritual tone for the day. This can be as structured as a set prayer or as spontaneous as speaking from the heart. Mindfully acknowledging God's presence in daily life can transform mundane tasks into opportunities for spiritual reflection and growth.

Another essential aspect of this incorporation is the practice of scripture reading. Dedicating time each day to read the Bible not only enhances understanding of God's word but also provides guidance and encouragement. By selecting a verse or passage that resonates, Christian singles can meditate on its meaning throughout the day. This practice can be woven into routines, such as during a lunch break or while commuting, allowing for deeper engagement with faith amidst a busy lifestyle.

Moreover, integrating faith into daily activities also involves creating a Christ-centered routine. This can include setting aside specific times for worship, whether through attending church services, participating in small groups, or engaging in personal devotionals. By establishing these routines, individuals cultivate a rhythm that prioritizes their spiritual well-being. Such intentionality not only nurtures personal faith but can also serve as a beacon for others, encouraging them to explore their own spiritual journeys.

Serving others is another powerful way to incorporate faith into daily life. Christian singles can seek out volunteer opportunities within their communities, allowing their faith to manifest through acts of kindness and service. Whether it's helping at a local food bank, mentoring youth, or participating in community clean-up efforts, these activities not only fulfill the call to serve but also provide a sense of belonging and purpose. Engaging in service fosters connections with others, creating a community of purposeful Christian singles who share similar values and goals.

Finally, embracing solitude can enhance the incorporation of faith into daily activities. Taking time for personal reflection allows individuals to deepen their spiritual lives and gain clarity on their purpose. Whether through journaling, nature walks, or quiet contemplation, solitude provides the space to listen for God's guidance. This practice encourages a profound understanding of one's spiritual gifts and how they can be utilized in daily life. By embracing both communal and solitary experiences, Christian singles can find fulfillment and joy in their everyday endeavors, rooted in their faith.

Engaging in Meaningful Conversations about Faith as a Single

Starting Conversations on Spiritual Topics

Starting conversations on spiritual topics can feel daunting for many Christian singles, yet these discussions are essential for deepening one's faith and building a supportive community. Engaging with others about spirituality provides an opportunity to explore shared beliefs, question doubts, and strengthen relationships. By initiating dialogues about faith, singles can foster connections that are not only meaningful but also purposeful, allowing everyone involved to grow together in their spiritual journeys.

One effective way to start these conversations is by sharing personal experiences related to faith. This could involve discussing a recent sermon that resonated, a book that has influenced spiritual growth, or even a challenge faced in one's walk with God. Such personal anecdotes can serve as a bridge to deeper discussions, encouraging others to share their own stories and insights. By creating a safe space where vulnerability is welcomed, singles can cultivate an environment rich in mutual understanding and support.

Another approach is to ask open-ended questions that invite reflection and dialogue. Questions like, "How do you see God's presence in your daily life?" or "What spiritual practices help you stay grounded in your faith?" can prompt thoughtful responses. These inquiries not only encourage others to think critically about their spirituality but also reveal diverse perspectives that can enhance one's understanding of faith. Engaging in this manner fosters a sense of community among singles, as they collectively navigate their spiritual paths.

In addition to personal sharing and questioning, utilizing resources like Bible studies or faith-based book clubs can facilitate deeper discussions. These structured environments provide a framework for meaningful conversations, allowing singles to explore spiritual topics in a focused setting. By studying scripture together or discussing Christian literature, participants can examine their beliefs and experiences in light of God's Word, thereby enriching their spiritual lives and strengthening their bonds with one another.

Finally, it's important to approach these conversations with an open heart and mind. Recognizing that everyone's journey is unique encourages respect for differing viewpoints and experiences. By being receptive to others' insights and willing to share one's own, Christian singles can create a dynamic of mutual growth and support. Embracing these conversations as opportunities for learning and connection can lead to a more fulfilling Christian single life, one grounded in purpose and community.

Building Deeper Connections through Faith Discussions

Building deeper connections through faith discussions can significantly enrich the lives of Christian singles, fostering a sense of community and belonging. Engaging in conversations about faith allows individuals to share their experiences and beliefs, creating an environment where vulnerability and honesty thrive. This openness not only strengthens existing relationships but also paves the way for new friendships rooted in shared values and spiritual growth. Through these discussions, singles can find encouragement and support as they navigate their unique journeys, ensuring they feel less isolated in their walk with God.

Faith discussions can also serve as a catalyst for personal growth and understanding. By exploring diverse perspectives within the Christian faith, singles can deepen their knowledge and appreciation for Scripture, theology, and Christian living. Engaging with others in meaningful conversations encourages critical thinking and reflection, prompting individuals to examine their beliefs and practices. This process can lead to a more profound faith experience, empowering singles to articulate their beliefs confidently and share their insights with others, thereby enhancing their spiritual journeys.

Moreover, these discussions can provide practical applications of faith in everyday life. Christian singles often seek ways to integrate their beliefs into their daily routines, and conversations centered around faith can reveal actionable steps to do just that. Whether discussing how to approach challenges at work, navigate dating with intention, or serve the community, these dialogues can offer valuable advice and inspiration. By exchanging ideas and strategies, singles can learn from each other's successes and setbacks, fostering a spirit of collaboration that enhances their collective journey.

In addition to personal growth, faith discussions can help build a supportive community among Christian singles. Establishing connections with like-minded individuals creates a network of support that can be invaluable during times of struggle or uncertainty. When singles come together to discuss their faith, they create an atmosphere of mutual encouragement, allowing them to celebrate victories and navigate challenges as a united front. This sense of community can lead to lasting friendships that provide both emotional support and spiritual accountability, essential components of a fulfilling single life.

Finally, engaging in faith discussions encourages singles to develop and utilize their spiritual gifts. As individuals share their insights and experiences, they often uncover unique talents and passions that can be used for service within the church and the broader community. By identifying and cultivating these gifts through collaboration and discussion, Christian singles can find purpose and fulfillment in their lives. Ultimately, building deeper connections through faith discussions not only enriches personal relationships but also enhances the overall experience of being a Christian single, fostering a life filled with joy, purpose, and community.

Chapter 3

Positioned by Purpose: Discovering God's Plan for Your Life

Understanding Your Divine Position

The Concept of Purpose in a Christian Context

The concept of purpose in a Christian context is deeply intertwined with the belief that God has a unique plan for each individual. For Christian singles, understanding this purpose can be a source of strength and direction, especially during times of transition or uncertainty. The Bible emphasizes that every person is created with intention, as seen in Jeremiah 29:11, where God declares His plans for prosperity and hope. This assurance provides a foundation for singles to explore their spiritual purpose, recognizing that they are not merely waiting for a partner but are actively engaged in fulfilling God's calling in their lives.

As singles navigate their personal growth, the pursuit of purpose often leads to self- discovery. This journey involves identifying individual gifts and talents that God has bestowed upon them. Each person possesses unique abilities and passions that can be harnessed to serve others and contribute to the community. By engaging in activities that align with their gifts, singles can experience a profound sense of fulfillment and connection to their divine purpose. This exploration not only enhances personal growth but also prepares individuals for future relationships, as they become more grounded in their identity and faith.

Faith-based career development is another significant aspect of understanding purpose in a Christian context. Singles often grapple with the intersection of their professional lives and spiritual calling. By seeking God's guidance in their career choices, they can align their work with their faith, finding opportunities that reflect their values and contribute to the greater good. This alignment fosters a sense of fulfillment, as individuals recognize their work as a form of ministry. Embracing a purpose-driven career can lead to greater satisfaction and a deeper understanding of how their professional lives fit into God's overarching plan.

Divine timing plays a crucial role in the life of a single Christian. Understanding that God orchestrates events and relationships in His perfect timing can alleviate feelings of anxiety or impatience. Each season of life brings its own lessons and opportunities for growth, and recognizing this can help singles embrace their current circumstances. Whether facing challenges or celebrating victories, acknowledging God's timing encourages individuals to trust in His plan, knowing that their purpose will unfold as they remain faithful. This perspective shifts the focus from a narrow view of purpose to a broader understanding of life's journey.

Finding meaning in adversity is a vital component of living a purposeful life. Challenges often serve as catalysts for growth, teaching resilience and deepening faith. For Christian singles, these experiences can illuminate aspects of their purpose that might not have been apparent otherwise. By seeking spiritual guidance during difficult times, individuals can glean insights that strengthen their character and clarify their mission. Sharing these stories of overcoming adversity within a community of believers fosters connection and encouragement, reminding everyone that they are not alone in their journey. Ultimately, a life centered on purpose and faith can transform challenges into opportunities for deeper engagement with God and His plans.

Recognizing Your Unique Place in God's Plan

Recognizing your unique place in God's plan begins with understanding that you are strategically positioned at this moment in your life for a specific reason. As a Christian single, it is vital to see your current state not as a period of lack or incompleteness, but as a season brimming with opportunities for spiritual growth and personal development. God has intentionally placed you where you are to equip you for the next steps in your journey. Embracing this perspective can transform feelings of isolation or uncertainty into a sense of purpose and belonging within His will.

In the realm of spiritual purpose and personal growth, acknowledging your unique place allows you to cultivate your individual gifts and talents. Each person is endowed with specific abilities that contribute to the body of Christ. These gifts are not only for personal fulfillment but are also meant to serve others and fulfill the greater mission of the Church. Engaging in self-discovery through prayer, worship, reflection, and community involvement can help illuminate your strengths. As you explore your capabilities, you begin to see how they align with God's purposes, empowering you to take confident steps forward in your faith journey.

Faith-based career development also plays a crucial role in recognizing your place in God's plan. Your professional path can be an extension of your spiritual journey, where your work becomes a platform for ministry. By seeking God's wisdom for your career decisions, you can find meaningful ways to integrate your faith with your professional aspirations. Understanding that your vocation is a calling can bring clarity and motivation, allowing you to navigate challenges while remaining anchored in your purpose. This alignment between faith and work encourages you to view your career as an avenue for expressing your God-given talents and contributing positively to the world around you.

God's timing and life transitions often present challenges that can lead to feelings of confusion or frustration. However, recognizing that every season of life serves a purpose can help you navigate these changes with grace. Trusting in God's timing allows you to embrace the lessons that come with each transition, whether it's moving to a new city, embarking on a new job, or shifting your focus in relationships. Each step is a part of His plan, designed to refine you and prepare you for what lies ahead. Fostering patience and faith during these periods can deepen your reliance on God and enhance your understanding of His greater purpose for your life.

Finding meaning in adversity is another essential aspect of recognizing your unique place in God's plan. Difficult experiences can serve as profound opportunities for growth and development, shaping your character and faith in ways that comfort and success cannot. By leaning into God's promises during tough times, you can discover resilience and strength that might otherwise remain hidden. Alongside this, building community through shared purpose can offer encouragement and support, reminding you that you are not alone in your journey. Sharing your story with others can not only inspire them but also reinforce your own understanding of how each piece of your life contributes to a larger narrative crafted by God.

The Journey of Spiritual Growth

Foundations of Faith and Personal Development

Foundations of faith serve as the bedrock for personal development, particularly for Christian singles navigating their unique journeys. Understanding that you have been strategically positioned by God instills a sense of purpose and direction. Each individual is called to explore their faith deeply, allowing it to inform their decisions and actions. This exploration is essential for personal growth, as it encourages you to seek God's guidance and wisdom in every aspect of your life, from relationships to career choices. By fostering a strong foundation in faith, you empower yourself to embrace the challenges and opportunities that come your way.

Spiritual purpose is intricately linked to personal growth. As you delve into your faith, you begin to uncover your individual gifts and talents. Each person possesses unique abilities that are meant to be utilized in service to others and in fulfillment of God's plan. For Christian singles, this discovery phase can be particularly transformative. It encourages introspection and self-awareness, allowing you to align your aspirations with God's vision for your life. Embracing your spiritual purpose not only enhances your personal development but also prepares you for future relationships, as you become more attuned to what you can offer and what you seek in a partner.

Faith-based career development is another critical aspect of advancing in life while remaining rooted in your beliefs. As you navigate your professional journey, it's vital to remember that your work can be an extension of your faith. Seeking positions that allow you to express your values and contribute positively to society can lead to greater job satisfaction and fulfillment. For Christian singles, this pursuit can be particularly enriching, as it opens doors to meet like-minded individuals who share similar goals and values. By integrating your faith with your career choices, you can create a life that reflects your beliefs while also achieving personal and professional success.

God's timing plays a significant role in life transitions, especially for those who may feel pressure to achieve certain milestones by societal standards. Understanding that God's timing is perfect can alleviate the anxiety often associated with being single. Embracing this concept encourages patience and trust in God's plan, allowing you to focus on personal development rather than societal expectations. Each phase of life, whether marked by waiting or action, has its purpose. By recognizing this divine orchestration, you can find peace and clarity during times of uncertainty, ultimately leading to a more purposeful existence.

Lastly, finding meaning in adversity is a crucial lesson in building a faith-centered life. Challenges often lead to personal growth and a deeper understanding of God's love and grace. As Christian singles face various life obstacles—whether in relationships, careers, or personal circumstances—these experiences can serve as catalysts for spiritual maturity. By leaning on your faith during tough times, you can cultivate resilience and wisdom. Additionally, sharing your stories of faith and purpose with others fosters a sense of community, reminding you that you are not alone in your journey. This collective strength can inspire and uplift, reinforcing the importance of living purposefully through faith.

Embracing Change as a Catalyst for Growth

Embracing change is often perceived as a daunting challenge, especially for Christian singles who may find themselves navigating the uncertainties of life alone. However, it is essential to recognize that change is not merely a disruptor but a catalyst for growth and transformation. In the context of faith-based living, understanding this principle can significantly alter how one perceives life transitions. God strategically places us in various situations to fulfill His divine purpose, and each change we face is an opportunity to align more closely with that purpose.

As you embark on your journey of personal growth, consider the role of divine timing in the changes you encounter. Each stage of life brings unique challenges and opportunities that are essential for spiritual development. The Bible tells us that there is a time for everything, and this includes seasons of transition. When you embrace these seasons, you open yourself up to God's guidance and the potential for profound personal and spiritual growth. Trusting in God's plan during these times can strengthen your faith and help you navigate life's challenges with grace and resilience.

In periods of adversity, finding meaning becomes crucial. Change can often lead to feelings of uncertainty or despair, but it is vital to seek God's purpose even in difficult circumstances. Inspirational stories of faith often highlight how individuals have transformed their adversities into opportunities for growth, helping them discover their unique gifts and talents. By reflecting on these experiences and recognizing that God can bring beauty from ashes, you can cultivate a mindset that embraces change as a necessary part of your journey toward fulfilling His plan for your life.

Additionally, building community through shared purpose can significantly enhance your experience of embracing change. Surrounding yourself with fellow believers who understand the importance of growth and transition can provide support and encouragement. These relationships can foster an environment where you can share your struggles and victories, allowing you to grow together in faith. Engaging with a community that values purpose-driven living can inspire you to step out of your comfort zone and embrace the changes that God orchestrates in your life.

Ultimately, embracing change requires a shift in perspective—seeing it not as a threat but as an opportunity to deepen your relationship with God. Each transition is a chance to reflect on your journey, reassess your goals, and seek His guidance for the future. As you learn to navigate life's challenges with spiritual insight, you will find that change, when aligned with God's plan, becomes a powerful tool for personal growth and purposefulness. By trusting in His timing and embracing the transformative power of change, you can live a life that is not only fulfilling but also deeply aligned with your God-given purpose.

Faith-Based Career Development

Aligning Career Choices with God's Will

Aligning career choices with God's will is a journey of faith that requires intentional reflection and discernment. For Christian singles, this process can be particularly meaningful as they navigate the complexities of career development while seeking to fulfill their spiritual purpose.

Understanding that God has strategically positioned each individual for a unique role in His grand design can offer clarity and motivation. By embracing the belief that their careers can be a reflection of God's will, singles can find not only direction but also a deeper sense of fulfillment.

One of the first steps in aligning career choices with God's will involves prayerful consideration of one's individual gifts and talents. Each person has been uniquely created with specific abilities that contribute to the greater good. By taking time to reflect on these gifts, Christian singles can identify career paths that not only resonate with their skills but also align with their spiritual values. This alignment fosters a sense of purpose, allowing individuals to become instruments of God's love and service in their workplaces and communities.

Additionally, understanding God's plan often requires acknowledging the importance of divine timing. Many singles may feel pressure to make quick career decisions, but trusting in God's timing can lead to opportunities that are more aligned with His will. Life transitions, such as job changes or new ventures, can serve as moments for spiritual growth and reflection. By waiting on the Lord and seeking His guidance, individuals can gain confidence that their career choices are part of a larger narrative crafted by God.

Navigating life's challenges through spiritual guidance is also essential in this pursuit. Adversity can often lead to doubt or confusion about one's career path; however, it can also serve as a powerful catalyst for growth. Embracing challenges with a faith-based perspective allows singles to learn valuable lessons and develop resilience. Sharing these experiences within a supportive community can provide encouragement and accountability, creating a network of individuals who are committed to living out their God-given purposes.

Ultimately, aligning career choices with God's will is an ongoing journey of discovery and growth. Christian singles are encouraged to remain open to the leading of the Holy Spirit, seeking opportunities where their faith and professional aspirations intersect. By actively engaging in a life that reflects God's purpose, individuals not only enhance their personal growth but also contribute positively to the world around them. This alignment not only brings individual fulfillment but also encourages a collective movement toward a life lived in accordance with divine purpose.

Identifying Opportunities for Service in the Workplace

Identifying opportunities for service in the workplace can be a transformative experience, particularly for Christian singles who are navigating their professional lives with a sense of purpose. Each workplace, regardless of its nature, is filled with potential for acts of service that not only benefit others but also align with God's plan for your life. Recognizing these opportunities begins with a mindset that seeks to serve rather than simply fulfill personal aspirations. Look for ways to contribute to the well-being of your colleagues, whether through acts of kindness, sharing wisdom, or offering support during challenging times.

One of the most effective ways to identify service opportunities is by paying attention to the needs around you. This requires active listening and observation. Colleagues may express struggles, whether related to workload, personal issues, or even spiritual questions. By being attuned to these needs, you can step in with assistance, encouragement, or a listening ear. Such actions not only demonstrate the love of Christ in a tangible way but also help foster an environment of support and community within your workplace.

Additionally, consider your unique gifts and talents as divine tools for service. God has equipped each of us with specific abilities and passions that can be utilized to uplift others. Take time to reflect on what you excel at and how those skills can be shared. Whether it's organizing events, mentoring a colleague, or initiating a prayer group, these activities can create meaningful connections and promote a culture of purpose- driven service. By leveraging your individual strengths, you not only serve others but also grow personally and spiritually.

Another critical aspect of identifying service opportunities is understanding the significance of divine timing. Life transitions, whether they involve promotions, changes in roles, or new projects, often open doors for service that may not have been visible before. Embrace these transitions as moments orchestrated by God, allowing you to step into roles that facilitate growth for both yourself and your coworkers. Being receptive to these changes can help you recognize when to lead initiatives or offer support in new ways, aligning your actions with God's timing.

Lastly, finding meaning in adversity can lead to profound opportunities for service. Challenges faced by yourself or your colleagues can often serve as a catalyst for compassion and understanding. When you navigate difficulties with faith, you not only strengthen your relationship with God but also become a beacon of hope for others. Sharing your experiences and how you have relied on faith during tough times can inspire those around you, creating a ripple effect of encouragement and service. By identifying these moments as opportunities, you fulfill your purpose while positively impacting the lives of those in your workplace.

The Importance of God's Timing

Trusting God's Timing in Life Transitions

Trusting God's timing in life transitions is a profound aspect of the Christian journey, particularly for singles navigating the complexities of relationships, careers, and personal growth. In a culture that often emphasizes immediate gratification and quick results, it can be challenging to embrace the waiting periods that God sometimes places in our lives. However, understanding that these times of transition are orchestrated by divine purpose allows us to cultivate patience and faith. Recognizing that God has strategically positioned us where we are for a reason gives us the confidence to trust in His plan, even when we cannot see the full picture.

As we experience various life transitions—whether it be moving to a new city, changing jobs, or contemplating new relationships—it's essential to reflect on the lessons these moments can teach us. Each transition serves as an opportunity for spiritual growth, pushing us to rely more deeply on our faith. When we are mindful of God's presence during these shifts, we can better discern how He is working in our lives. By focusing on our personal development and understanding our individual gifts and talents, we can use these transitions as a stepping stone toward fulfilling our God-given purpose.

Moreover, trusting in God's timing helps us navigate the uncertainty that often accompanies life changes. It can be easy to feel anxious or disheartened when things do not unfold as we envisioned.

However, Scripture reminds us that God's ways are higher than our ways, and His timing is perfect. Embracing this truth allows us to remain hopeful and expectant, knowing that the challenges we face are part of a greater plan. In moments of doubt, prayer and meditation can strengthen our resolve and remind us of God's faithfulness throughout history, encouraging us to lean into His guidance.

Building a supportive community can also play a crucial role in trusting God's timing. Connecting with fellow believers who share similar experiences can provide encouragement and reassurance during life transitions. Sharing our stories and challenges fosters a sense of belonging and reminds us that we are not alone in our journeys. Through fellowship, we can find inspiration in each other's faith stories, reinforcing the idea that God is actively working in our lives, even if we cannot always see it.

Ultimately, trusting God's timing in life transitions is about surrendering our plans and expectations to Him. It is an invitation to live purposefully, embracing each moment as part of a divine narrative. As Christian singles, recognizing that we are positioned by God for a unique purpose empowers us to approach life transitions with hope and anticipation. By remaining steadfast in faith, we can navigate the complexities of life with confidence, knowing that God is guiding us every step of the way toward our destined purpose.

Preparing for Change: A Spiritual Perspective

Preparing for change can often evoke feelings of uncertainty and anxiety, especially for Christian singles navigating the complexities of life transitions. However, viewing these changes through a spiritual lens can transform our understanding and approach. From a spiritual perspective, change is not merely a disruption; it is an integral part of God's divine plan for our lives. Embracing this concept allows individuals to recognize that every shift, whether anticipated or unexpected, serves a higher purpose in their journey toward fulfilling their God-given potential.

In this context, spiritual preparation for change involves cultivating a deeper relationship with God. Prayer and reflection become essential tools in seeking guidance and clarity. By engaging in regular communication with God, individuals can discern His voice amidst the noise of everyday life. This practice not only strengthens faith but also helps to foster an environment where one can receive divine wisdom on navigating the challenges that come with change. When faced with uncertainty, turning to scripture can provide reassurance, as many biblical narratives illustrate how God's people experienced transformations that ultimately led to greater fulfillment of His purpose.

Recognizing God's timing is another vital aspect of preparing for change. In the Christian faith, it is often emphasized that there is a season for everything, as articulated in Ecclesiastes 3. Understanding that God orchestrates life transitions helps individuals to surrender their need for control and trust in His plan. This perspective can alleviate the fear of the unknown, as it reassures believers that they are not merely at the mercy of life's circumstances but are part of a divine timeline designed for their growth and development. Embracing God's timing fosters patience and resilience while navigating the complexities of single life.

Moreover, change can serve as an opportunity for personal growth and the discovery of individual gifts and talents. When faced with new situations, individuals are often prompted to step outside their comfort zones, leading to the realization of abilities they may not have previously recognized. This self-discovery can be both empowering and affirming, as it aligns with the understanding that each person has been uniquely created by God with specific gifts intended for His purpose. Engaging in community and sharing experiences with others can further illuminate these gifts, as collaborative efforts often reveal strengths that were previously hidden.

Ultimately, preparing for change from a spiritual perspective enables individuals to find meaning in adversity. Challenges can serve as catalysts for spiritual development, prompting deeper reliance on God and fostering connections with others who share similar journeys. By embracing changes as part of God's purpose, Christian singles can cultivate a sense of hope and motivation, knowing that every experience contributes to their personal narrative of faith. In doing so, they not only prepare for the changes ahead but also thrive within them, living purposefully and fully aligned with God's plan for their lives.

Finding Meaning in Adversity

The Role of Trials in Strengthening Faith

Trials often serve as a crucible for faith, refining and strengthening it in ways that comfort and ease cannot. For Christian singles, navigating life's uncertainties can feel particularly daunting. However, these challenges are not merely obstacles but opportunities for growth and deeper understanding of God's purpose. Each trial faced is an invitation to trust in God's plan, fostering resilience in the face of adversity. By embracing these moments, individuals can develop a faith that is not only personal but also powerful enough to inspire others within their community.

The Bible is replete with examples of individuals whose faith was fortified through trials. Consider the story of Job, whose immense suffering ultimately led him to a greater understanding of God's sovereignty and faithfulness. His journey illustrates that trials can lead to a more profound relationship with God, one that transcends mere belief. For singles, reflecting on such stories can provide encouragement and perspective, reminding them that their struggles are not in vain but are part of a larger tapestry woven by divine hands. This understanding can transform how one views personal challenges, shifting the focus from despair to hope.

Additionally, trials often reveal personal gifts and talents that might otherwise remain dormant. When faced with adversity, individuals are pushed to tap into their inner resources and discover strengths they did not know they possessed. This process of discovery is crucial for personal growth and can guide singles in their faith-based career development. As they navigate professional landscapes, the lessons learned through trials can inform their choices, aligning their careers with their spiritual purpose. This alignment not only brings fulfillment but also enhances their ability to serve others, creating a ripple effect of positive impact in their communities.

Moreover, trials can serve as a catalyst for building relationships with others who share similar struggles. In times of difficulty, individuals often seek support from their faith community. This shared experience can foster a sense of belonging and deepen connections among members. By navigating life's challenges together, Christians can create a robust support system that reinforces their faith and purpose. Such communal bonds are vital, as they remind singles that they are not alone in their journey. Together, they can encourage one another, sharing insights and prayers that fortify their collective faith.

Finally, it is essential to recognize that trials are often a part of divine timing. God has a unique plan for each individual, and the trials faced at various stages of life are intricately woven into that plan. For Christian singles, understanding this can bring peace amid uncertainty. Rather than viewing challenges as setbacks, they can be seen as stepping stones toward fulfilling one's purpose. By surrendering to God's timing and trusting in His wisdom, individuals can cultivate a faith that not only withstands trials but thrives in them, ultimately leading to a more purposeful and meaningful life.

Transforming Challenges into Opportunities

Transforming challenges into opportunities is a fundamental aspect of understanding God's plan for your life as a Christian single. In every season of life, particularly in moments of trial, it can be easy to feel isolated or disheartened. However, recognizing that you are strategically placed by God allows you to view these challenges not as obstacles but as divine setups for growth and purpose. Embracing this perspective can lead to profound personal transformation, helping you to align more closely with your spiritual purpose.

One of the key ways to transform challenges into opportunities is by reframing your mindset. Instead of viewing difficulties as signs of failure or abandonment, consider them as invitations to deepen your faith. Scripture teaches us that trials produce perseverance, character, and hope (Romans 5:3-5). By approaching challenges with a spirit of curiosity and resilience, you can uncover valuable lessons about yourself and your relationship with God. This shift in mindset fosters spiritual growth and equips you for future encounters, making you more adaptable and prepared to seize opportunities that align with your divine purpose.

In the realm of faith-based career development, challenges often present unique opportunities for advancement and fulfillment. When faced with setbacks in your job or career path, instead of succumbing to despair, seek God's guidance through prayer and reflection. Consider how these experiences might be redirecting you towards a role that better fits your gifts and talents. By trusting in God's timing, you can discover new passions and avenues for service that align with your faith, ultimately leading to a more purposeful and satisfying career.

Finding meaning in adversity is another vital aspect of transforming challenges into opportunities. Many inspirational stories of faith and purpose illustrate how individuals have emerged stronger and more focused after facing significant difficulties. Sharing these narratives within your community can foster a sense of connection and support, reminding you that you are not alone in your struggles. Engaging with others who have navigated similar challenges can provide insights and encouragement, reinforcing the idea that God uses even the most painful experiences to shape your character and calling.

Lastly, purposeful living through faith requires an active commitment to seek out and cultivate the opportunities that arise from your challenges. Embrace the idea that every trial is an opportunity for growth, not just for yourself but also for those around you. As you navigate life's complexities, allow your faith to guide you in building a community that shares your values and purpose. By leveraging your individual gifts and talents to serve others, you can create a ripple effect that transforms not only your life but also the lives of those you encounter, fulfilling your God-given purpose in the process.

Living Purposefully through Faith

Cultivating a Heart for Service

Cultivating a heart for service is an essential element of recognizing and fulfilling God's purpose in your life. For Christian singles, this phase of life can serve as a unique opportunity to explore ways to serve others, deepen your faith, and grow personally. Service is not merely about volunteering time; it is an expression of love and compassion that reflects the heart of God. When you engage in service, you begin to understand how your individual gifts and talents can positively impact those around you, revealing the divine plan that God has for your life.

In your journey of cultivating a heart for service, it is important to first develop a posture of humility and willingness to learn. This means actively seeking opportunities to help others, whether through community outreach, church activities, or simply being there for friends and family. As you engage in service, you will likely encounter various challenges and obstacles. However, these experiences can become catalysts for personal growth and spiritual development. Embracing adversity can strengthen your character and enhance your understanding of God's unwavering presence in your life.

Moreover, serving others often leads to the discovery of your spiritual gifts. Each person is uniquely designed by God with specific talents that can be used for the greater good. As you become more involved in service, you may uncover hidden abilities and passions that align with God's purpose for you. This can be particularly encouraging for Christian singles who may feel uncertain about their direction. By actively participating in service, you not only contribute to your community but also gain clarity about your own path and how it aligns with God's plan.

Building community through shared purpose is another vital aspect of cultivating a heart for service. Engaging with like-minded individuals who share your faith and values fosters a sense of belonging and encouragement. When you serve alongside others, you create bonds that are rooted in a common mission to uplift and support those in need. This fellowship can provide invaluable support during life's transitions and challenges, reminding you that you are not alone in your journey. Together, you can navigate obstacles and celebrate victories, reinforcing the idea that service is a shared endeavor.

Ultimately, cultivating a heart for service is about embracing a lifestyle of purposeful living through faith. It invites you to step outside your comfort zone, lean into God's guidance, and trust in His divine timing. As you embark on this journey, remember that each act of service, no matter how small, is a reflection of God's love and purpose in your life. By committing to serve others, you not only fulfill your spiritual calling but also position yourself to be an instrument of change in the world around you.

Daily Practices for Purposeful Living

Daily practices for purposeful living are essential for Christian singles seeking to align their lives with God's plan. Establishing a routine that centers on spiritual growth can create a solid foundation for understanding your divine purpose. Start each day with intentional prayer and scripture reading to invite God's presence into your life. This practice not only deepens your relationship with Him but also provides clarity and direction. Consider journaling your thoughts during this time, reflecting on how the scriptures resonate with your current circumstances. This can help you identify patterns and insights that guide your journey toward discovering your unique gifts and talents.

Engaging with a community of like-minded believers is another vital practice for purposeful living. Look for local church groups or online communities that focus on spiritual growth and personal development. Sharing experiences, challenges, and triumphs with others can foster a sense of belonging and accountability. Additionally, participating in group activities, whether they are service projects or prayer meetings, allows you to explore your individual gifts in a supportive environment. Building relationships within the community not only enriches your faith but also enables you to navigate life's challenges with collective wisdom and encouragement.

Embrace the concept of God's timing in your daily life. Understand that every moment is orchestrated by God for a reason, and trust that He is guiding your steps even when the path seems unclear. Practicing mindfulness can help you remain present and open to the lessons life offers. Take time to reflect on the moments of adversity you face and recognize how they may be shaping you for greater purpose. This perspective encourages resilience and fosters a deeper understanding of God's plan, even in difficult times. Each challenge can be viewed as an opportunity for growth, leading you closer to your divine purpose.

Incorporating acts of service into your daily routine can significantly enhance your sense of purpose. Find opportunities to serve others, whether through volunteering, mentoring, or simply offering a listening ear to a friend in need. These acts of kindness not only align with biblical teachings but also help you discover the joy of living out your faith in practical ways. Serving others can reveal your strengths and passions, providing insight into how God has uniquely positioned you to make a difference in the world. As you engage in these practices, you may find that your own needs are met through the very act of giving.

Finally, cultivate an attitude of gratitude to reinforce your commitment to purposeful living. Each day, take time to acknowledge the blessings in your life, no matter how small. This practice shifts your focus from what is lacking to the abundance that surrounds you, fostering a sense of contentment and peace. Gratitude can enhance your spiritual well-being and strengthen your faith, reminding you that God is working in your life even in the mundane moments. By intentionally recognizing His hand at work, you align yourself more closely with His purpose, paving the way for a fulfilling and meaningful life as you continue on your journey of faith.

Navigating Life's Challenges with Spiritual Guidance

Seeking God's Wisdom in Difficult Times

Seeking God's wisdom during challenging times can be a transformative experience for Christian singles, as it invites personal growth and deeper understanding of one's spiritual journey. In moments of uncertainty or distress, turning to God for guidance allows individuals to align their lives with divine purpose. This process often involves prayer, meditation, and introspection, which can help clarify the path ahead. By earnestly seeking God's wisdom, singles can gain insight into their unique circumstances and discover the lessons and opportunities that adversity presents.

Navigating the complexities of life transitions is particularly relevant for Christian singles. These transitions may include changes in career, relationships, or personal goals. In seeking God's wisdom, individuals can find reassurance and direction during these times of change. By focusing on scripture and seeking counsel from spiritually mature friends or mentors, one can identify God's hand in their life. This guidance can illuminate the way forward, helping to reveal how each transition is part of a larger divine plan that contributes to personal and spiritual growth.

Moreover, seeking wisdom from God encourages singles to recognize their individual gifts and talents. Often, life's challenges prompt introspection, allowing individuals to assess their skills and passions in a new light. By leaning into their faith, they can better understand how their unique abilities can serve others and fulfill God's purpose for their lives. This realization can lead to fulfilling career opportunities and meaningful relationships, as singles learn to align their pursuits with their spiritual calling.

In times of adversity, it is essential to find meaning and purpose through faith. Difficult circumstances can often feel isolating, but by seeking God's wisdom, Christian singles can foster a sense of community and shared purpose. Engaging with others who are experiencing similar challenges provides a support network that encourages resilience and growth. These relationships can be a source of strength, reminding individuals that they are not alone in their struggles and that God is working through them to achieve greater things.

Ultimately, seeking God's wisdom in difficult times is a journey towards purposeful living and faith-based development. By embracing divine timing and recognizing that challenges can be opportunities for growth, Christian singles can cultivate a deeper relationship with God. This alignment with spiritual guidance not only assists in navigating life's challenges but also fosters a profound sense of fulfillment and peace. By trusting in God's plan, individuals can confidently move forward, knowing that their struggles are shaping them for a greater purpose, both in their personal lives and the lives of those around them.

The Power of Prayer in Overcoming Obstacles

The act of prayer serves as a profound channel through which Christian singles can connect with God, especially when faced with life's obstacles. In moments of trial, prayer becomes a source of strength and clarity, enabling individuals to navigate challenges with grace. It is during these times of struggle that one can genuinely experience the power of faith, as prayer invites divine intervention, offering guidance and reassurance. By committing to a consistent prayer life, singles can cultivate a deeper relationship with God, allowing His purpose to unfold in their lives, even amidst adversity.

Prayer not only provides comfort but also serves as a tool for personal growth and spiritual development. When seeking God's will through prayer, individuals are encouraged to reflect on their intentions and desires. This self-examination fosters an environment where personal gifts and talents can be recognized and nurtured. As singles engage in heartfelt conversations with God, they often discover insights into their unique purpose, which can lead to greater fulfillment in both their personal and spiritual lives. This transformative process can help them identify the obstacles that may be hindering their growth and empower them to overcome these challenges with renewed strength.

Faith-based career development is another area where the power of prayer manifests significantly. Singles often grapple with decisions regarding their professional paths, and seeking God's guidance through prayer can illuminate the right direction. By aligning their career aspirations with God's plan, individuals can find peace in their choices, knowing they are on a path designed for them. This alignment not only enhances their professional lives but also contributes to their overall sense of purpose, reinforcing the idea that their work can be an extension of their faith.

Divine timing plays a crucial role in the journey of Christian singles, particularly as they navigate life transitions. Prayer allows individuals to surrender their timelines to God, trusting that He knows what is best for them. This surrender fosters patience and resilience, equipping them to face uncertainties with confidence. As they learn to wait for God's timing, they can also build a supportive community with others who share similar faith-based aspirations, learning together how to embrace each season of life with purpose and hope.

Finally, prayer serves as a powerful reminder of the strength found in community. When Christian singles come together in prayer, they not only uplift one another but also deepen their understanding of God's plan in everyday life. Inspirational stories of faith and purpose emerge from these communal prayer experiences, reinforcing the notion that obstacles can be overcome collectively. As they share their journeys, singles can inspire one another to view challenges as opportunities for growth, ultimately leading to a more purposeful living through faith. In this way, prayer becomes a foundational element in overcoming obstacles, guiding individuals to discover their true purpose and meaning in life.

Understanding God's Plan in Everyday Life

Recognizing God's Hand in Daily Activities

Recognizing God's hand in our daily activities is essential for Christian singles seeking to understand their purpose and navigate life's challenges. Every moment, whether mundane or extraordinary, can serve as a reminder of God's presence and guidance. By cultivating an awareness of how God operates in our daily routines, we can align our actions and decisions with His divine plan. This awareness not only enhances our spiritual growth but also enriches our personal experiences, allowing us to see the significance in seemingly trivial encounters and tasks.

As you go about your day, consider the small blessings that often go unnoticed. A friendly conversation with a coworker, a moment of peace during your morning commute, or an encouraging message from a friend can all be interpreted as God's gentle nudges. These instances are not mere coincidences; they reflect God's intention to reveal His love and purpose in our lives. By recognizing these moments, we train ourselves to see beyond the surface and appreciate the divine orchestration at play, fostering a deeper connection with God and His plan for us.

Navigating life transitions can be particularly challenging, but understanding God's hand in these changes is crucial. Whether facing a new job opportunity, moving to a different city, or entering a new phase of life, these transitions are often laden with divine purpose. God uses these moments to shape us, refine our character, and guide us toward our destiny. By embracing these transitions and seeking God's guidance through prayer and reflection, we can trust that He is positioning us exactly where we need to be for our growth and development.

In times of adversity, it can be difficult to see God's hand at work. However, recognizing His presence during challenging moments is a testament to our faith. Adversity often brings opportunities for growth, resilience, and a greater understanding of our strengths and weaknesses. When we look for God's purpose in our struggles, we can find meaning and hope. Inspirational stories of others who have faced similar challenges can serve as powerful reminders of God's faithfulness and the transformative power of faith during difficult times.

Finally, building a community of like-minded individuals can significantly enhance our ability to recognize God's hand in our lives. Engaging with others who share our faith and purpose encourages us to share our experiences, insights, and gifts. This communal approach fosters a supportive environment where we can collectively discern God's direction and celebrate the unique ways, He works in each of our lives. By coming together, we not only strengthen our individual faith but also create a network of encouragement that helps us navigate life's challenges with spiritual guidance and purpose.

Living with Intention: Finding Joy in the Ordinary

Living with intention is a transformative approach that invites Christian singles to find joy in the ordinary moments of life. This intentionality begins with the understanding that God has strategically placed each individual exactly where they are for a specific reason and purpose. Recognizing that every day holds the opportunity for divine encounters can shift one's perspective. As singles navigate their unique paths, they can cultivate a mindset that seeks out the beauty and purpose in daily routines, relationships, and challenges. This awareness doesn't just enhance personal growth but also aligns with a broader spiritual purpose that resonates deeply within the Christian faith.

Joy often resides in the simple, everyday experiences that we sometimes overlook. By practicing mindfulness and gratitude, singles can uncover the richness of their current circumstances. Whether it's a quiet morning coffee, a heartfelt conversation with a friend, or moments of solitude spent in prayer, these ordinary experiences hold profound significance when viewed through the lens of faith. Embracing these moments as gifts from God encourages a deeper appreciation for life's blessings. As singles learn to find joy in the mundane, they can also develop resilience against life's inevitable challenges, seeing each trial as an opportunity to grow closer to God and strengthen their faith.

Faith-based career development can also play a crucial role in living with intention. When individuals approach their work with the mindset of service and purpose, they begin to see their careers not just as jobs but as platforms for fulfilling God's plan. By aligning their professional goals with their spiritual values, singles can create a sense of joy and fulfillment that transcends traditional measures of success. This alignment empowers them to navigate life transitions with confidence, trusting that God's timing is perfect and that each step taken is part of His divine plan. As they pursue their passions while remaining rooted in faith, they can inspire others in their community to do the same.

Navigating life's challenges can often feel daunting, but when approached with spiritual guidance, these experiences can lead to profound personal growth. Christian singles are encouraged to seek God's wisdom through prayer and scripture, allowing His guidance to illuminate their paths. Understanding that adversity can have purpose helps to foster resilience and a deeper connection to one's faith. By sharing their stories of overcoming obstacles, singles can build community with others who share similar struggles, fostering a sense of belonging and support that is instrumental in discovering individual gifts and talents.

Ultimately, living with intention is about more than just finding joy; it's about establishing a lifestyle that reflects a commitment to God's plan. By focusing on purposeful living through faith, Christian singles can cultivate a life that not only embraces the ordinary but also magnifies the extraordinary potential within themselves and their community. Each moment, no matter how small, can be infused with meaning when approached with a heart open to God's leading. By doing so, they embark on a journey of discovery that not only enriches their own lives but also serves as a beacon of hope and inspiration to others seeking to understand their purpose in God's grand design.

Building Community through Shared Purpose

The Importance of Fellowship and Support

Fellowship and support are vital components in the journey of Christian singles seeking to align their lives with God's purpose. In a world that often emphasizes individualism, the biblical call to community becomes even more significant. God designed each of us to thrive in relationships, providing an essential support system that encourages spiritual growth and personal development. Engaging in fellowship with other believers allows individuals to share their experiences, challenges, and triumphs, creating a rich tapestry of mutual encouragement and accountability.

The act of coming together in fellowship offers a unique opportunity to discover and embrace individual gifts and talents. When Christian singles participate in group activities, Bible studies, or service projects, they can uncover their strengths and passions in a supportive environment. This communal exploration not only enhances personal growth but also enriches the broader body of Christ. By using their unique gifts, individuals contribute to the community's mission and actively participate in God's plan, thus reinforcing their sense of purpose.

Moreover, the importance of support networks cannot be overstated, particularly during times of transition or adversity. Life's challenges can leave individuals feeling isolated and uncertain about their path. However, when surrounded by a community of faith, Christian singles can find solace and guidance through shared experiences. These connections provide a safe space for vulnerability and healing, allowing individuals to navigate through life's difficulties with the encouragement of others who understand their struggles and aspirations.

Fellowship also plays a crucial role in faith-based career development. As singles seek to understand their calling in the workplace, the insights and wisdom of fellow believers can illuminate potential paths and opportunities. Engaging in discussions with like- minded individuals can spark new ideas and provide clarity on one's vocation. The collective wisdom within a supportive community fosters an environment where individuals can explore their God-given talents and apply them effectively in their careers, aligning their professional lives with their spiritual journeys.

Finally, the shared purpose found in fellowship cultivates a deeper understanding of God's plan in everyday life. By actively participating in a community of faith, Christian singles can witness firsthand the diverse ways God is working in the lives of others. These inspirational stories of faith and purpose serve as powerful reminders that God is at work, even in seemingly mundane circumstances. As individuals embrace their place in the community and support one another, they collectively grow in faith, navigate life's challenges, and ultimately fulfill their God-given purpose.

Creating Meaningful Connections within the Church

Creating meaningful connections within the church is essential for Christian singles seeking to understand their purpose and navigate their spiritual journeys. The church community serves as a vital support system where individuals can share their experiences, grow in faith, and foster relationships that encourage personal and spiritual growth. By engaging with others who share similar values and beliefs, singles can create a network that not only uplifts them but also helps them discover and utilize their unique gifts and talents in service to God.

One of the most effective ways to build these connections is through active participation in church activities and ministries. Whether it be volunteering for outreach programs, joining a small group, or participating in church events, these opportunities allow singles to meet fellow congregants in a meaningful context. Engaging in shared service not only strengthens bonds but also fosters an environment where individuals can learn from one another, share their stories, and grow together in faith. This collaborative spirit can lead to lasting friendships and provide a sense of belonging that is crucial during life's transitions.

Moreover, meaningful connections can often emerge from shared experiences of adversity. The church can be a sanctuary for those facing life's challenges, providing a space for open dialogue and mutual support. When singles share their struggles and triumphs, they not only find comfort in one another but also gain insights into how God's plan unfolds through difficult times. These connections can be instrumental in helping individuals navigate their personal journeys, offering encouragement and spiritual guidance that reinforces the understanding of divine timing.

Building a community centered around shared purpose also allows for the exploration of faith-based career development. Singles can find mentorship and support from others who understand the intersection of faith and professional life. These interactions can lead to collaborative projects, networking opportunities, and the sharing of resources that align with their spiritual values. As individuals pursue their career paths, the church community can provide both accountability and inspiration, helping them to align their professional goals with their spiritual calling.

Ultimately, creating meaningful connections within the church enriches the lives of Christian singles and enhances their understanding of God's plan for them. Through the relationships formed in this environment, individuals are reminded that they are not alone in their journeys. By nurturing these connections, singles can experience profound personal growth, wisdom, and a deeper appreciation for their unique purpose within the broader tapestry of the church community. Each interaction serves as a reminder of God's love and intentional design, guiding them to live purposefully through their faith.

Discovering Your Individual Gifts and Talents

Identifying Spiritual Gifts through Reflection

Identifying spiritual gifts through reflection requires a deliberate and introspective approach. For Christian singles, this process can be particularly enriching, as it allows individuals to uncover their unique contributions to the world around them. Reflection begins with a quieting of the mind and heart, creating a space where one can hear the still, small voice of God. It is essential to create an environment conducive to seeking, whether through prayer, journaling, or meditative practices. This intentional focus can help clarify how God has uniquely equipped each individual with specific talents and abilities that serve a greater purpose in His divine plan.

As you engage in reflection, consider the experiences that have shaped your spiritual journey. Think about times when you felt a profound sense of fulfillment or joy while serving others or participating in church activities. These moments often illuminate the areas where your spiritual gifts lie. Reflecting on past experiences can reveal patterns and themes that may point to particular strengths, such as teaching, hospitality, or encouragement. This self-awareness not only enhances personal growth but also aligns your passions with God's calling for your life.

Another critical aspect of identifying spiritual gifts involves seeking feedback from trusted friends and mentors within your faith community. Often, others can see the gifts in us that we may overlook or underestimate. Engaging in conversations about your strengths and areas of interest can provide valuable insights. Additionally, participating in group activities or volunteering can expose you to various roles, helping you discern where you thrive and feel the most connected to God's work. This communal aspect of reflection emphasizes that discovering spiritual gifts is not a solitary journey but one that flourishes within the context of community.

Furthermore, prayer plays a pivotal role in the discernment process. Asking God for clarity and guidance can open your heart and mind to recognize the gifts He has placed within you. It is essential to remain open to the possibility that your spiritual gifts may manifest in unexpected ways or call you to new paths that you had not previously considered. Allowing your prayer life to guide your reflection can lead to profound revelations about your purpose and how you can serve others in meaningful ways.

Finally, embracing the idea of lifelong growth is vital in the journey of identifying and utilizing spiritual gifts. As you reflect and learn, remain open to the evolving nature of your gifts. Life transitions and challenges often provide opportunities for growth and deeper understanding of God's plan. By committing to a life of purposeful living through faith, you can navigate these changes with grace, continually seeking to align your talents with your calling. This ongoing process not only enriches your own life but also contributes to building a community that thrives on shared purpose and support.

Utilizing Your Talents for God's Glory

Utilizing your talents for God's glory begins with recognizing that each of us has been endowed with unique gifts and abilities. As Christian singles, it is essential to understand that these talents are not merely for personal advancement but are meant to serve a higher purpose. When you embrace your God-given abilities and seek ways to apply them, you align yourself with His divine plan for your life. This alignment is foundational in fulfilling your spiritual purpose and encourages personal growth as you step outside your comfort zone to serve others.

In the journey of faith-based career development, identifying and honing your talents is crucial. Whether you excel in communication, creativity, or leadership, these skills can be utilized in various contexts, from your workplace to community service. Your professional life is a platform to showcase God's glory, and it is vital to approach your career with the mindset of serving rather than merely earning. Engaging in meaningful work not only fulfills your personal aspirations but also contributes to the greater good, reflecting the love and grace of God in all you do.

Divine timing plays a significant role in how and when you utilize your talents. As you navigate life's transitions, remember that God orchestrates events for His purpose. Trust that the challenges you face may be opportunities for growth and the discovery of new talents. When you remain open to His guiding hand, you may find that your skills are revealed or sharpened in unexpected ways. Embracing these moments allows you to remain flexible and responsive to God's call, ensuring that you are prepared to act when the time is right.

Finding meaning in adversity can also unveil your hidden talents. Difficult experiences often push individuals to discover strengths they were unaware of. Reflecting on past hardships can provide insight into how you can use your experiences to bless others. By sharing your journey and the lessons learned, you not only offer hope to those facing similar trials but also honor God by demonstrating His faithfulness in your life. This process of transformation is integral to purposeful living through faith, as it reinforces the idea that your struggles can serve a greater purpose.

Lastly, building community through shared purpose enhances the impact of your talents. Engaging with others who share your values and vision creates an environment where collective strengths can flourish. Encourage and support one another in recognizing and utilizing individual gifts for the benefit of the community. Inspirational stories abound of individuals who have come together, leveraging their talents to fulfill God's mission. As you cultivate these relationships, you will find that your journey becomes richer and more meaningful, further confirming that you are indeed positioned by purpose in every aspect of your life.

Inspirational Stories of Faith and Purpose

Testimonies of Transformation

Testimonies of transformation offer a powerful glimpse into how individuals, particularly Christian singles, have experienced profound changes in their lives through faith and purpose. These stories often reveal how God has strategically positioned them in unique circumstances to fulfill His divine plan. For many, the journey begins during a season of waiting or uncertainty, where they grapple with loneliness or questions about their future. However, through prayer and community support, they discover that these moments are not mere pauses in life, but essential times of preparation and growth.

One notable testimony comes from a young woman who faced significant challenges after a difficult breakup. Initially, she felt lost and unsure of her direction. However, through engaging in local church activities and seeking mentorship, she began to uncover her gifts in teaching and community engagement. This process not only brought her healing but also revealed her calling to work with youth in her community. Her transformation illustrates how adversity can lead to self-discovery and a renewed sense of purpose, aligning with God's plan for her life.

Another inspiring story involves a man who, after losing his job, found himself at a crossroads. Instead of succumbing to despair, he leaned into his faith, seeking God's guidance through prayer and scripture. During this challenging period, he felt called to volunteer at a local food bank, where he not only provided support to those in need but also discovered his passion for service and leadership. His experience highlights the significance of divine timing in life transitions, showcasing how being open to God's direction can lead to unexpected opportunities that align with one's spiritual purpose.

Moreover, many testimonies emphasize the value of building a community through shared purpose. Singles often find strength and encouragement in fellowship, where they can discuss their struggles and triumphs. One couple, who eventually married, shared how they met during a church retreat focused on discovering individual gifts and talents. Their connection blossomed not only from shared faith but also from a mutual desire to pursue their God-given purposes. This narrative underscores the importance of surrounding oneself with like-minded individuals who can inspire and uplift during times of personal growth and exploration.

Lastly, these testimonies of transformation serve as a reminder that God's plan unfolds in everyday life, often in the most unexpected ways. Many individuals recount how seemingly mundane experiences, such as a casual conversation or a chance encounter, led to significant revelations about their purpose. These stories encourage Christian singles to remain open to divine guidance, trusting that their current position is not random but part of a greater design. By embracing their journeys, they can navigate life's challenges with faith, finding new meaning and direction along the way.

Lessons Learned from Faithful Lives Lessons learned from the lives of faithful individuals can provide profound insight and inspiration for Christian singles navigating their unique journeys. Throughout scripture and history, we find examples of men and women who exemplified unwavering faith while pursuing their divine purpose. These stories illuminate the importance of recognizing God's hand in every season of life, particularly in times of waiting and uncertainty. By understanding the lessons from these faithful lives, individuals can better discern their paths and embrace the purpose for which they were created.

One significant lesson is the value of patience and trust in God's timing. Figures like Abraham and Sarah waited decades for the fulfillment of God's promise to have a child. Their journey was fraught with challenges and moments of doubt, yet they ultimately learned to trust in God's plan. For Christian singles, this serves as a reminder that divine timing often involves periods of preparation and growth. Embracing this time can lead to personal development and spiritual maturity, equipping them for future roles in their communities and families.

Another essential lesson is the importance of community and shared purpose. The lives of faithful individuals often highlight how collaboration and support among believers can amplify their impact. For instance, the early church thrived as members came together in unity, sharing their gifts and talents for the common good. Christian singles can take inspiration from this model by seeking out fellowship and building relationships with others who share their spiritual goals. Such connections can provide encouragement, accountability, and a sense of belonging, all of which are vital during life's transitions.

Faith-based career development is also a key theme among the faithful. Joseph's journey from slavery to leadership in Egypt exemplifies how God can use seemingly adverse circumstances to position individuals for higher purposes. His ability to interpret dreams not only advanced his career but also saved nations from famine. Christian singles can glean from this by recognizing that their current jobs or callings may serve a greater purpose in God's plan. By focusing on their individual gifts and talents, they can actively seek opportunities that align with their values and contribute to the greater good.

Lastly, finding meaning in adversity is a powerful lesson observed in the lives of those who remained steadfast in their faith. Job's story illustrates that suffering does not negate purpose; rather, it can deepen one's understanding of God's character and lead to personal transformation. For Christian singles facing challenges, these narratives provide hope and perspective. They remind individuals that struggles can cultivate resilience and a stronger reliance on God, ultimately revealing their purpose through trials. By learning from the faithful, singles can approach their lives with renewed hope, confident that they are positioned by God for a reason.

Chapter 4

Trusting God's Timing: Guides to Surrendering control

 Understanding Divine Timing

The Concept of Time in Scripture

The concept of time in Scripture is intricately woven into the fabric of faith, offering profound insights for Christian singles navigating the complexities of life. Throughout the Bible, time is not merely a sequence of events but a divine orchestration of moments that reflect God's sovereignty and purpose. This perspective encourages believers to view their individual timelines as part of a greater narrative crafted by God, where patience and trust become essential virtues. Understanding this divine timing can inspire singles to embrace their unique journeys, knowing that God's plans often unfold in ways that are beyond human comprehension.

Scripture presents time as a gift from God, where every moment holds significance. Ecclesiastes 3:1 reminds us that "for everything, there is a season, and a time for every matter under heaven." This verse encapsulates the essence of divine timing, reassuring singles that their wait for relationships or life changes is not in vain. Each season serves a purpose, whether it involves preparation, healing, or growth. Recognizing this can alleviate the pressure to rush into decisions or relationships, fostering a mindset that values the process of waiting as an opportunity for personal development and spiritual maturity.

Moreover, the stories of biblical figures provide powerful examples of surrendering control to God's timing. Consider the life of Abraham, who waited for decades for the fulfillment of God's promise regarding his descendants. His journey illustrates the lessons of faith and perseverance amidst uncertainty. For singles, reflecting on such narratives can offer encouragement to trust God's timing, even when immediate answers or resolutions seem distant. In moments of doubt, recalling the faithfulness demonstrated in these stories can help cultivate a heart that is willing to surrender to God's plans, reinforcing the belief that His timing is ultimately perfect.

In times of waiting, it is essential to cultivate a practice of prayer and patience. Philippians 4:6-7 encourages believers to present their requests to God, assuring them that through prayer, they can experience peace that surpasses all understanding. This peace is crucial for singles who may face anxiety about their future or feel pressure from societal expectations. By embracing prayer as a means to communicate with God, singles can develop a deeper relationship with Him, reinforcing their trust in His timing. This spiritual discipline not only nurtures faith but also fosters a sense of calm amid life's uncertainties.

Ultimately, embracing the concept of time in Scripture invites Christian singles to shift their focus from control to trust. By meditating on verses that highlight God's faithfulness and timing, such as Jeremiah 29:11, which affirms that God has plans for hope and a future, individuals can find reassurance in the unknown. This journey of surrendering control is not about passivity but actively engaging with God through faith, prayer, and reflection. As singles learn to trust God's perfect timing, they can experience profound peace and fulfillment, knowing that their lives are part of a beautifully orchestrated divine timeline.

God's Perfect Timing vs. Human Timelines

God's perfect timing often stands in stark contrast to human timelines, especially for Christian singles navigating the complexities of life and relationships. In our fast-paced world, where instant gratification is the norm, trusting in God's timing requires a shift in perspective. Scripture reminds us in Ecclesiastes 3:1 that "To everything, there is a season, and a time for every matter under heaven." This verse encourages us to recognize that God has a divine schedule that is not bound by our limited understanding or expectations. Embracing this truth can be a source of peace, allowing us to relinquish control over our timelines and trust in God's greater plan.

When we look at biblical stories, we see many instances where God's timing was crucial to fulfilling His promises. For example, consider the story of Abraham and Sarah, who waited decades for the birth of their son Isaac. Despite their doubts and attempts to take control, God's promise was fulfilled at the perfect moment. This narrative teaches us that waiting, though challenging, is often a part of God's design. Romans 8:28 reassures us that "all things work together for good for those who are called according to His purpose." This calls us to trust that even in our waiting, God is orchestrating events for our ultimate benefit.

In moments of uncertainty, it's easy to feel anxious about our future, particularly when it comes to relationships and marriage. Philippians 4:6-7 offers comfort, stating, "Do not be anxious about anything, but in every situation, by prayer and petition, with thanksgiving, present your requests to God." This passage highlights the importance of communication with God through prayer, allowing us to express our fears and desires while also cultivating a heart of surrender. Trusting God with our timelines involves recognizing His sovereignty and understanding that our plans may not align with His perfect will.

The journey of surrender is further illustrated in the life of Joseph, who faced numerous setbacks yet remained faithful to God's vision for his life. His story demonstrates that even when circumstances seem unfavorable, God is working behind the scenes to fulfill His purposes. Genesis 50:20 encapsulates this sentiment: "You intended to harm me, but God intended it for good." As singles, we can draw strength from this narrative, knowing that our current season may be preparing us for a future filled with hope and promise.

Ultimately, cultivating a trusting relationship with God involves both prayer and patience. Daily devotions and scripture readings can help reinforce the importance of surrendering our timelines to Him. Isaiah 40:31 encourages us to "wait for the Lord," promising that those who do will renew their strength. By focusing on our faith instead of our fears, we can find peace in uncertainty, embracing the journey of trust as we learn to let go and let God lead us in His perfect timing.

Surrendering Control

The Call to Surrender in the Bible

The concept of surrendering control is woven throughout the Bible, providing a profound framework for Christian singles navigating the complexities of life and relationships. In moments of uncertainty, the scriptures remind us that surrender is not merely an act of giving up, but an invitation to trust in God's divine timing. One of the most significant biblical passages that encapsulates this call to surrender is Proverbs 3:5-6, which encourages believers to "trust in the Lord with all your heart and lean not on your own understanding." This scripture serves as a foundation for understanding that our plans may not align with God's purpose, urging us to seek His guidance and wisdom instead.

The story of Abraham and Sarah is a powerful testament to the journey of surrender and the challenges that often accompany it. Despite receiving God's promise of descendants, they faced years of waiting, leading to feelings of impatience and doubt. Their decision to take control by seeking alternatives resulted in complications that echoed through generations. However, when they ultimately surrendered to God's timing, they witnessed the miraculous fulfillment of His promise with the birth of Isaac. This narrative illustrates how surrendering control can lead to the realization of God's promises, even when the wait feels interminable.

In the New Testament, the life of Jesus exemplifies the essence of surrender. His prayer in the Garden of Gethsemane reflects a deep understanding of the struggle between human desire and divine will. Jesus expressed His anguish but ultimately submitted to the Father's plan, saying, "Not my will, but yours be done" (Luke 22:42). This moment of surrender not only highlights the importance of seeking God's will over our own but also reassures us that surrendering control can lead to profound peace, even amidst turmoil. For singles, this serves as a reminder that trusting God's plan, even when it diverges from personal expectations, leads to a deeper relationship with Him.

Finding peace in uncertainty is a recurring theme throughout scripture, particularly in passages like Philippians 4:6-7, which urges believers not to be anxious but to present their requests to God. The reassurance of God's peace guarding our hearts and minds comes as we practice surrender in our daily lives. For Christian singles, this means cultivating a habit of prayer, sharing fears and desires with God, and waiting patiently for His answers. In doing so, they can experience a tranquility that surpasses understanding, allowing them to navigate the complexities of singleness with grace.

Ultimately, the call to surrender in the Bible invites Christian singles to embrace a journey of faith that prioritizes trust over control. By reflecting on scriptural stories of surrender and the experiences of biblical figures, individuals can find encouragement to let go of anxiety and embrace the divine timeline laid out for them. Through daily devotions and prayer, they can develop a heart of surrender, fostering a deeper relationship with God and discovering peace in the uncertainties of life. Surrendering control is not a passive act; it is a courageous step towards embracing God's purpose and timing, leading to fulfillment beyond what we could imagine.

Recognizing the Need to Let Go

Recognizing the need to let go is a crucial step in the journey of surrendering control and trusting in God's divine timing. For many Christian singles, the desire for a partner and a fulfilling relationship can lead to feelings of anxiety, impatience, and even desperation. It is essential to understand that holding tightly to our plans and timelines can hinder the beautiful work God is doing in our lives. The Bible teaches us that our ways are not God's ways, and recognizing the need to relinquish control is the first step toward embracing His perfect plan for us.

Scripture reminds us repeatedly of the importance of trusting God's timing. Proverbs 3:5-6 encourages us to "Trust in the Lord with all your heart and lean not on your own understanding; in all your ways acknowledge Him, and He will make your paths straight." This verse reassures us that surrendering our control allows God to guide us in ways we may not have considered. It is through acknowledging His sovereignty that we can release our burdens and anxieties about the future. Recognizing the need to let go of our expectations opens our hearts to the possibilities that God has in store for us.

Letting go also involves embracing the uncertainty that often accompanies our lives. Ecclesiastes 3:1 states, "There is a time for everything, and a season for every activity under the heavens." As Christian singles, we may feel pressure to conform to societal timelines regarding relationships and marriage, but God has His own perfect timing. The stories of biblical figures like Abraham and Sarah remind us that waiting can be part of God's plan. Their journey illustrates that trusting God often requires patience and faith, even when the timeline seems delayed.

In moments of doubt and uncertainty, prayer becomes a powerful tool for fostering trust. Philippians 4:6-7 encourages us to "not be anxious about anything, but in every situation, by prayer and petition, with thanksgiving, present your requests to God." Engaging in prayer not only helps us articulate our fears and desires but also cultivates a heart of surrender. As we pray, we invite God into our uncertainties, allowing Him to replace our anxiety with peace that surpasses all understanding. This practice of surrendering through prayer reinforces our dependence on God's timing rather than our own.

Ultimately, recognizing the need to let go is about cultivating a relationship with God based on trust and faith. Jeremiah 29:11 assures us, "For I know the plans I have for you, declares the Lord, plans to prosper you and not to harm you, plans to give you hope and a future." Embracing this promise helps us shift our focus from what we lack to the abundant life God desires for us. As we surrender our control, we begin to experience the joy and peace that come from trusting in His divine purpose, paving the way for His blessings to manifest in our lives.

Embracing Divine Timing

Biblical Examples of Divine Timing

In the journey of faith, understanding divine timing can significantly impact our lives, especially for Christian singles navigating the complexities of relationships and personal aspirations. The Bible is filled with examples that illustrate how God's timing is often different from our own expectations. One prominent example is found in the story of Abraham and Sarah. God promised them a child when they were well beyond the age of bearing children. Despite their initial doubt and attempts to take matters into their own hands by having Abraham's father a child with Hagar, it was only when they were fully surrendered to God's promise that Isaac was born. This story teaches us the importance of patience and trust in God's timing, reminding us that His plans are always perfect, even when they seem delayed.

Another powerful example is the life of Joseph. Sold into slavery by his brothers, Joseph faced years of hardship and imprisonment before eventually rising to power in Egypt. Throughout his trials, Joseph maintained his faith in God's plan. When he finally reconciled with his brothers and revealed his identity, he expressed profound insight into divine timing: "You intended to harm me, but God intended it for good." This narrative encourages Christian singles to recognize that periods of waiting or suffering may serve a larger purpose in God's divine plan, cultivating resilience and faith in the process.

Ruth is another biblical figure who exemplifies trust in divine timing. After the death of her husband, Ruth chose to remain with her mother-in-law, Naomi, demonstrating loyalty and faith in uncertain circumstances. Her journey led her to Boaz, who would become her husband, ultimately placing her in the lineage of David and Jesus. Ruth's story illustrates that surrendering control and trusting in God's timing can lead to unexpected blessings and significant outcomes that align with His greater purpose for our lives.

The story of David also highlights the theme of divine timing. Anointed as king while still a shepherd boy, David had to endure years of fleeing from King Saul, who sought to kill him. Despite being promised the throne, David waited patiently for God to fulfill His promise. His experiences taught him valuable lessons about humility, dependence on God, and the importance of waiting for the right moment. For Christian singles, David's life serves as a reminder that God's promises may take time to manifest, and that preparation during the waiting period can be crucial for achieving His intended purpose.

Lastly, the New Testament provides the ultimate example of divine timing in the life of Jesus. His ministry began at the appointed time, as foretold in scripture, and He fulfilled His mission of salvation through His death and resurrection in perfect accordance with God's plan. In John 7:6, Jesus states, "My time is not yet here." This emphasizes that even Christ, in His earthly ministry, adhered to divine timing. For those feeling anxious about their future, this encourages a mindset of faith over fear. Embracing divine timing allows Christian singles to cultivate a deeper relationship with God, trusting that He is orchestrating every detail of their lives according to His perfect will.

Daily Practices for Embracing God's Timing

Embracing God's timing in our daily lives requires intentional practices that align our hearts and minds with His divine schedule. As Christian singles, we often find ourselves grappling with the pressure of societal expectations regarding relationships and marriage. To cultivate a sense of peace and surrender, it is essential to establish daily practices that remind us of God's perfect timing. Reflecting on scriptures such as Ecclesiastes 3:1, which reminds us that "To everything, there is a season," can help us understand that our lives unfold in accordance with divine purpose rather than human urgency.

One of the most powerful daily practices involves prayer and meditation on God's Word. Setting aside time each day to connect with God through prayer allows us to express our desires while also seeking His guidance. Incorporating verses like Philippians 4:6-7, which encourages us not to be anxious but to bring our requests to God, can foster a sense of peace amidst uncertainty. Journaling our prayers and thoughts can also enhance this practice, serving as a tangible reminder of how God is working in our lives, even when we cannot see immediate results.

Another vital practice is to immerse ourselves in biblical stories of trust and surrender. Characters like Abraham, who waited decades for God's promise of a son, and Ruth, who followed Naomi into the unknown, exemplify the beauty of waiting on the Lord. By reflecting on their journeys, we gain insight into the importance of patience and faithfulness. We can read and meditate on these stories, allowing them to inspire us to remain steadfast in our trust, as highlighted in Hebrews 10:36, which states, "You need to persevere so that when you have done the will of God, you will receive what he has promised."

Cultivating a heart of surrender also involves practical steps such as seeking community and support from fellow believers. Engaging in groups where sharing testimonies of faith and waiting on God's timing is encouraged can create a sense of belonging and reassurance. As we share our struggles and victories, we remind one another of God's faithfulness. Romans 12:12 encourages us to "Rejoice in hope, be patient in tribulation, be constant in prayer," which serves as a foundation for building each other up within the body of Christ.

Finally, developing a mindset of gratitude can significantly impact our ability to embrace God's timing. Each day, we can take time to reflect on the blessings we have, even in the waiting. Colossians 3:15 encourages us to "Let the peace of Christ rule in your hearts," which can be achieved through gratitude. By acknowledging what God has already done, we shift our focus from anxiety about the future to appreciation for the present. This practice not only strengthens our faith but also cultivates a spirit of surrender that acknowledges God's perfect plan for our lives.

Biblical Stories of Trust and Surrender

Abraham and Sarah: Trusting God's Promise

Abraham and Sarah's journey is a powerful testament to the essence of trusting God's promises, especially for those navigating the complexities of being single and seeking divine direction. Their story, rooted in Genesis, reveals the challenges of waiting for God's timing amidst life's uncertainties. When God promised Abraham that he would be the father of many nations, it came with a significant burden: he and Sarah were childless and advanced in age. This aspect of their narrative resonates deeply with Christian singles who often grapple with the pressure of societal expectations and personal desires, reminding them that divine plans often unfold in unexpected ways.

As they waited for the promised child, Abraham and Sarah faced moments of doubt and impatience. Sarah, in her struggle to conceive, took matters into her own hands by giving her maid, Hagar, to Abraham, resulting in the birth of Ishmael. This decision serves as a poignant reminder of the pitfalls of attempting to control outcomes rather than surrendering to God's timing. For singles, it underscores the importance of patience and faith in God's plan, even when immediate circumstances seem unfulfilling or contrary to their hopes. The scripture in Isaiah 40:31 encourages believers to "wait for the Lord" as it promises that those who do will renew their strength.

God's response to their impatience came with a reaffirmation of His promise. In Genesis 18:14, the Lord asks, "Is anything too hard for the Lord?" This rhetorical question challenges both

Abraham and Sarah, as well as modern believers, to reflect on their faith in God's capabilities. For Christian singles, this passage can serve as a powerful motivator to relinquish control over their timelines and trust in God's supreme authority. It encourages individuals to remember that divine delays are not denials but opportunities for spiritual growth and deeper reliance on God.

The culmination of Abraham and Sarah's story is the miraculous birth of Isaac, fulfilling God's promise despite their doubts. This moment illustrates that God's timing is often different from human expectations. It highlights the beauty of trusting in a divine timeline that surpasses human understanding. For those who feel anxious about their future—be it in relationships, careers, or personal goals—this narrative offers reassurance that faith in God's promises can bring about transformation, even in seemingly impossible situations.

Ultimately, Abraham and Sarah's story is one of redemption and grace, emphasizing the importance of cultivating a heart of surrender. It invites Christian singles to embrace prayer as a means of developing trust and patience, finding peace in uncertainty. Philippians 4:6-7 reminds believers to present their requests to God, allowing His peace to guard their hearts and minds. By reflecting on the faith journey of Abraham and Sarah, individuals can learn to let go of their need for control, embracing the fullness of God's plan with confidence and hope.

Joseph: From Pit to Palace

Joseph's journey from the pit to the palace serves as a profound example of trusting God's divine timing, especially for those navigating the uncertainties of single life. Sold into slavery by his brothers and thrown into a pit, Joseph's circumstances appeared bleak. However, in Genesis 37:19-20, we see that God's purpose was at work even in his darkest moments. The betrayal he faced would ultimately lead him to a greater purpose. For Christian singles, Joseph's story emphasizes that surrendering control does not mean inactivity; rather, it invites a deep trust in God's overarching plan.

As Joseph found himself in Potiphar's house, he remained faithful despite his circumstances. Genesis 39:2-3 highlights that "the Lord was with Joseph," granting him favor. This illustrates the importance of remaining steadfast and diligent in our current situations, even when they do not align with our expectations. For singles feeling stuck or overlooked, Joseph's story encourages us to embrace where we are now while trusting that God is preparing us for future opportunities. Like Joseph, we can cultivate our skills and character in the waiting period, knowing it contributes to our growth.

When faced with false accusations and imprisonment, Joseph continued to exhibit a spirit of service and integrity. Genesis 39:21 assures us that "the Lord was with Joseph" even in prison, highlighting that our value in God's eyes is not diminished by our circumstances. This is a powerful reminder for singles battling feelings of inadequacy or loneliness. Trusting God's timeline means recognizing that every season serves a purpose. In times of waiting, we are often being refined, much like Joseph, who would eventually rise to prominence.

Joseph's rise to power in Egypt was not immediate; it required patience and unwavering faith. Genesis 41:14 captures the moment when Pharaoh called for Joseph, reminding us that God's timing is perfect. God orchestrated events in Joseph's life that seemed random at first but led to his appointed position. For those who feel pressure to rush into relationships or make hasty decisions, Joseph's experience teaches us to wait for God's timing. Trusting in His plan can transform our waiting period into a season of preparation.

Ultimately, Joseph's story culminates in reconciliation with his brothers, showcasing that surrender leads to restoration and growth. Genesis 50:20 emphasizes that what was meant for evil, God intended for good. As Christian singles, we can find hope in knowing that God can turn our trials into triumphs. By surrendering control and trusting in God's timeline, we position ourselves to experience His blessings in ways we might never have imagined. Embracing this journey of trust allows us to discover peace amid uncertainty, knowing that God's plans for us are always good.

Finding Peace in Uncertainty Scriptures for Times of Waiting

In moments of waiting, it is essential to anchor ourselves in the truth of God's Word. Scripture provides profound insights that remind us to trust in God's perfect timing, especially as Christian singles navigating the complexities of life. Isaiah 40:31 serves as a powerful reminder: "But those who hope in the Lord will renew their strength. They will soar on wings like eagles; they will run and not grow weary; they will walk and not be faint." This verse emphasizes that waiting is not a passive endeavor; it is an active engagement of hope and trust, allowing God to renew our strength as we remain patient in His presence.

The story of Abraham and Sarah is a biblical illustration of trusting God when faced with seemingly impossible circumstances. God promised Abraham countless descendants, yet they waited many years for the fulfillment of that promise. Genesis 21:1-2 states, "Now the Lord was gracious to Sarah as he had said, and the Lord did for Sarah what he had promised. Sarah became pregnant and bore a son." Their journey teaches us that God's promises are reliable even when the timeline does not align with our expectations. Reflecting on these narratives can help Christian singles to embrace their own periods of waiting with faith, knowing that God's plans are often unfolding in ways we cannot immediately see.

In the New Testament, James 1:2-4 encourages us to view trials and periods of waiting as opportunities for growth: "Consider it pure joy, my brothers and sisters, whenever you face trials of many kinds, because you know that the testing of your faith produces perseverance." This perspective shift is crucial for singles who may feel frustration or anxiety during their waiting periods. Rather than succumbing to despair, they can find joy in the process of becoming stronger and more resilient in their faith.

Another scripture that resonates during times of uncertainty is Philippians 4:6-7, which reminds us to present our requests to God with thanksgiving: "Do not be anxious about anything, but in every situation, by prayer and petition, with thanksgiving, present your requests to God." This passage offers a path to peace amidst anxiety. Christian singles can practice this by regularly bringing their concerns and desires to God in prayer, trusting that His peace will guard their hearts and minds as they wait.

Ultimately, trusting God's timing requires a heart of surrender and a willingness to let go of control. Proverbs 3:5-6 provides a foundational principle for this journey: "Trust in the Lord with all your heart and lean not on your own understanding; in all your ways submit to him, and he will make your paths straight." Embracing this scripture empowers singles to release their need for immediate answers and instead lean into God's perfect plan, allowing Him to guide their steps in His timing. Through prayer, reflection on His Word, and a commitment to surrender, Christian singles can find peace and purpose in their waiting seasons.

Cultivating Peace through Prayer

Cultivating peace through prayer is essential for Christian singles navigating the uncertainties of life. Prayer serves as a powerful tool to connect with God, allowing individuals to express their fears, hopes, and desires. In moments when life feels overwhelming, bringing these feelings to God in prayer can provide clarity and assurance. Philippians 4:6-7 reminds us to not be anxious but to present our requests to God, assuring us that His peace will guard our hearts and minds. This is especially relevant for singles who may feel pressure regarding relationships and their future.

When we engage in prayer, we invite God into our circumstances, recognizing that we don't have to navigate life alone. This act of surrender enables us to let go of control and trust in His divine timing. Jesus encouraged His followers in Matthew 7:7 to ask, seek, and knock, emphasizing that God is always ready to respond to our prayers. As singles, it is vital to remember that God hears our prayers, and through them, we can cultivate a deeper relationship with Him, which fosters peace amidst uncertainty.

Incorporating scripture into our prayer life can enhance our communication with God. Verses such as Jeremiah 29:11, which speaks of God's plans to prosper us and not to harm us, remind us that His intentions are always for our good. By meditating on such promises, we can align our prayers with God's will, reinforcing our trust in His plan. This practice not only brings comfort but also helps us to focus on the positive aspects of our journey, rather than fixating on what we lack.

Moreover, prayer fosters patience, encouraging us to wait on God's timing. In Isaiah 40:31, we find encouragement that those who hope in the Lord will renew their strength. This promise is particularly relevant for singles who may feel weary from waiting for their ideal partner or life circumstances to unfold. Through prayer, we can cultivate a heart that is patient and trusting, learning to embrace the journey rather than rushing to the destination.

Ultimately, cultivating peace through prayer involves an ongoing commitment to surrender and trust. It requires us to daily bring our concerns before God and to be open to His guidance. As we deepen our prayer life, we not only find peace for ourselves but also grow in our understanding of God's character and His unwavering promise to provide for us. By leaning into prayer, Christian singles can navigate the complexities of their lives with faith, knowing that they are securely held in God's perfect timing.

Prayer and Patience

Developing a Prayer Life Focused on Trust

Developing a prayer life focused on trust is essential for Christian singles who desire to surrender control and embrace God's divine timing. Prayer serves as a pivotal channel for communication with God, allowing individuals to express their concerns, hopes, and desires while also reinforcing their faith in His plan. Through prayer, one can cultivate a deep sense of trust that transcends the uncertainties of life. Philippians 4:6-7 instructs believers to present their requests to God, assuring them that a peace that surpasses all understanding will guard their hearts and minds. This peace comes from a commitment to trust in God's timing rather than their own.

Incorporating scripture into daily prayers can enhance the focus on trust. Selecting verses that emphasize God's faithfulness, such as Isaiah 26:3, which promises perfect peace to those who trust in Him, can provide reassurance during moments of doubt. This practice not only grounds prayers in biblical truth but also serves as a reminder of God's unchanging nature. As Christian singles pray, they should seek to align their desires with God's will, asking for guidance and the strength to let go of their own timelines. This alignment fosters a deeper relationship with God, reinforcing the belief that His plans are ultimately for their good.

In addition to personal prayer, communal prayer can also play a significant role in developing trust. Engaging with a community of believers allows for shared experiences and testimonies of faith. When singles gather for prayer, they can encourage one another to trust God's timing through shared stories of surrender. These gatherings can be uplifting, as they remind individuals that they are not alone in their struggles. Hebrews 10:24-25 encourages believers to spur one another on toward love and good deeds, and prayer groups can serve as a vital support system for those seeking to strengthen their trust in God.

Patience is an integral aspect of prayer focused on trust. Just as the psalmist declares in Psalm 27:14 to "wait for the Lord; be strong and take heart," Christian singles must recognize that waiting on God is part of the journey. Developing a prayer life that emphasizes patience allows individuals to embrace seasons of waiting without losing hope. This waiting period can be transformed into an opportunity for spiritual growth, where trust is nurtured through consistent prayer and reflection on God's word. As they wait, singles can find comfort in knowing that their prayers are heard and that God is working behind the scenes.

Finally, creating a routine of prayer that emphasizes trust can lead to profound transformation. Setting aside dedicated time each day for prayer and meditation on scripture can cultivate a habit of surrender. This practice invites God into every aspect of life, fostering an ongoing dialogue built on trust rather than anxiety. As singles immerse themselves in prayer, they will find that their fears of uncertainty diminish, replaced by a growing assurance in God's perfect timing. Proverbs 3:5-6 serves as a guiding principle, encouraging believers to trust in the Lord with all their hearts and lean not on their own understanding. Through this journey, Christian singles can develop a prayer life that not only focuses on trust but ultimately transforms their relationship with God.

The Role of Patience in Surrender

The essence of patience in the journey of surrender is deeply rooted in the Christian faith. Patience is not merely the act of waiting; it is an active trust in God's timing and His divine plan for our lives. As Christian singles navigate the complexities of relationships and personal aspirations, understanding patience as a virtue becomes crucial. In James 1:2-4, believers are encouraged to consider it pure joy when facing trials, knowing that the testing of faith develops perseverance. This scripture emphasizes that patience is a process, one that refines and shapes our character as we learn to rely on God's timing rather than our own.

Surrendering control, particularly in the realm of relationships, often requires a deep sense of patience. Many singles may find themselves wondering when their time will come or questioning why God seems silent in their prayers. However, Isaiah 40:31 reassures us that those who hope in the Lord will renew their strength; they will soar on wings like eagles. This verse highlights that patience is not a passive state but a hopeful anticipation of God's promises. By trusting in His plan and timing, we can cultivate a heart that is ready to receive what God has in store for us, rather than being consumed by anxiety and impatience.

Biblical narratives provide powerful examples of individuals who exemplified patience in their surrender to God's will. Consider the story of Abraham, who waited many years for the fulfillment of God's promise of a son. His journey was fraught with moments of doubt and impatience, yet he ultimately learned to trust God's timing. Genesis 21:1-2 illustrates the moment when God fulfilled His promise, underscoring that divine timing often surpasses human understanding. These stories serve as reminders for Christian singles that the path to surrendering control is often marked by waiting, but it is during these times that God prepares our hearts for His blessings.

In moments of uncertainty, the call to be patient can feel overwhelming. However, Philippians 4:6-7 encourages believers to present their requests to God with thanksgiving, promising that the peace of God will guard their hearts and minds. This peace is a vital component of patience, as it allows us to trust that God is in control, even when circumstances do not align with our expectations. Through prayer and meditation on scripture, singles can develop a deeper sense of patience, learning to embrace the unknown while resting in the assurance that God's plans are always for their good.

Ultimately, patience is a critical element of surrendering control to God. It requires faith, trust, and the willingness to wait on His timing. As Christian singles navigate their journeys, cultivating patience will not only enhance their relationship with God but also prepare them for the blessings that He has ordained. Through scripture, prayer, and reflection on biblical stories, they can learn to embrace the waiting period as a transformative experience that deepens their faith and trust in God's perfect plan.

Faith Over Fear

Overcoming Doubts with Scripture

Overcoming doubts can be one of the most challenging aspects of a Christian single's journey, especially when it comes to trusting God's timing. Scripture serves as a powerful tool to combat these doubts, providing reminders of God's promises and faithfulness. In moments of uncertainty, turning to verses that highlight God's unwavering presence can help reinforce the belief that He is in control, even when life appears to be at a standstill or doesn't unfold as we had envisioned.

One of the most reassuring passages in the Bible is Jeremiah 29:11, which states, "For I know the plans I have for you, declares the Lord, plans to prosper you and not to harm you, plans to give you hope and a future." This verse emphasizes that God has a divine plan for each of us, designed with our best interests in mind. When doubts arise regarding our relationships or life choices, recalling this promise can help shift our focus from fear and uncertainty to an expectation of hope and fulfillment, trusting that God knows what we truly need.

Additionally, Philippians 4:6-7 offers encouragement when anxiety threatens to overwhelm us: "Do not be anxious about anything, but in every situation, by prayer and petition, with thanksgiving, present your requests to God. And the peace of God, which transcends all understanding, will guard your hearts and your minds in Christ Jesus." This passage reminds us to bring our worries to God through prayer, fostering a sense of peace that is not dependent on our circumstances. By surrendering our concerns to Him, we can cultivate a heart of surrender, allowing His peace to envelop us and dispel the doubts that often cloud our minds.

The story of Abraham and Sarah serves as a poignant example of navigating doubt while waiting on God's timing. Despite receiving the promise of a child, they faced years of waiting and uncertainty, leading to moments of doubt and attempts to take control of the situation. Yet, when they ultimately surrendered to God's timing, they witnessed His miraculous fulfillment of the promise. This biblical narrative illustrates that even the most faithful can struggle with doubt, but it is through surrender and trust that we can experience God's perfect timing and plans for our lives.

Incorporating these scriptures into daily life can create a foundation for overcoming doubts and embracing the journey of surrender. By meditating on God's Word, praying for guidance, and sharing our struggles with a supportive community, we can strengthen our faith and learn to trust God's timing wholeheartedly. Each moment spent in scripture not only reassures us of God's promises but also equips us with the courage to let go of our control and embrace the divine path laid out before us.

Encouragement from the Psalms

The Book of Psalms offers a rich tapestry of emotional expression, providing comfort and encouragement for those navigating the complexities of life. For Christian singles grappling with the uncertainties of relationships and personal timelines, Psalms serves as a reminder of God's faithfulness and the importance of surrendering control. Psalm 37:5 proclaims, "Commit your way to the Lord; trust in him, and he will act." This verse invites individuals to relinquish their anxieties about the future, encouraging them to place their trust in God's perfect timing. By actively committing their plans to God in prayer, singles can cultivate a sense of peace, knowing that He is at work behind the scenes.

In moments of doubt and impatience, the Psalms remind us of God's unwavering presence. Psalm 46:10 states, "Be still, and know that I am God." This verse encourages believers to pause and reflect on God's sovereignty, especially when life feels chaotic or unclear. For singles, this can be a powerful prompt to let go of the need to control every aspect of their lives. Instead of rushing into decisions or relationships, they can take a step back, embrace stillness, and develop a deeper relationship with God. This stillness is not just a cessation of activity but an active waiting on God, trusting that His plans are far better than any they could orchestrate on their own.

Furthermore, the Psalms highlight the importance of patience as a component of faith. Psalm 27:14 encourages, "Wait for the Lord; be strong, and let your heart take courage; wait for the Lord!" This verse emphasizes that waiting is not a passive activity but a time of strength building and courage cultivation. For singles, waiting on God's timing allows for personal growth and preparation for future relationships. It is during these moments of waiting that individuals can develop qualities such as patience, resilience, and trust—traits essential for any healthy partnership.

The Psalms also provide reassurance during times of anxiety and fear. Psalm 55:22 advises, "Cast your burden on the Lord, and he will sustain you; he will never permit the righteous to be moved." This promise serves as a balm for the anxious heart, reminding singles that they do not have to carry their burdens alone. By entrusting their concerns to God, they can experience the relief that comes from knowing He is actively working on their behalf. This act of surrender fosters a deeper reliance on God's timing, enabling them to navigate the uncertainties of life with greater peace and assurance.

Ultimately, the encouragement found in the Psalms calls Christian singles to embrace a posture of surrender, trusting in God's divine plan. Psalm 31:15 states, "My times are in your hand." This verse encapsulates the essence of surrendering control and trusting God's timeline. As singles learn to align their desires with God's will, they open themselves up to the beauty of His unfolding purpose in their lives. By immersing themselves in the truths of the Psalms, they can find solace and strength, anchoring their faith in the promise that God is always present, always faithful, and always in control.

Trusting God's Purpose

Understanding God's Plans for Us

Understanding God's plans for us can be a profound journey, especially for Christian singles navigating the complexities of life and relationships. The Bible offers numerous insights into understanding divine timing and God's purpose. In Jeremiah 29:11, we are reminded, "For I know the plans I have for you, declares the Lord, plans to prosper you and not to harm you, plans to give you hope and a future." This verse reassures us that God's plans are inherently good, crafted with love and intention. Embracing this truth can transform our perspective, allowing us to view our current circumstances, including our single status, as part of a larger divine narrative.

In moments of uncertainty and waiting, it is essential to seek comfort in scripture. Psalms 27:14 encourages us, "Wait for the Lord; be strong and take heart and wait for the Lord." This call to patience aligns with the understanding that God's timing is perfect, even when it feels like life is not unfolding as we desire. Trusting in His timeline fosters a sense of peace, allowing us to let go of anxiety and the need for control. By embracing divine timing, we can cultivate a heart that is open to God's leading, trusting that He is orchestrating every detail of our lives for our ultimate good.

Biblical stories serve as powerful reminders of surrender and trust in God's plans. Consider the story of Joseph, who faced numerous trials before fulfilling his destiny. Despite being sold into slavery and imprisoned, he remained faithful. In Genesis 50:20, Joseph reflects on his journey, stating, "You intended to harm me, but God intended it for good." This illustrates that our struggles may have a purpose beyond our understanding. As Christian singles, we can draw inspiration from such narratives, recognizing that delays and detours are often part of a divine plan that leads to greater fulfillment.

Developing a trusting relationship with God requires intentional prayer and reflection. Philippians 4:6-7 guides us, urging us not to be anxious but to bring our requests to God in prayer. This practice of surrendering our desires and fears can replace anxiety with the peace that surpasses all understanding. It is through consistent communication with God that we learn to trust His plans. Engaging with scripture daily can reinforce this trust, reminding us of His promises and faithfulness throughout history.

Ultimately, understanding God's plans for us is about recognizing that we are not alone in this journey. As we cultivate a heart of surrender, we can find solace in the knowledge that God is with us, guiding our paths. Isaiah 30:21 reassures us, "Whether you turn to the right or to the left, your ears will hear a voice behind you, saying, 'This is the way; walk in it.'" By surrendering control and trusting in God's timeline, we can navigate our lives with hope and anticipation, knowing that every step is part of a divine purpose.

Aligning Our Desires with God's Will

Aligning our desires with God's will is a journey that requires intentionality, reflection, and a deep understanding of scripture. For Christian singles, this alignment often involves navigating the complexities of relationships, career aspirations, and personal growth, all while remaining anchored in faith. The Bible offers profound insights that encourage us to seek God's will above our own desires. Proverbs 3:5-6 reminds us to trust in the Lord with all our hearts and lean not on our own understanding; in all our ways, we are to acknowledge Him, and He will direct our paths. This scripture serves as a foundational principle for ensuring that our desires align with God's greater plans.

The challenge often lies in the tension between our immediate desires and God's ultimate purpose for our lives. It is natural to yearn for companionship, stability, and fulfillment, but these desires can sometimes lead us away from God's best for us. James 4:3 cautions us that we may not receive because we ask with wrong motives. Therefore, it is essential to reflect on our intentions behind our desires. Are we seeking fulfillment for ourselves, or are we genuinely looking to glorify God in our pursuits? This self- examination can lead to a transformation of our hearts, allowing us to desire what God desires.

Prayer is a powerful tool in aligning our desires with God's will. In Philippians 4:6-7, Paul encourages us not to be anxious but to present our requests to God in prayer and supplication with thanksgiving. By consistently bringing our desires before God, we invite Him to shape them according to His will. This practice fosters a relationship of trust, where we learn to listen for His guidance and discern the path, He has laid out for us. As we pray, we may find that our desires begin to shift, aligning more closely with God's purpose, leading us to peace and confidence in His timing.

Moreover, the stories of biblical figures who exemplified trust and surrender can inspire us as we navigate our own desires. Consider the story of Hannah in 1 Samuel 1, who fervently prayed for a child, ultimately surrendering her desires to God's will. Her faithfulness and patience led to the birth of Samuel, who became a significant leader in Israel. This narrative reminds us that surrendering our desires is not a passive act; it is an active engagement with God, trusting that He knows what is best for us. Embracing this mindset allows us to release our anxiety and embrace the uncertainty of life with faith.

Finally, cultivating a heart of surrender is a daily practice that involves gratitude, reflection, and a willingness to let go of control. Romans 12:2 encourages us to not conform to the patterns of this world but to be transformed by the renewing of our minds. By focusing on God's Word and seeking His will, we can cultivate an attitude of surrender that aligns our desires with His divine plan. Trusting God's timing, especially in moments of waiting, equips us with the patience and resilience necessary to embrace His path for our lives. As we learn to let go and let God, we find that our desires become intertwined with His purpose, leading us to a fulfilling and meaningful journey as Christian singles.

The Journey of Surrender

Personal Testimonies of Trust

In the journey of faith, personal testimonies often serve as powerful reminders of the transformative power of trust. Many Christian singles have experienced moments when they had to surrender their control and rely solely on God's timing. One such testimony comes from Grace, yes, I spent years feeling anxious about my single status, I really beg God for my kingdom spouse. Despite of my prayers and efforts to find the man God made specifically for me, I often felt lost and discouraged and it leads me to write this book. However, during a period of deep reflection, I turned to Proverbs 3:5-6, which encourages believers to trust in the Lord with all their heart and not to lean on their own understanding. This scripture resonated with me, leading to a profound realization: I needed to let go of my tightly held plans and embrace the uncertainty of God's timing.

John's story reflects a similar theme of surrender and trust. After a painful breakup, he found himself questioning his worth and future. In his pain, he discovered the promise of Jeremiah 29:11, which reassures us that God has plans to prosper us and not to harm us, giving us hope and a future. As he meditated on this verse, John learned to shift his focus from his immediate desires to God's overarching purpose for his life. This shift allowed him to find peace in uncertainty, understanding that God's timeline may not align with his but is ultimately for his good. Through prayer and patience, John cultivated a deeper relationship with God, paving the way for healing and renewed hope.

Another testimony comes from Emily, who faced a crossroads in her life. At 35, the pressure to marry weighed heavily on her. Despite societal expectations, she felt a strong conviction to trust God's timeline. She drew strength from Psalm 27:14, which encourages believers to wait for the

Lord and be strong. Emily began to view her singlehood not as a waiting period but as a unique opportunity for growth and service. Embracing this perspective, she dedicated herself to community service and personal development, allowing her faith to flourish. In surrendering her control, she found joy and purpose, realizing that God was preparing her for a future beyond her imagination.

David's journey illustrates the importance of faith over fear. After years of struggling with anxiety about relationships, he learned to anchor his trust in God through Isaiah 41:10, which reassures us of God's presence and strength in times of fear. David began to replace his anxious thoughts with affirmations of faith, developing a habit of prayer that centered on trusting God's plan rather than his own. This transformation did not happen overnight; it was a gradual process of surrendering his fears and choosing to believe in God's goodness. Through this journey, he discovered that peace comes from trusting in God's character rather than the uncertainty of his circumstances.

These personal testimonies collectively highlight the essence of trusting God's timing and surrendering control. They remind Christian singles that they are not alone in their struggles and that God is ever- present in their journeys. By embracing divine timing, reflecting on scripture, and sharing stories of faith and resilience, believers can cultivate a heart of surrender. In doing so, they open themselves up to the incredible possibilities that God has in store, learning to find peace in the uncertainty and joy in the wait.

Insights from Biblical Characters

Biblical characters offer profound insights into the practice of surrendering control and trusting in God's perfect timing. The story of Abraham is a prime example. Called by God to leave his homeland and family, Abraham faced uncertainty and fear. Despite the promise of a great nation arising from his lineage, years passed without fulfillment. Yet, Abraham's journey teaches us the importance of faith and patience. His willingness to trust God's plan, even when it seemed delayed, illustrates the essence of surrender. Scripture highlights that Abraham believed God's promises, and it was credited to him as righteousness, emphasizing the value of unwavering faith amid life's unpredictability.

Another compelling figure is Joseph, whose life exemplifies resilience and trust in God's timing. Sold into slavery by his brothers, Joseph encountered numerous hardships, including wrongful imprisonment. However, he remained steadfast in his faith and integrity. Eventually, his trials led him to a position of power in Egypt, where he could save his family during a famine. Joseph's story reminds us that what may appear to be setbacks can serve a greater purpose in God's divine plan. His unwavering trust transformed his suffering into a vessel for God's glory, illustrating the profound truth that surrendering control can lead to extraordinary outcomes.

The life of Ruth also provides significant lessons on surrender and divine timing. As a widow in a foreign land, Ruth chose to follow her mother-in-law Naomi back to Bethlehem, demonstrating loyalty and faith. Her decision to glean in the fields of Boaz, a relative of Naomi, exemplifies her proactive yet humble approach to trusting God. Ruth's eventual marriage to Boaz was not just a personal blessing; it positioned her within the lineage of Christ. This narrative encourages

Christian singles to remain steadfast in faith, knowing that God's plans may unfold in unexpected ways, often beyond what we can envision for ourselves.

The story of Esther further illustrates the significance of timing and the role of divine providence. As a Jewish woman who became queen, Esther faced a critical moment when her people were threatened. Her courage to approach the king without being summoned, risking her life, showcases the power of trusting God's timing and purpose. Esther's declaration, "For such a time as this," reminds us that each moment is significant in God's grand design. Her story encourages singles to recognize their unique positions and to trust that God has placed them where they are for a reason, urging them to act with faith when opportunities arise.

Finally, the life of David offers a rich tapestry of surrender and trust in God's timeline. Anointed as king while still a shepherd boy, David spent years fleeing from King Saul before he assumed the throne. His psalms reflect deep emotions of despair, hope, and trust in God's sovereignty. David's journey emphasizes that even when circumstances seem dire, surrendering control to God can lead to fulfillment of His promises. His life illustrates that waiting on God often cultivates a deeper relationship with Him, reminding Christian singles that patience, prayer, and trust are vital components of their faith journey.

Cultivating a Heart of Surrender

Daily Devotions for Trusting God

Daily devotions play a crucial role in cultivating a heart that surrenders control and trusts in God's divine timing, especially for Christian singles navigating the complexities of life and relationships. Engaging in daily scripture reading and prayer invites God's presence into our daily routines, fostering a deeper connection with Him. As we turn to the Bible, we find numerous verses that encourage us to release our need for control and embrace God's plans, which are often beyond our understanding. For instance, Proverbs 3:5-6 reminds us to trust in the Lord with all our hearts and not lean on our own understanding, but instead acknowledge Him in all our ways. This commitment to daily devotion can transform our perspective, helping us recognize that God's timing is perfect.

In moments of uncertainty, it is vital to seek peace through scripture. Philippians 4:6-7 offers reassurance that through prayer and supplication with thanksgiving, we can present our requests to God, and His peace will guard our hearts. Incorporating this practice into our daily life allows us to express our fears and anxieties while trusting that God has a plan for our future. As we meditate on these verses, we begin to understand that our timelines may not align with God's, yet His ways are higher than ours, as stated in Isaiah 55:8-9. This acknowledgment fosters a sense of comfort and peace, guiding us through the unpredictable seasons of life.

Letting go and letting God requires intentionality. Biblical stories of trust and surrender, such as Abraham's journey to Canaan or Mary's acceptance of her role as the mother of Jesus, provide powerful examples of faith in action. These narratives remind us that surrendering control often leads to divine blessings and fulfillment of God's promises. By reflecting on these stories during our daily devotions, we can learn to emulate their trust and obedience, even when the path ahead seems unclear. Each account reinforces the message that God's plans, though sometimes mysterious, are always for our good and His glory.

Prayer and patience are essential components of developing trust in God's timing. Psalm 27:14 encourages us to wait for the Lord and be strong; our hearts should take courage as we wait. Establishing a consistent prayer routine allows us to communicate our desires and frustrations to God while patiently waiting for His response. Through regular prayer, we build a trusting relationship with God, learning to lean on Him during times of doubt. Patience is not merely a passive state but an active commitment to trust in God's process, recognizing that He is working all things together for our good, as highlighted in Romans 8:28.

Finally, cultivating a heart of surrender is a journey that requires daily devotion, scriptural reflection, and community support. Surrounding ourselves with fellow believers who share similar struggles can provide encouragement and accountability. As we continue to trust God's purpose for our lives, we can find strength in the knowledge that we are not alone. Engaging with daily devotions not only deepens our relationship with God but also equips us to face the challenges of singleness with grace and faith. In doing so, we embrace the beautiful truth that surrendering control to God leads to a life filled with hope, joy, and divine purpose.

Scriptures to Meditate On

In the journey of trusting God's timeline, scriptures serve as powerful tools to ground our faith and encourage our hearts. For Christian singles navigating the complexities of life and relationships, meditating on biblical verses can provide profound insights into surrendering control and embracing divine timing. The Word of God offers both comfort and direction, reminding us that our plans are often not aligned with His divine purpose. By reflecting on specific passages, we can cultivate a mindset that prioritizes faith over fear, allowing God's timing to guide our lives.

One pivotal scripture to meditate on is Jeremiah 29:11, where God assures us, "For I know the plans I have for you, declares the Lord, plans to prosper you and not to harm you, plans to give you hope and a future." This verse emphasizes that God has a purpose for each of us, one that transcends our immediate desires and timelines. When we internalize this promise, we can find peace in knowing that God's plans are inherently good, even when life feels uncertain. This assurance can help singles relinquish the urge to control their circumstances and instead trust in the unfolding of God's perfect timing.

Another scripture that resonates deeply with the theme of surrender is Proverbs 3:5-6, which counsel us to "Trust in the Lord with all your heart and lean not on your own understanding; in all your ways submit to Him, and He will make your paths straight." These verses remind us that our understanding is limited, and reliance on our own reasoning often leads to anxiety and frustration. By submitting our plans to God, we open ourselves to His guidance and direction. For singles, this can mean letting go of the pressure to find a partner according to a self-imposed timeline and instead allowing God to lead them to the right person at the right time.

Philippians 4:6-7 offers another essential reminder during times of uncertainty: "Do not be anxious about anything, but in every situation, by prayer and petition, with thanksgiving, present your requests to God. And the peace of God, which transcends all understanding, will guard your hearts and your minds in Christ Jesus." In moments of doubt or anxiety, these verses encourage us to bring our worries before God. Through prayer, we can develop a deeper trust in His plans while experiencing the peace that comes from surrendering our concerns to Him. This practice is especially vital for singles who may grapple with feelings of loneliness or impatience regarding their relationship status.

Lastly, Isaiah 40:31 reminds us of the strength we gain through waiting upon the Lord: "But those who hope in the Lord will renew their strength. They will soar on wings like eagles; they will run and not grow weary; they will walk and not be faint." This passage illustrates the transformative power of hope and patience in our spiritual journey. When we actively choose to hope in God's promises, we find renewed strength and resilience, enabling us to navigate the waiting periods of life with grace. By meditating on these scriptures, Christian singles can foster a heart of surrender, embracing God's perfect timing while trusting that He is working all things together for their good.

Overcoming Anxiety with Faith

Biblical Verses for Anxiety Relief

Finding peace in moments of anxiety is a journey that many Christian singles face as they navigate their lives and relationships. The pressures of societal expectations, particularly regarding marriage and companionship, can create overwhelming feelings of uncertainty and fear. However, the Bible offers numerous verses that encourage believers to surrender their worries and trust in God's perfect timing. By meditating on these scriptures, individuals can cultivate a heart of peace and reassurance amid life's challenges.

Philippians 4:6-7 is a powerful reminder of God's promise to provide peace that surpasses all understanding. This passage encourages believers to bring their anxieties to God through prayer and supplication. It emphasizes the importance of communicating with God about our fears and concerns. By doing so, we not only express our trust in Him but also open ourselves to receive His divine peace. As Christian singles, this verse serves as a call to replace anxiety with prayer, allowing God's tranquility to guard our hearts and minds.

Another comforting scripture is Psalm 55:22, which states, "Cast your burden on the Lord, and He will sustain you." This verse reassures believers that they do not have to carry the weight of their worries alone. Surrendering our burdens to God involves an act of faith, trusting that He will take care of our needs and provide the strength to endure. For many singles, this means letting go of the need to control their relationship status and instead, focusing on building a deeper relationship with God, who knows their desires and needs intimately.

Matthew 6:34 further emphasizes the importance of living in the present by reminding us not to worry about tomorrow. This verse encourages believers to focus on today and to trust that God will provide for their needs in His timing. For Christian singles, this can be a liberating truth, releasing the pressure to rush into relationships or anxiously await their future. By embracing this mindset, individuals can find joy in their current season and trust that God is orchestrating their journey according to His divine plan.

Lastly, 1 Peter 5:7 encourages believers to cast all their anxieties on God because He cares for them. This verse serves as a powerful affirmation of God's love and concern for His children. It reassures Christian singles that they do not have to navigate anxiety alone; instead, they can rely on God's unwavering support. By continually surrendering their worries to Him, individuals can cultivate a mindset of trust and patience, allowing God's purpose to unfold in their lives. Embracing these biblical truths equips singles with the strength to overcome anxiety and fosters a deeper reliance on God's perfect timing.

Practical Steps to Trust God More

To trust God more deeply, begin by immersing yourself in Scripture. The Bible is filled with promises of God's faithfulness and His perfect timing. Verses such as Jeremiah 29:11 remind us that God has plans for our lives, plans for hope and a future. By consistently reading and meditating on these verses, you can reinforce your understanding of God's character and His commitment to guide you. This practice not only strengthens your faith but also helps you internalize the truth that God's timing is ultimately for your good.

Another essential step is to cultivate a habit of prayer. Prayer is a powerful means of communicating with God and surrendering your worries and desires to Him. Philippians 4:6-7 encourages believers to present their requests to God with thanksgiving, promising that His peace will guard their hearts and minds. Establishing a regular prayer routine allows you to express your fears and hopes, creating space for God to work in your heart. Over time, this practice fosters a deeper trust in His timing and plans.

Additionally, surrounding yourself with a community of fellow believers can significantly enhance your journey of trust. Engaging in discussions, attending Bible studies, or participating in church activities can provide encouragement and accountability. Proverbs 27:17 states that iron sharpens iron, emphasizing the importance of mutual support in spiritual growth. Sharing your struggles and victories with others who understand your journey can help you see God's faithfulness reflected in their lives, reinforcing your own trust in Him.

Practicing gratitude is another practical step towards trusting God more. Keeping a journal of blessings can shift your focus from what you lack to the abundance God has already provided. In 1 Thessalonians 5:16-18, believers are urged to rejoice always and give thanks in all circumstances. By acknowledging God's past provision and the countless ways He has been faithful, you can build a reservoir of trust that sustains you during uncertain times.

Finally, embrace the process of waiting as an opportunity for growth. The Bible is replete with examples of individuals who had to wait on God's timing, such as Abraham and Sarah, who received the promise of a child after years of waiting. Reflecting on these stories can help you see that waiting is not a passive endeavor but an active trust in God's sovereignty. As you learn to be patient and to lean into His presence during these times, you will find that your faith deepens and your ability to trust God grows stronger.

Building a Trusting Relationship with God

Scriptural Steps to Deepen Your Faith

In the journey of faith, particularly for Christian singles navigating the complexities of life and relationships, the scriptures offer profound guidance on deepening trust in God's perfect timing. One essential step is immersing oneself in the Word of God. Regular reading and meditation on scriptures such as Jeremiah 29:11, which reminds us that God has plans for our future, can provide reassurance during moments of uncertainty. This practice not only strengthens faith but also cultivates a mindset of surrender, allowing individuals to recognize that God's timeline often differs from their own expectations.

Prayer is another fundamental aspect of deepening faith. Philippians 4:6-7 encourages believers to present their requests to God with thanksgiving, promising that His peace will guard their hearts and minds. Through prayer, singles can express their desires, worries, and hopes, fostering a deeper relationship with God. This communication helps to shift focus from control over circumstances to trust in God's sovereignty, creating space for His peace to flourish amidst life's challenges. Engaging in consistent prayer also reinforces the understanding that God's timing is perfect, even when it feels del ay ed.

Incorporating biblical stories of trust and surrender can serve as powerful examples for Christian singles. The narrative of Abraham, who waited for years for the fulfillment of God's promise of a son, illustrates the importance of patience and faith. Romans 4:20-21 highlights Abraham's unwavering belief in God's promises, which can inspire individuals to remain steadfast in their own journeys. Reflecting on such stories encourages singles to embrace their own waiting periods as opportunities for growth and reliance on God's plans.

Another vital step is surrounding oneself with a community of believers who can provide support and encouragement. Hebrews 10:24-25 emphasizes the importance of gathering together and encouraging one another in faith. This fellowship can be particularly beneficial for singles as they navigate their unique challenges. Sharing experiences and testimonies of how others have trusted in God's timing can reinforce personal faith and serve as reminders that they are not alone in their journey of surrender.

Lastly, developing a heart of gratitude can significantly impact how one perceives their circumstances. 1 Thessalonians 5:16-18 calls believers to rejoice always, pray continually, and give thanks in all circumstances. By cultivating gratitude, singles can shift their focus from what they lack to the blessings already present in their lives. This attitude not only fosters a deeper trust in God's provision but also reinforces the belief that He is at work in every situation, ultimately leading to a more profound surrender to His divine timing.

The Importance of Community in Surrender

Community plays an essential role in the journey of surrender for Christian singles. Engaging with others who share similar beliefs and experiences can provide support and encouragement in the process of letting go of control and trusting God's timing. In moments of uncertainty, the shared understanding of struggles and triumphs can foster a sense of belonging, reminding individuals that they are not alone in their faith journey. The Bible emphasizes the importance of community in several instances, from the early church in Acts to the letters of Paul, which highlight the need for fellowship and mutual support.

Scripture offers numerous examples of how community can strengthen our faith. For instance, in Ecclesiastes 4:9-10, we are reminded that "two are better than one," as they can help each other in times of need. This verse illustrates that during the challenging times of surrendering control, having a supportive community can provide the encouragement needed to persevere. Whether through prayer groups, Bible studies, or simple gatherings, Christian singles can find solace in the fellowship of others who also seek to trust God's divine timing.

Moreover, community can serve as a source of accountability. When individuals are surrounded by fellow believers, it becomes easier to stay committed to their journey of surrender. Sharing personal struggles and victories with trusted friends can facilitate honest conversations about faith and doubt. Hebrews 10:24-25 encourages believers to "consider how to stir up one another to love and good works," emphasizing the importance of coming together to uplift each other. This accountability can help singles remain focused on their spiritual growth and reliance on God.

In addition to providing support and accountability, community can also offer diverse perspectives on surrendering to God's plans. Different experiences and testimonies can illuminate various aspects of faith and trust. Proverbs 27:17 states, "Iron sharpens iron, and one man sharpens another." Engaging with others can lead to deeper insights into God's character and His timing. Through sharing stories of waiting and trusting, individuals can find hope and inspiration to continue their journey, no matter how difficult it may seem.

Ultimately, the importance of community in the process of surrendering lies in its ability to foster an environment of love, encouragement, and growth. Christian singles can find strength in the collective faith of those around them, reminding them that surrendering control is not just a personal battle but a communal journey. By seeking out and nurturing these relationships, individuals can cultivate a heart of surrender, learning to embrace divine timing as they navigate the complexities of life and faith together.

Living in Trust

Making Daily Choices that Reflect Trust

Making daily choices that reflect trust in God's plan is essential for Christian singles navigating the complexities of life and relationships. Each decision, no matter how small, can either anchor us in faith or pull us into doubt. As we face choices related to our careers, friendships, and potential romantic relationships, we are called to align our actions with our beliefs. Philippians 4:6-7 reminds us not to be anxious about anything, but in every situation, by prayer and petition, with thanksgiving, present our requests to God. This scripture encourages us to approach our daily choices with a heart of gratitude and trust, acknowledging that God is actively involved in our lives.

Embracing divine timing means recognizing that God's schedule does not always align with our desires. Isaiah 55:8-9 teaches us that God's thoughts and ways are higher than ours, reminding us that what we perceive as delays may actually be divine preparations. When faced with uncertainty or waiting, it is crucial to lean into faith rather than frustration. Choosing to trust God's timing can transform moments of waiting into opportunities for growth and reflection. Instead of rushing decisions, we can take time to pray and seek scripture, allowing God to guide us in ways that align with His perfect plan.

Letting go and letting God is a recurring theme in biblical stories, demonstrating how trust is cultivated through surrender. The story of Abraham exemplifies this beautifully; despite the uncertainties surrounding God's promise, Abraham chose to step out in faith, believing in a future he could not yet see (Genesis 12). As we make daily choices, we can reflect on such testimonies, understanding that our willingness to surrender control opens doors for God to work in our lives. By embracing our role as active participants in His plan, we can find peace even when the path forward seems unclear.

In moments of anxiety, turning to scripture can offer profound comfort and guidance. 1 Peter 5:7 encourages us to cast all our anxieties on Him because He cares for us. Incorporating prayer into our decision-making processes allows us to release our fears and replace them with faith. This practice not only reinforces our relationship with God but also fosters a sense of peace that transcends our circumstances. When we acknowledge our limitations and trust God's purposes, we become more resilient and open to His leading.

As we cultivate a heart of surrender, daily devotions can serve as a powerful tool for reinforcing our commitment to trust. Engaging with scriptures such as Jeremiah 29:11, which assures us of God's plans for our future, helps us to internalize the truth that we are not navigating life alone. By consistently reflecting on these promises and integrating them into our choices, we build a trusting relationship with God. This journey of surrender is not always easy, but it is one that leads to deeper faith, greater peace, and the assurance that God's timing is always worth the wait.

Celebrating God's Faithfulness in Your Life

Celebrating God's faithfulness in your life is a powerful practice that can transform your perspective as a Christian single. Recognizing moments when God has shown His unwavering love and support reinforces the promise found in Hebrews 10:23, which encourages believers to hold unswervingly to the hope we profess, for He who promised is faithful. Reflecting on these experiences helps to cultivate a heart of gratitude and reminds us to trust God's timeline, even when it feels uncertain. By intentionally acknowledging God's past faithfulness, we can build a stronger foundation for our future, knowing that He is always working in our lives.

As you navigate the journey of singleness, it is essential to remember that God's timing is perfect. The story of Joseph in Genesis illustrates this beautifully. Joseph faced numerous challenges and delays in his life, but each setback was part of God's larger plan to position him for greatness. Embracing this truth can provide comfort when life doesn't go as planned. Romans 8:28 reassures us that all things work together for good for those who love God. By celebrating the little victories and recognizing God's hand in your life, you can foster an attitude of trust and patience.

Prayer plays a pivotal role in celebrating God's faithfulness. As you commit to praying regularly, incorporate moments of thanksgiving into your conversations with God. Philippians 4:6-7 encourages us not to be anxious but to present our requests to God with thanksgiving. By doing so, you open your heart to experience His peace and presence. Documenting your prayers and the ways God answers them can serve as a powerful reminder of His faithfulness. When you look back on these records, you will see how God has been at work, reinforcing your trust in His divine plan.

In times of uncertainty, it's crucial to turn to Scripture for guidance and encouragement. Verses such as Isaiah 41:10 remind us not to fear, for God is with us. As you face moments of doubt or anxiety about your future, immerse yourself in the Word. Let the stories of biblical figures who trusted God's timing inspire you. Whether it's the faith of Abraham, the perseverance of Job, or the unwavering trust of Ruth, each story offers insight into the beauty of surrendering control and relying on God's faithfulness.

Ultimately, celebrating God's faithfulness is about recognizing His presence in every aspect of your life. It invites you to share your journey with others, fostering a community of support and encouragement among fellow believers. As you celebrate how God has worked in your life, you can also encourage others to see His faithfulness in their own journeys. Your testimony can serve as a beacon of hope, reminding those around you that trusting God, especially in times of waiting, leads to a deeper relationship with Him and a more profound sense of peace.

Chapter 5

The Single Life: Embracing God's Plan Beyond Marriage

The Single Life as God's Design

Singleness is Not a Problem to Solve

Singleness is often viewed through the lens of societal pressures, where the emphasis is placed on finding a partner as the ultimate goal in life. However, it is essential for Christian singles to recognize that singleness is not a problem to be solved but rather a divine calling. The Bible presents numerous instances where individuals thrived in their singleness, demonstrating that fulfillment and purpose can be found outside of marriage. Embracing this perspective allows singles to focus on their unique contributions to the Kingdom of God, rather than viewing their status as a deficiency.

In 1 Corinthians 7:7, the Apostle Paul highlights the gift of singleness, stating, "I wish that all of you were as I am. But each of you has your own gift from God; one has this gift, another has that." This scripture underscores the importance of recognizing singleness as a divine gift rather than a burden. Each person is equipped with distinct talents and callings, and for many, this season of life allows for greater freedom to pursue God's purpose without the distractions that can accompany marriage. Understanding this can shift the mindset from seeing singleness as a temporary state to embracing it as a crucial part of one's spiritual journey.

The story of Ruth and Naomi offers valuable lessons on building a fulfilled life in singleness. Ruth's loyalty and commitment to Naomi exemplify the strength of deep, meaningful relationships that can exist outside of romantic partnerships. Their narrative illustrates that companionship and support among friends can fulfill emotional and spiritual needs, emphasizing the importance of community in the single life. In Ecclesiastes 4:9-12, we see that "two are better than one," highlighting how mutual support and companionship enrich our lives, regardless of marital status.

Personal growth during the single years is crucial for future relationships and overall well-being. Biblical examples, such as Daniel and Esther, demonstrate how individuals can develop their character and skills while serving God. By investing time in spiritual disciplines, pursuing education, and honing talents, singles can prepare themselves for whatever God has planned for their future. This growth fosters a sense of contentment, as articulated in Philippians 4:11-13, where Paul speaks of learning to be content in all circumstances. This contentment is rooted in a deep relationship with Christ, allowing singles to find joy and purpose in their current season.

Lastly, understanding God's timing is vital for navigating the single life. Jeremiah 29:11 reassures us that God has specific plans for each of us, plans that are for our welfare and not for harm. Trusting in His timing helps alleviate the pressure to rush into relationships or feel inadequate in one's current status. Instead, singles are encouraged to seek first the Kingdom of God, as instructed in Matthew 6:33, and to cultivate a relationship with Him that brings peace and fulfillment. By focusing on God's presence, as promised in Psalm 16:11, singles can navigate feelings of loneliness and find joy in their relationship with the Lord, redefining their understanding of what it means to live a fulfilled life in Christ.

Marriage is Not the Solution

Marriage is often portrayed as the ultimate goal in life, especially within many Christian circles. However, the idea that marriage is a solution to personal fulfillment or happiness can lead to misguided expectations and disappointments. The Bible does not frame singleness as a problem to be solved but rather as a unique state of life filled with opportunities for growth, service, and deeper relationship with God. In 1 Corinthians 7:7, Paul emphasizes that both marriage and singleness are gifts from God, each with their own advantages and callings. It is crucial for singles to recognize that their worth and purpose are not contingent upon marital status.

Embracing singleness as a divine calling can transform how one perceives this period of life. The Scriptures provide numerous examples of individuals who thrived in their singleness, such as the prophetess Anna, who dedicated her life to serving God in the temple (Luke 2:36-38). These biblical accounts highlight that being single allows for a unique focus on one's relationship with God and the freedom to pursue His calling without the distractions that can accompany marriage. By viewing singleness as a divine purpose, Christian singles can cultivate a mindset that celebrates this season rather than viewing it as a temporary deficiency.

In 1 Corinthians 7:7, Paul articulates the implications of singleness, recognizing it as a gift. This perspective encourages individuals to appreciate the opportunities for personal growth, creativity, and self-development that come with being single. For example, the story of Ruth and Naomi illustrates how strong relationships can flourish outside of marriage. Their bond showcases the importance of community and support, which can provide a sense of fulfillment and belonging. Singles can derive immense joy and purpose from investing in friendships and community, knowing that these relationships are valuable and significant.

Ecclesiastes 4:9-12 reminds us of the power of companionship, emphasizing that two are better than one. In the context of single life, this verse underscores the importance of building a supportive community. Friends can serve as a vital source of encouragement and accountability, helping each other navigate the challenges of loneliness and uncertainty. By fostering deep connections, singles can experience the richness of companionship, reflecting the love of Christ in their relationships without the necessity of romantic involvement.

Ultimately, contentment in Christ is foundational for singles. Philippians 4:11-13 teaches that true fulfillment comes from relying on God rather than circumstances or relationships. Learning to find joy in God's presence, as expressed in Psalm 16:11, allows individuals to navigate loneliness while cultivating a sense of wholeness. As singles embrace their season of life, trusting in God's timing as outlined in Jeremiah 29:11, they can redefine their understanding of relationships and purpose, finding peace and direction that transcends the cultural narrative that equates marriage with happiness.

Embracing Singleness as a Divine Calling

Biblical Perspectives on Purpose

Biblical perspectives on purpose provide a profound framework for understanding the significance of singleness in the life of a Christian. The Bible teaches that each individual has a unique calling and purpose, independent of marital status. In 1 Corinthians 7:7, Paul emphasizes that singleness is a gift, suggesting that being single allows for undivided devotion to the Lord. This perspective challenges the notion that marriage is the ultimate goal, instead highlighting that God has a specific plan for everyone, whether single or married. Embracing this divine calling can lead to a fulfilling life rooted in serving God and others.

One of the most compelling examples of purpose in singleness is found in the story of Ruth and Naomi. Their relationship illustrates the importance of community and mutual support in the journey of life. Ruth's commitment to Naomi not only provided companionship but also demonstrated how single individuals can fulfill God's purpose through relationships with others. As Ruth chose to remain with Naomi, she became part of God's larger plan, ultimately leading to her role in the lineage of David and, subsequently, Jesus. This narrative reinforces that singleness can be a time of significant contribution and impact within the community of faith.

The implications of 1 Corinthians 7:7 extend beyond the acknowledgment of singleness as a gift; they also encourage personal growth and development. Biblical examples like Joseph and Daniel illustrate how single individuals can pursue their God-given talents and callings. Joseph's journey from slavery to becoming a leader in Egypt showcases the importance of perseverance and faithfulness to God's purpose, even in challenging circumstances. Similarly, Daniel's commitment to his faith in a foreign land highlights the power of integrity and devotion to God, serving as a reminder that fulfillment comes from living out one's purpose, regardless of marital status.

Furthermore, the Bible emphasizes the importance of spiritual wholeness before considering marriage. Matthew 6:33 instructs believers to seek first the kingdom of God, which underscores the necessity of personal relationship with Christ. For Christian singles, this pursuit of spiritual maturity is vital in building a solid foundation for future relationships. Engaging deeply in one's faith not only fosters personal growth but also prepares individuals to enter into healthy partnerships when the time is right. A strong spiritual life ensures that future relationships are grounded in shared faith and values, enhancing the potential for lasting connections.

Lastly, navigating feelings of loneliness can be particularly challenging for singles. Psalm 16:11 reassures believers that true joy and fulfillment are found in God's presence. Engaging in prayer, worship, and community can help alleviate feelings of isolation. By cultivating a deep relationship with God and surrounding oneself with supportive friends, singles can experience joy in their current season of life. This reliance on God not only brings comfort but also emphasizes that one's worth and purpose are not contingent upon marital status but are rooted in being a beloved child of God.

The Beauty of Being Set Apart

The beauty of being set apart lies in the unique opportunity to cultivate a deep and personal relationship with God. In a world that often equates worth with marital status, it is essential for Christian singles to embrace the truth that singleness is not a problem to be solved but a divine calling. The Bible offers numerous examples of individuals who were called to serve God in their singleness, demonstrating that this season can be filled with purpose and fulfillment. By recognizing that God has crafted a unique plan for each individual, singles can find joy and significance in their current state, knowing they are not lacking but rather positioned for specific assignments in His kingdom.

1 Corinthians 7:7 reminds us that singleness can be considered a gift. Paul emphasizes that not everyone is called to marry; some are called to be single for the sake of the kingdom. This perspective challenges the societal norm that suggests marriage is the ultimate goal in life. Instead, it invites singles to explore their gifts and talents, seeking to use them in service to others and to God. Embracing this calling can lead to a life of abundance, where individuals can focus on spiritual growth, personal development, and making a positive impact within their communities without the distractions that often accompany married life.

The story of Ruth and Naomi illustrates the beauty of building a fulfilled life in singleness through strong, supportive relationships. Despite their circumstances, both women exemplified loyalty, faithfulness, and resilience. Their journey reveals that singles can find purpose and strength in community, reflecting the teachings of Ecclesiastes 4:9-12, which emphasizes the value of companionship and mutual support. In the context of singleness, this means fostering deep, meaningful friendships that can provide encouragement and accountability, ultimately enriching the single life.

Personal growth is another vital aspect of being set apart. Biblical figures such as Joseph and David exemplified how God used their seasons of waiting and preparation to shape their character and fulfill His plans. In singleness, individuals have the opportunity to invest in their personal and spiritual development, focusing on areas such as education, career, and ministry. This growth not only enhances one's life but also prepares the heart for future relationships, aligning with the principle found in Matthew 6:33, which encourages prioritizing God's kingdom and righteousness above all else.

Finally, finding contentment in Christ is crucial for singles navigating the complexities of life. Philippians 4:11-13 teaches that true fulfillment comes from a deep reliance on God rather than external circumstances. In moments of loneliness or longing for companionship, singles can turn to God's presence for comfort and joy, as highlighted in Psalm 16:11. By redefining their understanding of relationships and anchoring their identity in Christ, singles can embrace their unique journey, trusting that God's timing is perfect and that He has a meaningful plan for their lives, as assured in Jeremiah 29:11.

The Gift of Singleness

Understanding 1 Corinthians 7:7

1 Corinthians 7:7 presents a profound perspective on the gift of singleness, emphasizing that both marriage and singleness are divine gifts from God. The Apostle Paul acknowledges that each state has its unique advantages and challenges. For Christian singles, understanding this verse is crucial as it reframes the narrative around singleness as a purposeful and valued phase of life rather than a mere waiting period for marriage. Paul expresses his desire that all may be as he is, highlighting the freedom and opportunities that come with being unmarried. This perspective encourages singles to embrace their current state as a calling and a chance for personal and spiritual growth.

In the context of singleness, the verse conveys that being single is not a deficiency or a problem to be solved. Instead, it is an opportunity for individuals to dedicate themselves fully to the Lord's work without the distractions that often come with marriage. This understanding is vital for Christian singles who may feel societal pressure to pursue marriage as the ultimate goal. Paul points out that each person has their own gift from God, suggesting that singleness can be just as fulfilling and significant as marriage. Embracing this gift allows singles to focus on their relationship with God, fostering a deeper understanding of their identity in Christ.

Furthermore, Paul's message in 1 Corinthians 7:7 encourages singles to cultivate a spirit of contentment in their current circumstances. It challenges the narrative that fulfillment can only be found in romantic relationships, urging individuals to seek satisfaction in their relationship with God. This aligns with other biblical teachings, such as Philippians 4:11-13, where Paul emphasizes contentment in every situation. By internalizing this principle, singles can build a life rich in purpose and joy, finding fulfillment in their unique calling and the opportunities it presents.

Additionally, understanding 1 Corinthians 7:7 can help singles build strong, healthy relationships within their community. As Paul highlights the value of both marital and single states, it is essential for singles to engage with others, forming meaningful friendships and support systems. The biblical story of Ruth and Naomi illustrates the power of companionship and mutual support, showing that deep, fulfilling relationships can exist outside of romantic contexts. These connections can provide encouragement, accountability, and a sense of belonging, reinforcing the notion that community plays a vital role in the single life.

Ultimately, embracing the message of 1 Corinthians 7:7 equips Christian singles to navigate their journey with confidence and purpose. It reinforces the idea that singleness is not a waiting room but a vibrant and dynamic season of life filled with potential. By cultivating a deeper relationship with God, fostering community, and seeking personal growth, singles can truly embrace their divine calling. This understanding leads to a life characterized by joy, fulfillment, and a steadfast trust in God's perfect timing for their future, whatever that may hold.

Implications for Today's Singles The implications for today's singles within the context of embracing God's plan beyond marriage are profound and multifaceted. In a culture that often equates singleness with a problem to be solved, it is essential to recognize that this state of life is not a deficiency but rather a unique calling filled with divine purpose. The Bible provides a framework that encourages singles to view their lives through the lens of God's intentions. Scriptures such as 1 Corinthians 7:7 remind us that singleness is a gift, allowing individuals to serve God and others with undivided attention, fostering a deeper relationship with Him and a greater impact on their communities.

Embracing singleness as a divine calling encourages individuals to seek their purpose in Christ rather than in societal expectations. The story of Ruth and Naomi illustrates this beautifully, showcasing how God can work through relationships and circumstances to fulfill His promises. Ruth's commitment to Naomi and her faithfulness to God led to a transformative journey, ultimately resulting in blessings that extended beyond their immediate situation. Singles today can learn from this narrative to cultivate meaningful relationships and seek God's direction in their lives, understanding that their contributions to the world can be as significant as those of married individuals.

The gift of singleness, as articulated in 1 Corinthians 7:7, emphasizes the importance of personal growth and self-development. It challenges singles to invest in their spiritual, emotional, and intellectual lives, equipping them for future relationships or fulfilling lives independent of marital status. Biblical examples of self-development, such as Daniel and his unwavering commitment to God amid challenges, serve as reminders that personal growth is a continuous journey. By prioritizing their relationship with God and developing their gifts, singles can build a fulfilled life that resonates with purpose and joy.

Community plays a critical role in the lives of singles. Ecclesiastes 4:9-12 highlights the value of companionship, illustrating how mutual support strengthens individuals. For those navigating the complexities of singleness, building a robust network of friends and mentors can provide encouragement and accountability. The importance of fostering authentic relationships cannot be overstated; these connections can alleviate feelings of loneliness and isolation, helping individuals to experience the fullness of life that God desires for them. Engaging in community also allows singles to share their unique insights and gifts, contributing to the body of Christ in meaningful ways.

Ultimately, understanding and accepting God's timing is crucial for singles. Jeremiah 29:11 assures believers that God has plans for their lives, filled with hope and a future. By trusting in His timing and remaining content in their current circumstances, singles can foster a sense of peace and purpose. Philippians 4:11-13 encourages contentment, reminding individuals that true fulfillment is found in Christ, regardless of marital status. As singles navigate their journey, cultivating joy in God's presence, redefining relationships, and embracing their unique roles within the community will empower them to live fully and authentically, embodying the essence of God's plan for their lives.

Building a Fulfilled Life in Singleness

Lessons from Ruth and Naomi

In the narrative of Ruth and Naomi, we find profound lessons that resonate with the journey of Christian singles today. Their story begins with hardship, illustrating that life can bring unexpected challenges. Naomi, widowed and bereft, faced a daunting future. Yet, rather than succumbing to despair, she models resilience. This teaches us that embracing our current season—whether singleness or another—is vital. The Bible encourages us to recognize that every chapter in our lives serves a purpose, urging us to seek God's will even in times of uncertainty.

Ruth's decision to stay with Naomi exemplifies the beauty of loyalty and the importance of community. In a world that often emphasizes individualism, Ruth's commitment reminds us that relationships matter. For Christian singles, cultivating deep, supportive friendships can provide a sense of belonging and purpose. Proverbs 27:17 states, "As iron sharpens iron, so one person sharpens another." Engaging in meaningful relationships helps us grow spiritually and emotionally, fostering a community where we can thrive while single.

The bond between Ruth and Naomi further demonstrates the concept of divine providence. As Ruth gleaned in Boaz's fields, she unknowingly stepped into God's plan, which ultimately led to her becoming part of the lineage of Christ. This narrative encourages singles to remain open to God's leading, trusting that He orchestrates events for our good. Often, singles may feel overlooked or uncertain about their future, but Ruth's story reassures us that God sees us and has a purpose for our lives, even when we cannot see the full picture.

Additionally, the characters of Ruth and Naomi illustrate the importance of selflessness and sacrificial love. Ruth's willingness to care for Naomi highlights that fulfillment does not solely come from romantic relationships or marriage. Instead, investing in others and serving our communities can bring joy and purpose in our singleness. In John 15:13, Jesus reminds us that "greater love has no one than this: to lay down one's life for one's friends." This love can manifest in various ways, enriching our lives and the lives of those around us.

Ultimately, the story of Ruth and Naomi encourages singles to embrace their unique calling. By focusing on spiritual growth, community, and service, we can find fulfillment in our current season. As we navigate life, it is essential to remember that singleness is not a problem to be solved but an opportunity to grow in faith and purpose. Embracing God's plan can lead to profound experiences that shape our character and deepen our relationship with Him, preparing us for whatever lies ahead.

Cultivating Purposeful Relationships

Cultivating purposeful relationships is essential for Christian singles who are navigating a season of life that challenges societal norms surrounding marriage. The belief that singleness is not a problem to be solved but a divine calling is fundamental to understanding how to engage meaningfully with others. Relationships should not be viewed solely through the lens of potential romantic connections but as opportunities for fellowship, support, and spiritual growth. By embracing the truth that one's worth and purpose in life are anchored in their identity in Christ, singles can cultivate relationships that reflect God's love and intention for community.

The apostle Paul, in 1 Corinthians 7:7, acknowledges the gift of singleness, stating that each person has their own calling. This scripture invites singles to recognize that their current state is not a limitation but an opportunity to deepen their relationships with God and others. Purposeful relationships can be formed through shared interests, spiritual growth, and mutual support. By focusing on building connections that are rooted in faith, singles can create a community that encourages one another to grow in their relationship with Christ, ultimately enhancing their sense of purpose and belonging.

Lessons from biblical figures such as Ruth and Naomi illustrate the importance of cultivating deep, meaningful relationships in singleness. Their story highlights the beauty of loyalty, support, and encouragement in friendship. Ruth's commitment to Naomi showcases how relationships can be a source of strength during difficult times. For Christian singles, these relationships can provide a safe space to navigate life's challenges, celebrate successes, and seek counsel from those who share similar values. By investing in such purposeful relationships, singles can enrich their lives and reflect God's love in tangible ways.

Community plays a vital role in the life of a single believer, as emphasized in Ecclesiastes 4:9-12. This passage highlights the strength found in companionship and the importance of support systems. For singles, engaging with a community of believers fosters a sense of belonging and accountability. These relationships can help combat feelings of loneliness and isolation, which are often prevalent in single life. By participating in church activities, small groups, or volunteer opportunities, singles can build connections that offer encouragement, prayer support, and shared experiences, reinforcing the idea that they are not alone on their journey.

Finally, cultivating purposeful relationships requires a commitment to personal growth and spiritual wholeness. Matthew 6:33 reminds believers to seek first the Kingdom of God and His righteousness. This principle encourages singles to prioritize their relationship with God, which will naturally enhance their interactions with others. As they grow in their faith and understanding of their identity in Christ, they can approach relationships from a place of contentment, joy, and fulfillment. By focusing on spiritual growth, singles can redefine their relationships, understanding that friendship and community are integral parts of living a fulfilled life, regardless of marital status.

The Role of Community in Single Life

Insights from Ecclesiastes 4:9-12

Ecclesiastes 4:9-12 offers profound insights into the significance of companionship, emphasizing that two are better than one. This passage serves as a reminder to Christian singles that while the journey of singleness may sometimes feel isolating, it can also be a time for building meaningful relationships and fostering a sense of community. The verses illustrate the value of partnership not solely in the context of marriage but in the broader scope of friendship and mutual support. Embracing such relationships can enhance the single life, providing encouragement and strength during challenging times.

The context of Ecclesiastes reveals that life can be filled with toil and struggle. The author highlights the importance of having companions to share burdens and joys alike. For singles, this insight underscores the need for intentional connections within their communities. Building friendships that reflect the love of Christ can lead to spiritual growth and fulfillment, demonstrating that being single does not equate to being alone. Rather, it is an opportunity to cultivate deep, supportive relationships that mirror the biblical call to love and serve one another.

Moreover, the passage emphasizes the strength found in unity. In verse 12, we read that a threefold cord is not quickly broken, which can be interpreted as the importance of including God in relationships. Singles can take this to heart by inviting God into their friendships and community life. When friendships are grounded in faith, they become sources of resilience and encouragement. This understanding helps singles to see their relationships not just as social connections but as divine partnerships that can strengthen their faith journey.

The insights from Ecclesiastes also encourage singles to actively seek out community. This may involve engaging in church activities, participating in small groups, or volunteering. Each of these avenues provides opportunities to connect with others who share similar values and beliefs. The act of reaching out can foster an environment where individuals support one another in their respective journeys, creating a sense of belonging that is vital for emotional and spiritual well-being.

Lastly, embracing the teachings of Ecclesiastes can lead to a more profound understanding of one's purpose during the single season. As singles build relationships, they can discover their unique roles within the body of Christ. Each interaction can serve as a reminder that God has a plan for their lives, which includes the cultivation of deep, meaningful connections. Recognizing the beauty of these relationships can empower singles to view their current state not as a waiting period for marriage but as an integral part of their divine calling.

Building a Supportive Network

In the journey of embracing singleness as a divine calling, building a supportive network becomes essential for Christian singles. This network does not merely serve as a social safety net; it reflects the love and community that Christ exemplified during His time on earth. Ecclesiastes 4:9-12 underscores the strength found in companionship, emphasizing that two are better than one. Engaging with other believers who share similar values and experiences can provide encouragement, accountability, and a sense of belonging. Creating a community that nurtures spiritual growth and mutual support can help singles navigate the complexities of life while reinforcing that their worth is not contingent upon marital status.

A supportive network fosters an environment where individuals can explore their God- given purpose. In 1 Corinthians 7:7, Paul acknowledges the gift of singleness, highlighting that each state—married or single—has its unique advantages for serving God. By surrounding themselves with fellow Christians who appreciate and embrace their current season of life, singles can cultivate a deeper understanding of their calling. Mentorship, shared experiences, and collective prayer can turn a focus on the "problem" of singleness into a celebration of the opportunities for growth and service available during this time.

The biblical narrative of Ruth and Naomi provides a profound example of friendship and support in a single woman's life. Their relationship exemplifies how community can be a source of strength and direction. Ruth's loyalty to Naomi not only led her to her own divine purpose but also demonstrated the power of companionship in times of uncertainty. By forging meaningful relationships similar to Ruth and Naomi's, Christian singles can create bonds that encourage them to seek God's will while also offering the kind of support that strengthens faith and resolves loneliness.

Navigating the feelings of loneliness can be challenging, but a supportive network provides the necessary tools for finding joy in God's presence, as outlined in Psalm 16:11. This scripture reassures believers that true fulfillment and joy are found in a relationship with God. Engaging with a community allows singles to share their struggles and successes, reminding each other of the joy that comes from pursuing God first. Such connections can lead to deeper spiritual insights and personal growth, reinforcing the importance of being rooted in Christ.

Finally, the importance of spiritual wholeness before marriage cannot be overstated, as highlighted in Matthew 6:33. When Christian singles prioritize their relationship with God and build a supportive network, they lay the foundation for a fulfilled life. Trusting in God's timing, as mentioned in Jeremiah 29:11, encourages singles to embrace their current status while preparing for whatever future He has in store. Through communal support, singles can learn to redefine their relationships and find fulfillment in friendships, reinforcing the truth that their identity and purpose are grounded in Christ, not in their marital status.

Personal Growth in Singleness

Biblical Examples of Self-Development

Biblical narratives are rich with examples of individuals who embraced self-development during their seasons of singleness. These stories serve as powerful reminders that personal growth and purpose can flourish outside of marriage. The life of Joseph, for instance, showcases how he developed character and leadership skills while enduring hardships as a single man. Sold into slavery by his brothers, Joseph remained faithful to God, which ultimately led him to rise to power in Egypt. His journey illustrates that even in the most challenging circumstances, God can shape our character and prepare us for future roles that align with His divine purpose.

Another compelling example is that of David, who spent significant time as a shepherd before becoming king. During his years in the fields, David honed his skills, developed his relationship with God, and learned valuable lessons about leadership and faithfulness. His time in solitude was not wasted; instead, it was a period of preparation for the greater calling ahead. David's psalms reflect his deep reliance on God and a commitment to personal growth, emphasizing that self-development often stems from a close relationship with the Creator, which is accessible to all, regardless of marital status.

Esther's story further highlights the transformative power of self-development in a single life context. As a young woman, Esther was thrust into a challenging situation that required courage, wisdom, and faith. Her preparation involved not only physical beauty but also spiritual readiness, as she fasted and sought God's guidance before taking action to save her people. Esther exemplifies how singles can engage in personal development through prayer, seeking wisdom, and embracing their unique roles in God's plan, reinforcing the idea that God can use individuals in profound ways, even when they are single.

The Apostle Paul also provides a model for self-development through his own life and teachings. In 1 Corinthians 7:7, he acknowledges the gift of singleness and encourages others to embrace it. Paul's dedication to his mission, extensive travels, and writings demonstrate how he maximized his time as a single man to advance the gospel and grow spiritually. His letters reflect a deep understanding of contentment and purpose, reminding Christian singles that their value and calling are not diminished by their marital status but can be enhanced through dedication to God's work.

Lastly, the story of Timothy showcases the importance of mentorship and community in self-development. Raised by a strong mother and grandmother, Timothy grew in faith and knowledge under their influence and the guidance of Paul. This illustrates that the development of character and spiritual maturity can flourish within a supportive community. For singles, investing in relationships that foster growth and accountability is essential. In every example, the Bible encourages singles to view their season of life as an opportunity for growth, learning, and preparation for the future, reinforcing the belief that God has a unique and purposeful plan for each individual.

Strategies for Growing Spiritually and Emotionally

Spiritual and emotional growth is essential for Christian singles who are navigating their unique journey. Embracing the truth that singleness is not a problem to be solved, but rather a divine calling, allows individuals to focus on cultivating their relationship with God. This growth begins with a commitment to personal prayer and scripture study, establishing a foundation of faith that nurtures spiritual maturity. Engaging with the Word of God not only provides guidance and wisdom but also fosters a deeper understanding of one's identity in Christ. As believers seek God earnestly, they can experience transformative changes in their hearts and minds.

In addition to personal devotion, community plays a vital role in spiritual and emotional growth. The Bible emphasizes the importance of fellowship, as seen in Ecclesiastes 4:9- 12, which highlights how two are better than one. Building relationships with other believers provides encouragement, accountability, and opportunities for shared experiences in faith. Christian singles can benefit from participating in small groups, church events, and mentorship programs, which can facilitate deeper connections and provide a support network. These relationships serve as a reminder that they are not alone in their journey, fostering a sense of belonging and purpose.

Understanding and embracing the gift of singleness, as articulated in 1 Corinthians 7:7, allows individuals to recognize their unique position in God's plan. This perspective encourages singles to use their time and resources for personal development and service to others. By engaging in volunteer work, pursuing education, or developing new skills, Christians can cultivate a sense of fulfillment and purpose. The stories of biblical figures, such as Ruth and Naomi, demonstrate the importance of using one's circumstances for God's glory and the potential for spiritual growth through service and dedication.

Contentment is another crucial aspect of spiritual and emotional growth. Philippians 4:11-13 speaks to finding joy and peace in all circumstances. Learning to be content with one's current state fosters resilience and gratitude, allowing singles to appreciate the blessings in their lives. Practicing gratitude can shift focus from feelings of loneliness to recognizing God's goodness. Engaging in daily reflections, journaling, or sharing testimonies with others can help cultivate a mindset of thankfulness, reinforcing the belief that God is sufficient in every season of life.

Finally, trusting in God's timing is fundamental for emotional well-being. Jeremiah 29:11 assures believers that God has a plan for their lives, filled with hope and a future. Singles can find peace in the knowledge that their current season is part of a larger divine narrative. This understanding encourages patience and a willingness to wait for God's perfect timing, rather than succumbing to societal pressures regarding marriage. By focusing on spiritual wholeness and developing a strong relationship with God, Christian singles can navigate their journey with confidence, knowing they are fulfilling their God- given purpose while embracing the beauty of singleness.

Contentment in Christ

Exploring Philippians 4:11-13 for Singles

Philippians 4:11-13 offers profound insights into the nature of contentment, particularly relevant for singles navigating their unique journey. The Apostle Paul, writing from a place of imprisonment, emphasizes that contentment is not dependent on external circumstances but rather on an internal relationship with Christ. For Christian singles, this passage serves as a reminder that fulfillment and joy do not hinge on marital status but can be found in a deepening relationship with God. Understanding this truth can reshape how singles perceive their current situation, moving from a mindset of lack to one of abundance in Christ.

In verse 11, Paul states that he has learned to be content in whatever state he finds himself. This learning process is crucial for singles who may struggle with feelings of inadequacy or societal pressure to marry. Embracing singleness as a divine calling allows individuals to focus on personal growth, spiritual development, and the discovery of purpose outside the confines of marital expectations. The journey of learning contentment can lead to a more profound understanding of one's identity in Christ, fostering a sense of peace that is not easily shaken by life's challenges.

Verse 12 expands on the idea of experiencing both abundance and need. For singles, this means recognizing that life can bring various seasons, each with its own set of blessings and trials. Whether feeling fulfilled in a vibrant community or facing moments of loneliness, it's essential to see these experiences as opportunities for growth. By trusting in God's provision, singles can cultivate resilience and adaptability, which are invaluable traits for navigating life with grace and confidence.

The powerful declaration in verse 13, "I can do all things through Christ who strengthens me," encapsulates the essence of empowerment in Christ. For singles, this assurance is transformative. It encourages individuals to pursue their passions, serve others, and engage in life fully, knowing that their strength derives from a source greater than themselves. This perspective shifts the narrative from viewing singleness as a limitation to embracing it as a platform for God's work, where extraordinary things can be accomplished through reliance on Him.

Ultimately, exploring Philippians 4:11-13 invites singles to redefine their relationship with contentment and purpose. By anchoring their identity in Christ and recognizing the value of their current season, they can cultivate a life rich with meaning and joy. This biblical perspective not only affirms that singleness is not a problem to be solved but highlights it as an opportunity for divine empowerment, personal growth, and a deeper connection with God, reinforcing that every phase of life holds its unique purpose within His grand design.

Finding Joy in Your Current Season

Finding joy in your current season is essential for Christian singles who often grapple with societal pressures that equate marital status with fulfillment. It is vital to recognize that singleness is not a problem to be solved, but rather a unique and valuable stage in life that God has designed for each individual. In 1 Corinthians 7:7, Paul articulates that singleness can be a gift, allowing for a deeper focus on God's work and purpose. Embracing this perspective can lead to a joyful acceptance of one's current season, fostering a sense of purpose that transcends societal expectations.

The biblical narrative provides numerous examples of individuals who found fulfillment in their singleness. Consider Ruth and Naomi, whose journey highlights the importance of community and mutual support. Their relationship exemplifies how deep, meaningful connections can provide joy and fulfillment without the necessity of romantic involvement. In Ecclesiastes 4:9-12, we are reminded that two are better than one, indicating that community plays a critical role in nurturing joy during the single season. Building such relationships can cultivate a sense of belonging and purpose, reinforcing the idea that life can be rich and rewarding outside of marriage.

Personal growth is another vital aspect to explore while navigating the journey of singleness. The Bible offers numerous examples of self-development, encouraging individuals to invest in their spiritual and personal growth. This is particularly evident in the lives of biblical figures who thrived in their single status by pursuing their relationship with God. Philippians 4:11-13 teaches contentment, emphasizing that true joy and fulfillment come from reliance on Christ rather than external circumstances. This understanding can empower singles to find joy in their current season, cultivating gratitude for the opportunities and experiences available to them.

Navigating loneliness is a common struggle for many singles, yet it provides an opportunity to deepen one's relationship with God. Psalm 16:11 reassures believers that in God's presence there is fullness of joy. By seeking intimacy with God, singles can experience a profound sense of joy that transcends their circumstances. This relationship can serve as a foundation for their identity and worth, allowing them to face loneliness with a renewed perspective that God is always with them.

Understanding God's timing is also crucial in finding joy during the season of singleness. Jeremiah 29:11 reminds us that God has plans for our lives, and trusting in His timing can alleviate the pressure to rush into relationships. Embracing this truth allows singles to focus on personal growth, spiritual wholeness, and the joy that comes from living in the present. By aligning their desires with God's plan, they can cultivate a fulfilling and joyful life, recognizing that this season is not merely a waiting period, but a beautiful opportunity for growth and purpose.

The Importance of Spiritual Wholeness Before Marriage

Understanding Matthew 6:33 Principles

Understanding Matthew 6:33 Principles emphasizes the call for Christian singles to prioritize their relationship with God above all else. This verse encourages believers to seek God's kingdom and righteousness first, assuring them that all other needs will be provided. For singles, this principle serves as a foundational truth that reshapes their perspective on life and relationships. Rather than viewing singleness as a deficiency or a waiting period for marriage, it can be recognized as a unique opportunity to cultivate a deeper relationship with God.

The practice of seeking God's kingdom involves actively engaging in spiritual growth and pursuing a life aligned with His will. Christian singles are encouraged to invest time in prayer, study of the Scriptures, and involvement in their faith communities. This pursuit not only strengthens their spiritual foundation but also fosters personal development. By focusing on their relationship with God, singles can experience a sense of purpose and fulfillment that transcends societal pressures regarding marriage and relationships.

Embracing God's righteousness means aligning one's values and actions with His teachings. For many singles, this involves reassessing their desires and motivations in the context of their faith. By understanding and living out biblical principles, individuals can cultivate a lifestyle that reflects God's character. This journey of righteousness fosters self-awareness and equips singles to make decisions that honor God, whether in their personal lives, friendships, or potential future relationships.

Furthermore, Matthew 6:33 reassures singles that God is aware of their needs and desires. This understanding brings comfort and alleviates the anxiety that often accompanies the single life. By trusting in God's provision, singles can focus on living fully in the present rather than fixating on future uncertainties. This trust can lead to a more contented life, as individuals learn to find joy and satisfaction in their current circumstances, embracing the fullness of life that God offers.

Ultimately, the principles found in Matthew 6:33 encourage singles to view their season of life as an opportunity for divine purpose and growth. By prioritizing their relationship with God, aligning their lives with His righteousness, and trusting in His provision, Christian singles can navigate their journey with confidence and hope. This approach not only enriches their personal lives but also prepares them for future relationships, grounded in solid faith and a clear understanding of their identity in Christ.

Preparing Your Heart for Future Relationships

Preparing your heart for future relationships is a vital step for Christian singles who desire to embrace their current season of life while remaining open to God's plan for their future. The Bible teaches that singleness is not a problem to be solved, but rather a divine calling filled with purpose and potential. It is essential to view this time not as a waiting period but as a unique opportunity to grow spiritually, emotionally, and relationally. By understanding and embracing the gift of singleness, individuals can cultivate a heart that is prepared for future relationships, grounded in faith and God's promises.

One foundational aspect of preparing your heart is to foster a deep sense of spiritual wholeness. Matthew 6:33 encourages believers to seek first the kingdom of God. This principle emphasizes the importance of prioritizing one's relationship with God above all else. When you focus on spiritual growth and pursue God's will for your life, you become more aligned with His purpose. This alignment not only enriches your personal faith journey but also equips you to enter future relationships from a place of strength and clarity. By nurturing your spiritual life, you cultivate a heart that is ready to engage in healthy, Christ-centered relationships.

Understanding the implications of 1 Corinthians 7:7, which refers to singleness as a gift, can transform how you view your current status. Recognizing that God has infused this season with purpose allows you to build a fulfilled life, similar to the relationship between Ruth and Naomi. Their story exemplifies loyalty, support, and spiritual growth. Through their bond, they navigated challenges and embraced God's timing. By investing in friendships and community, you can mirror this model, establishing a network of support that prepares you emotionally for future romantic relationships while deepening your understanding of love and commitment.

As you prepare your heart, it is also critical to reflect on contentment in Christ, as expressed in Philippians 4:11-13. Learning to find joy and satisfaction in your relationship with God is essential. This contentment fosters resilience against the loneliness that can sometimes permeate the single life. Psalm 16:11 reminds us that joy is found in God's presence. By cultivating a life rich in spiritual fulfillment, you create a solid foundation that allows you to approach future relationships with a healthy mindset and heart free from unrealistic expectations or dependency on another person for happiness.

Lastly, it is vital to trust in God's timing for your life, as Jeremiah 29:11 assures us of His plans to prosper and not to harm us. Preparing your heart means recognizing that each season of life serves a divine purpose, and that includes the waiting periods. Embracing this truth allows you to navigate your single life with hope and anticipation. By fostering relationships grounded in friendship and love, as encouraged by John 15:13, you can create a supportive environment that not only prepares you for future partnerships but also reflects the love of Christ to those around you. In doing so, you align your heart with God's greater plan, ensuring that you are ready to embrace future relationships when the time is right.

Navigating Loneliness

Finding Joy in God's Presence (Psalm 16:11)

Finding joy in God's presence is a profound aspect of the Christian single life, particularly emphasized in Psalm 16:11, which states, "You make known to me the path of life; in your presence there is fullness of joy; at your right hand are pleasures forevermore." This verse encapsulates the essence of finding true fulfillment and joy not in our circumstances or relationships, but in a deep and abiding relationship with God. For singles, this realization invites a transformative perspective, allowing them to embrace their season of life as an opportunity for spiritual growth and intimacy with the Creator.

In a culture that often equates happiness with romantic relationships, it is essential for singles to understand that their worth and joy are not contingent upon marital status. The Bible teaches that God's presence offers a joy that surpasses all understanding and is not limited by external factors. By cultivating a relationship with God through prayer, worship, and the study of His Word, individuals can discover a deeper sense of joy that transcends their current situation. This joy is a gift from God, rooted in His love and faithfulness, and it invites singles to shift their focus from what they lack to the abundant life promised in Christ.

Moreover, Psalm 16:11 assures us that in God's presence, we can find direction and clarity for our lives. Singles often grapple with questions about their future and purpose, but the assurance that God reveals the path of life encourages believers to lean into their faith. This divine guidance is not only about finding a partner but about discovering one's unique calling and purpose within the context of God's plan. Embracing this perspective allows singles to view their lives as meaningful and significant, contributing to the Kingdom of God in various capacities, whether through service, ministry, or personal development.

Community also plays a vital role in experiencing joy in God's presence. As seen in Ecclesiastes 4:9-12, the support and encouragement from fellow believers can enhance the joy found in a relationship with God. Single individuals should seek out friendships that foster spiritual growth, accountability, and mutual encouragement. Being part of a community that shares faith can serve as a reminder of the joy that comes from God and provide opportunities for deeper engagement with His presence through collective worship, study, and fellowship.

Ultimately, navigating loneliness is a reality for many singles, but it is crucial to remember that God's presence is always available. Philippians 4:11-13 teaches us about contentment, and this contentment can be found in the assurance of God's constant companionship. As singles lean into their relationship with God and find joy in His presence, they cultivate a fulfilling life that honors their current season. This journey not only enriches their own lives but also prepares them for future relationships, grounded in spiritual wholeness and a profound understanding of joy that originates from God alone.

Practical Ways to Combat Loneliness

Combatting loneliness as a Christian single can be approached through practical strategies rooted in biblical truths. First, it is essential to cultivate a vibrant relationship with God. Spending time in prayer, studying Scripture, and engaging in worship can fill the void that loneliness often creates. Psalm 16:11 assures us that in God's presence, there is fullness of joy. This joy is not contingent upon our relationship status but is a gift from the Lord that can sustain us in times of solitude. By prioritizing our spiritual life, we can find comfort and companionship in our walk with Christ.

Another effective way to combat loneliness is to actively seek community. Ecclesiastes 4:9-12 highlights the importance of companionship, stating that two are better than one. Engaging in church activities, small groups, or volunteer opportunities can help build meaningful connections with others who share similar values. These relationships not only provide support but also create a sense of belonging, reminding us that we are part of a larger body of believers. Embracing community allows us to experience fellowship and love, mitigating feelings of isolation.

Additionally, focusing on personal growth can transform loneliness into an opportunity for self-discovery and development. The story of Ruth and Naomi illustrates how relationships can flourish through shared purpose and mutual encouragement. As singles, we can dedicate our time to learning new skills, pursuing hobbies, or furthering our education. This commitment to personal growth not only enriches our lives but can also prepare us for future relationships, reinforcing the idea that our value is not diminished by our current status.

Moreover, redefining our understanding of relationships is crucial. John 15:13 teaches us about the depth of friendship, emphasizing that true love involves self-sacrifice. By investing in friendships, we create a supportive network that can help alleviate loneliness. Prioritizing deep, authentic connections rather than superficial interactions foster a more profound sense of belonging. These friendships allow us to experience love in various forms, reinforcing the community aspect of our Christian faith.

Finally, it is vital to embrace contentment in Christ, as emphasized in Philippians 4:11- 13. Recognizing that our worth is found in our relationship with God, rather than our relationship status, can help us navigate feelings of loneliness. By focusing on gratitude and the blessings in our lives, we can cultivate a mindset that appreciates the present moment. Trusting in God's plan for our lives, as outlined in Jeremiah 29:11, assures us that we are not alone and that His timing is perfect. Embracing this perspective can transform loneliness into a season of growth, preparation, and deeper reliance on God's faithfulness.

Redefining Relationships

Friendship and Singleness in the Context of John 15:13

Friendship, as described in John 15:13, emphasizes the profound love that exists within true connections, where one lays down their life for another. In the context of singleness, this verse invites Christian singles to redefine how they view relationships, particularly friendships. Rather than seeing singleness as a deficiency or a state to be escaped, it becomes a season rich with opportunities for deep, meaningful friendships that reflect Christ's love. This understanding allows singles to cultivate relationships that are not merely supportive but transformative, fostering a community that embodies the sacrificial love mentioned in Scripture.

Furthermore, friendships during singleness can serve as a powerful platform for personal growth and spiritual development. The bonds formed with friends can encourage individuals to pursue their God-given potential, providing a safe space for accountability and encouragement. In this environment, singles can explore their identities in Christ, gaining insights and perspectives that they might not encounter in more traditional marital relationships. As they invest in these friendships, they build a support system that reflects the biblical principle of Ecclesiastes 4:9-12, which highlights the strength found in companionship and mutual support.

In understanding the gift of singleness as outlined in 1 Corinthians 7:7, it becomes evident that friendships can fulfill many emotional and spiritual needs typically associated with romantic relationships. By embracing the single life, individuals can focus on cultivating authentic friendships that enrich their lives and foster a sense of belonging. These connections allow singles to share their experiences, joys, and struggles, ultimately creating a community that mirrors the love of Christ. This perspective shifts the narrative from viewing singleness as a waiting period for marriage to recognizing it as a divine calling filled with purpose.

Moreover, the importance of community cannot be overstated. Friendships formed during singleness can offer support during times of loneliness and discouragement. In navigating the complexities of life, friends can remind each other of the joy found in God's presence, as highlighted in Psalm 16:11. By leaning on one another, singles can experience a deeper understanding of God's love and faithfulness, allowing them to find joy and contentment in their current season. This relational dynamic reinforces the idea that while marriage may complement one's life, it is not the sole source of fulfillment.

Ultimately, friendship in the context of singleness serves as a vital reminder of God's design for relational living. As singles lean into the sacrificial love described in John 15:13, they not only fulfill their calling to love others but also create a vibrant community that reflects the heart of God. By embracing friendships as a gift and a vital component of their journey, Christian singles can experience the richness of life God intends, cultivating a deeper relationship with Him and with one another, all while preparing their hearts for whatever the future may hold.

Building Meaningful Connections

Building meaningful connections is an essential aspect of the single life, especially for Christian singles who seek to embrace their journey as a divine calling. In this context, it is important to remember that singleness is not a problem to be solved, nor is marriage the ultimate solution. Instead, God has a unique purpose for each individual, as highlighted in 1 Corinthians 7:7, where Paul speaks of singleness as a gift. This perspective encourages singles to seek fulfillment and joy in their current state, recognizing that their worth is not defined by their relationship status but by their identity in Christ.

The biblical narrative of Ruth and Naomi offers profound insights into building meaningful connections. Their relationship exemplifies loyalty, support, and mutual respect, demonstrating how friendships can provide emotional and spiritual nourishment. Ruth's commitment to Naomi, as expressed in Ruth 1:16-17, serves as a reminder that deep connections can enrich our lives and help us navigate the complexities of singleness. By cultivating such relationships, singles can experience the blessings of companionship and mutual encouragement, fostering a sense of belonging within the community of faith.

Community plays a pivotal role in the life of a single person, as emphasized in Ecclesiastes 4:9-12. This scripture highlights the value of companionship, stating that two are better than one for they have a good return for their labor. In a world where loneliness can be prevalent, engaging with a community of believers provides opportunities for connection, support, and shared experiences. Whether through church involvement, small groups, or volunteer opportunities, singles can find fulfillment in building relationships that reflect Christ's love and serve a greater purpose.

Personal growth is another vital aspect of building meaningful connections while embracing singleness. Biblical figures like Joseph and David demonstrate that periods of waiting and solitude can lead to significant personal development. By investing time in prayer, studying scripture, and pursuing hobbies or education, singles can cultivate skills and attributes that enhance their lives and prepare them for future relationships. This commitment to growth not only enriches their individual lives but also positions them to contribute positively to the lives of others.

Lastly, embracing contentment in Christ is foundational in the journey of building meaningful connections. Philippians 4:11-13 teaches that true contentment comes from relying on God's provision and presence, regardless of circumstances. Understanding that fulfillment is rooted in our relationship with Christ allows singles to approach friendships and potential relationships from a place of wholeness rather than neediness. By prioritizing spiritual wholeness and trusting in

God's timing, as highlighted in Jeremiah 29:11, singles can build meaningful connections that reflect the love of Christ and contribute to a rich, fulfilled life.

Understanding God's Timing Trusting

His Plan for Your Life (Jeremiah 29:11)

Trusting in God's plan for your life is a fundamental perspective that resonates deeply with singles navigating their journey. Jeremiah 29:11 assures us that God has a plan filled with hope and a future for each of us. This promise is especially significant for those who are single, as it reminds us that our current state is not a detour from God's purpose but rather an integral part of His design. Embracing this truth allows singles to look beyond societal pressures regarding marriage and instead focus on the unique calling and opportunities that come with this season of life.

Understanding that singleness is a divine calling can transform how we view our circumstances. Just as God has a purpose for our lives, He also has a specific role for us during this time of singleness. This can mean dedicating ourselves to personal growth, engaging in community service, or nurturing friendships that reflect Christ's love. By trusting in His plan, we can find fulfillment in our current situation and recognize that our value is not determined by our relationship status but by our identity in Christ.

The implications of 1 Corinthians 7:7 highlight the gift of singleness, emphasizing that it is not merely a waiting period for marriage but a season rich with potential. This Scripture encourages us to see our time as singles as an opportunity to cultivate our relationship with God and develop our gifts. By trusting His plan, we open ourselves to new experiences and deeper connections with others, fostering a sense of purpose that transcends the desire for a romantic relationship.

Lessons from biblical figures like Ruth and Naomi illustrate the importance of community and support during the single journey. Their relationship exemplifies how companionship and encouragement can help us navigate life's challenges. Ecclesiastes 4:9-12 reminds us that two are better than one, and as we trust in God's plan, we can build strong, supportive networks that enhance our lives. Engaging with a community of faith can provide the encouragement needed to embrace our singleness and pursue God's calling with confidence.

Ultimately, trusting in God's timing reinforces the importance of spiritual wholeness before marriage. Matthew 6:33 urges us to seek first the kingdom of God, emphasizing that fulfillment comes from aligning our lives with His will. Contentment in Christ, as explored in Philippians 4:11-13, allows us to find joy in our circumstances, knowing that God's plan is perfect. By anchoring ourselves in these truths, we can navigate our single lives with assurance, understanding that every step we take is part of a greater purpose crafted by our Creator.

Embracing the Journey of Singleness

Embracing the journey of singleness is an essential aspect of understanding one's identity in Christ and recognizing that being single is not merely a problem to be solved. The world often portrays marriage as the ultimate goal, but Scripture reveals that singleness can be a divine calling filled with purpose. 1 Corinthians 7:7 reminds us that both marriage and singleness are gifts from God, each with unique opportunities for growth and service. By reframing our perspective, we can see that our worth does not depend on our relationship status but on our identity as beloved children of God.

Exploring singleness through a biblical lens highlights its significance in God's plan. The lives of individuals such as Ruth and Naomi illustrate that meaningful relationships can flourish even outside of marriage. Their story teaches us that companionship, support, and love are not restricted to romantic partnerships. Instead, we can foster deep connections within our communities and with fellow believers, enriching our lives and helping us fulfill our God-given purposes. Embracing singleness means recognizing that every season of life, including this one, is filled with potential and divine appointments.

1 Corinthians 7:7 also emphasizes the idea of singleness as a gift, suggesting that it provides unique opportunities for personal and spiritual growth. During this time, singles can devote themselves to deepening their relationship with God, exploring their passions, and developing their skills. This period can serve as a foundation for spiritual wholeness and maturity, preparing individuals for future relationships. By focusing on self-development and aligning with God's will, singles can cultivate a fulfilled life that glorifies Him.

Community plays a crucial role in navigating the single life, as highlighted in Ecclesiastes 4:9-12. These verses remind us that two are better than one, emphasizing the importance of companionship and support. Engaging with fellow believers allows singles to share experiences, offer encouragement, and grow together in faith. This sense of belonging can alleviate feelings of loneliness and isolation, reinforcing the idea that we are not meant to journey through life alone. Building relationships within the church community can provide a strong support network, helping individuals thrive in their singleness.

Ultimately, contentment in Christ is the foundation for embracing the journey of singleness. Philippians 4:11-13 illustrates the importance of finding joy and sufficiency in God, regardless of circumstances. Trusting in His plan for our lives, as stated in Jeremiah 29:11, encourages singles to wait patiently for God's timing. By redefining relationships and understanding the value of friendship, as depicted in John 15:13, singles can build rich, fulfilling lives that honor God. Embracing the journey of singleness is not just about waiting for marriage but about flourishing in the present, fully engaging in the life God has called us to live.

Chapter 6: Anchored in Trust: Navigating Doubt with God's Promises

 Understanding Doubt

The Nature of Doubt

The experience of doubt is a universal aspect of the human journey, particularly for Christian singles navigating the complexities of faith and relationships. Doubt often arises in moments when God's presence seems distant, and His plans appear unclear. It is during these times that believers are called to rely on their faith, trusting in God's character rather than solely on their circumstances. Understanding the nature of doubt can help singles to recognize it as a natural part of their spiritual growth, rather than a sign of weakness or failure.

Doubt can manifest in various forms, from questioning one's faith to grappling with feelings of isolation and uncertainty. For many singles, this can be especially challenging as they face societal pressures regarding relationships and marriage. In these moments, it is essential to remember that doubt does not equate to a lack of faith. Instead, it can serve as a catalyst for deeper understanding and stronger beliefs. Embracing doubt allows individuals to confront their fears, examine their beliefs more closely, and ultimately draw closer to God in the process.

During difficult times, trusting God can feel like an uphill battle. However, it is essential to acknowledge that faith is not the absence of doubt but the decision to trust God despite it. When life becomes overwhelming, and the path ahead is clouded, singles are encouraged to lean into their faith community. Surrounding oneself with supportive friends and fellow believers can provide the encouragement and perspective needed to navigate these turbulent seasons. Engaging in conversations about doubt and faith can foster a sense of belonging and remind individuals they are not alone in their struggles.

Finding peace in uncertainty often requires intentional practices that draw one closer to God. Journaling can be a powerful tool for reflection, helping to clarify thoughts and emotions during times of doubt. Writing about feelings can create space for prayer and meditation, allowing individuals to process their experiences and seek God's guidance. Additionally, establishing prayer practices can foster a sense of connection with God, even when feelings of disconnection arise. These spiritual disciplines can cultivate emotional resilience, enabling singles to weather the storms of doubt with grace and strength.

Ultimately, stories of hope and faith restoration serve as reminders that doubt is not the end of the journey but a part of it. Many believers have experienced profound growth and transformation through their struggles with doubt. Sharing these testimonies within the community can inspire others, providing reassurance that God is faithful even in the midst of uncertainty. By anchoring themselves in trust and embracing the nature of doubt, Christian singles can navigate their journeys with renewed hope, knowing that God's promises are steadfast and true.

Biblical Perspectives on Doubt

Doubt is a common experience for many Christians, including singles navigating life's complexities. The Bible acknowledges this struggle, presenting various figures who faced doubt yet emerged with stronger faith. For instance, Thomas, one of Jesus' disciples, is often remembered for his skepticism when he insisted on seeing the resurrected Christ before believing. This story illustrates that doubt does not disqualify us from being part of God's narrative. Instead, it can serve as a catalyst for deeper understanding and connection with God, reminding us that even the most devoted followers have moments of uncertainty.

In times of doubt, it is crucial to remember that God's character remains unchanged. The Scriptures provide numerous assurances of God's love and faithfulness, even when His presence seems hidden. Hebrews 11:1 defines faith as "the assurance of things hoped for, the conviction of things not seen." This verse encourages believers to trust God's promises, especially in seasons of uncertainty. For Christian singles, this means leaning into faith practices such as prayer and meditation, which can cultivate a sense of peace and clarity amid doubts about relationships, career paths, and personal worth.

Moreover, the Book of Psalms is rich with expressions of doubt and despair, yet it also reveals a pathway to restoration and hope. Many Psalms articulate feelings of abandonment and confusion, ultimately leading to declarations of trust in God. For singles experiencing loneliness or uncertainty in their spiritual journey, these ancient songs can provide comfort. By journaling their thoughts and feelings, they can mirror the Psalms' raw honesty, allowing space for vulnerability while exploring God's faithfulness through prayer and reflection.

Community support plays a vital role in overcoming doubt. The early church exemplified the importance of fellowship, as believers shared their struggles and encouraged one another. For singles, seeking out a community—whether through small groups or church events—can provide the necessary support during times of doubt. Engaging in discussions about faith struggles can foster deeper connections and remind individuals that they are not alone in their experiences. This shared journey can also offer diverse perspectives on how others have navigated their doubts, enriching one's faith experience.

Lastly, it is essential to recognize that doubt can be a powerful tool for spiritual growth. The Bible often portrays doubt as an opportunity for believers to deepen their relationship with God. By embracing doubt and questioning our faith, we can invite God into our uncertainties, allowing Him to reveal more of His character and purpose. Prayer practices that focus on openness and honesty can transform feelings of disconnection into avenues for deeper intimacy with God. As singles reflect on their experiences and seek God's heart, they can find assurance that their doubts do not diminish their faith; instead, they can lead to profound spiritual resilience and growth.

The Importance of Trusting God

The journey of faith can often feel daunting, especially for Christian singles navigating the complexities of life. In moments when circumstances are overwhelming, and the path ahead seems unclear, it becomes crucial to remember the essence of trusting God. This trust is not merely a passive resignation to fate but an active, dynamic relationship with the Creator who knows us intimately. Embracing the belief that God's heart is always for us, even when we cannot see His hand at work, can transform our experience of doubt into a profound opportunity for spiritual growth.

Trusting God during difficult times is foundational to maintaining emotional resilience. When challenges arise, whether in relationships, career aspirations, or personal struggles, it is easy to succumb to feelings of anxiety and despair. Yet, scripture reminds us that faith is often birthed in the soil of adversity. By anchoring our trust in God's promises, we can cultivate a sense of peace that surpasses understanding. This peace acts as a refuge, allowing us to navigate uncertainty with grace and confidence, knowing that our circumstances do not define our worth or purpose.

In seasons of doubt, community support plays a pivotal role in reinforcing our trust in God. Engaging with fellow believers provides a safe space to share struggles and receive encouragement. Stories of hope and faith restoration from others can inspire us to persevere, reminding us that we are not alone in our journey. As we connect with others, we can also reflect on our own experiences through journaling, which serves as a powerful tool for spiritual clarity. Writing about our feelings and reflections can illuminate our understanding of God's faithfulness, even in moments when we feel disconnected from Him.

Prayer practices are essential in fostering a deeper relationship with God, especially when we encounter feelings of disconnection. Setting aside intentional time for prayer, whether through structured methods or spontaneous conversations, allows us to express our doubts and fears. It is in these honest dialogues that we can invite God into our uncertainties, seeking His guidance and comfort. As we cultivate a prayer life rooted in trust, we become more attuned to His presence and the gentle nudges of the Holy Spirit, guiding us through our trials.

Ultimately, trusting God is a journey of spiritual growth that requires patience and perseverance. In every season of life, whether filled with joy or marked by struggle, we are invited to deepen our understanding of His character. By placing our trust in God, we move from a mindset of fear and uncertainty to one of hope and assurance. As we anchor ourselves in this trust, we not only find peace in our own lives but also serve as a beacon of hope for others, encouraging them to navigate their own doubts with faith.

God's Promises in Difficult Times

Recognizing God's Presence

Recognizing God's presence, especially in times of uncertainty, can be a profound challenge for Christian singles navigating the complexities of their lives. Many find themselves in seasons where the divine seems distant, leading to feelings of doubt and confusion. However, it is essential to remember that God's presence is not always linked to visible signs or immediate answers. Trusting in God's heart, even when we cannot see His hands at work, is a crucial aspect of developing a resilient faith that can withstand life's trials.

In moments of doubt, recognizing God's presence often begins with cultivating an awareness of His promises. Scripture is filled with assurances that God is always with us, even when we face adversity. For singles who may feel isolated or uncertain about their future, engaging with these promises can provide a foundation of hope. Journaling can be a helpful tool during these times, allowing individuals to reflect on their spiritual journey, document their struggles, and record moments when they sensed God's presence. This practice not only fosters clarity but also helps to reinforce the understanding that God is actively involved in their lives, even when circumstances suggest otherwise.

Community support is another vital aspect of recognizing God's presence. Engaging with fellow believers can provide encouragement and accountability during difficult seasons. When doubt creeps in, sharing experiences with others can illuminate the ways God is working in their lives, offering perspectives that may have been overlooked. Whether through small groups, church gatherings, or online forums, building connections within a faith community can help reinforce the truth that none of us walk this path alone. These relationships can serve as reminders of God's faithfulness and can lead to moments of collective worship, where individuals can experience His presence together.

Prayer practices are also essential for bridging the gap when feeling disconnected from God. Establishing a routine that includes different forms of prayer—such as contemplative prayer, written prayers, or spontaneous conversations with God—can help cultivate a deeper sense of connection. During prayer, individuals can express their doubts, fears, and desires, while also opening their hearts to receive God's comfort and guidance. Learning to listen during these moments can lead to a profound recognition of His presence, even amid uncertainty.

Finally, stories of hope and faith restoration can be incredibly powerful in reinforcing the belief that God is always near. Many individuals have experienced significant growth through adversity, emerging with a stronger and more resilient faith. Sharing these testimonies can inspire others who may feel lost or overwhelmed, reminding them that God is at work in their lives, even when it is difficult to see. As Christian singles navigate their unique journeys, embracing the truth that God's presence is constant can transform doubt into a deeper trust, ultimately leading to spiritual growth and emotional resilience.

Promises of Provision and Protection

In the journey of faith, especially for Christian singles, the concept of provision and protection is often intertwined with moments of uncertainty and doubt. When life presents challenges that obscure the vision of God's hand at work, it is essential to anchor oneself in the promise that God remains a steadfast protector and provider. This assurance is foundational to building emotional resilience and fosters a deeper connection with God, even amidst adversity. Reflecting on the biblical narratives, we can find numerous examples of individuals who faced daunting trials yet experienced divine provision and protection, serving as reminders of God's unwavering faithfulness.

As we navigate the complexities of life, whether it be through the challenges of relationships, career uncertainties, or personal struggles, it can be easy to feel isolated and vulnerable. However, God's promises extend beyond mere words; they are a call to trust in His character. In seasons when we feel abandoned or overlooked, it is crucial to remember that God's heart is always aligned with our well-being. Embracing this truth can lead to spiritual growth, as we learn to rely not on our understanding or circumstances but on the unchanging nature of God. Journaling during these times can provide clarity, allowing individuals to articulate their fears and recognize God's past provisions.

Prayer serves as a vital practice for reconnecting with God when feelings of disconnection arise. It is during these moments of intimate communication that we can seek reassurance and experience the peace that surpasses all understanding. By bringing our doubts and uncertainties to God in prayer, we open ourselves to receive His guidance and comfort. Community support plays a crucial role in this process as well. Engaging with fellow believers who can share their own stories of faith restoration fosters an environment where trust can be nurtured, and collective strength is found in vulnerability.

The Bible is rich with promises of provision and protection that can anchor us in times of doubt. Philippians 4:19 reminds us that God will meet all our needs according to the riches of His glory. This promise serves as a beacon of hope, encouraging Christian singles to trust that God knows their desires and is actively working for their good. In moments of anxiety, reflecting on such scriptures can provide encouragement and a reminder that they are not alone in their struggles. Each promise becomes a tool for cultivating faith and resilience, enabling individuals to face challenges with a renewed spirit.

Ultimately, embracing the promises of provision and protection invites Christian singles to cultivate a life grounded in trust. This journey is not solely about waiting for visible answers or immediate resolutions but about developing a deeper relationship with God through faith. As they learn to lean into His heart during uncertain seasons, they can find solace in the assurance that God is with them, guiding their paths and providing for their needs. Through prayer, community, and the practice of journaling, they can transform their doubts into testimonies of faith, discovering that even in the midst of uncertainty, God's promises remain true and steadfast.

Clinging to Hope Through Scripture

Clinging to hope through Scripture is a vital practice for Christian singles navigating the complexities of faith and uncertainty. The Bible serves as a reservoir of promises and reassurances that can uplift and guide individuals during challenging times. When life's circumstances seem overwhelming, scripture provides a foundation of truth that reminds believers of God's unwavering presence and faithfulness. Verses such as Jeremiah 29:11, which speaks of God's plans for hope and a future, can become anchors that help maintain perspective amid life's storms.

In seasons of doubt, it can be easy to feel isolated and question God's intentions. However, Scripture invites believers to engage with their doubts rather than suppress them. The Psalms, for example, are filled with cries of anguish and moments of despair, yet they also reflect a deep trust in God's character. By journaling these feelings alongside corresponding verses, individuals can process their emotions and find clarity. This practice not only fosters emotional resilience but also deepens one's understanding of God's faithfulness through personal reflection.

Additionally, prayer practices can be instrumental in reconnecting with God during times of disconnection. Engaging in prayerful meditation on specific scriptures allows for a personal dialogue with God. This approach facilitates a deeper understanding of His nature and helps cultivate a sense of peace. For instance, Philippians 4:6-7 encourages believers to present their requests to God, promising that His peace will guard their hearts. Such verses can serve as prompts for prayer, inviting individuals to express their worries and receive comfort in return.

Community support can also play a crucial role during faith crises. Connecting with fellow believers who share similar struggles can provide encouragement and a sense of belonging. Participating in group Bible studies or support groups allows for the sharing of personal stories and insights, reinforcing the idea that one is not alone in their journey. These communal experiences not only strengthen faith but also remind individuals of the collective hope found in God's promises.

Ultimately, clinging to hope through Scripture is about embracing God's word as a source of strength and assurance. Whether through personal reflection, prayer, or community involvement, the journey of faith is enriched by the understanding that God's heart remains steadfast, even when His hands seem hidden. By immersing oneself in Scripture, Christian singles can cultivate a resilient spirit, navigating doubt with a renewed sense of hope and trust in God's eternal promises.

Trusting God When You Can't See His Hand

Faith Beyond Sight

Faith often requires us to navigate through seasons where God's presence feels distant, and His plans seem unclear. For Christian singles, this experience can be particularly challenging. In moments of uncertainty, trusting in God's heart rather than relying solely on visible signs becomes crucial. The scriptures remind us that we walk by faith, not by sight, emphasizing the importance of believing in God's goodness even when circumstances suggest otherwise. Holding on to this truth can provide comfort and strength during times of doubt and despair.

Difficult times can serve as fertile ground for spiritual growth. When faced with adversity, singles often grapple with feelings of isolation and confusion. However, these challenges can also lead to a deeper understanding of God's character. By leaning into prayer and seeking His presence, individuals can find clarity and peace. Journaling about these experiences can be a powerful tool for reflection, helping to articulate feelings and discover how God has moved even when He felt absent. This practice fosters emotional resilience, allowing singles to process their doubts while anchoring their faith in God's promises.

Finding community support is essential for navigating faith crises. Engaging with fellow believers can provide encouragement and shared experiences that remind us we are not alone in our struggles. Whether through church groups, online forums, or close friendships, connecting with others who understand the journey can bolster our faith. Sharing stories of hope and restoration within these communities can serve as a powerful reminder of God's faithfulness. These narratives not only inspire but also help individuals see how God works in the lives of others, reinforcing the truth that He is actively involved in our lives, even when it's hard to perceive.

Incorporating specific prayer practices can also help bridge the gap when feeling disconnected. Simple prayers of surrender, gratitude, and petition can invite the Holy Spirit to work in our hearts.

Engaging in contemplative prayer or using scripture as a guide for prayer can create a deeper sense of connection with God. During challenging times, these practices remind us to focus on God's eternal promises rather than our temporary circumstances. By consistently seeking God in prayer, singles can cultivate a sense of peace that transcends their current situations, allowing faith to flourish amidst uncertainty.

Ultimately, faith beyond sight is about trusting in God's heart even when His hands seem hidden. This journey is not without its difficulties, but it is also filled with opportunities for growth and deeper intimacy with Him. As you navigate your own seasons of doubt, remember that each struggle is a stepping stone toward a more profound faith. Embrace the process, lean on your community, and allow your experiences to deepen your trust in God's unwavering love and faithfulness. The path may be challenging, but it can lead to a richer, more resilient faith that carries you through every trial.

Examples from the Bible

The Bible is replete with stories that illustrate the importance of trusting God even when circumstances seem dire or when His presence feels distant. For Christian singles navigating the complexities of life and faith, these examples serve as powerful reminders that doubt and uncertainty are not new experiences in the journey of faith. They highlight how individuals faced with adversity found strength and reassurance through their trust in God's character and promises.

One of the most compelling examples is the story of Job, a man who endured immense suffering and loss. Despite his unimaginable trials, Job remained steadfast in his faith, declaring, "Though he slays me, yet will I hope in him." This profound statement reveals a deep trust in God's goodness, even when circumstances suggested otherwise. For singles grappling with feelings of isolation or doubt, Job's story underscores the importance of maintaining hope and trusting God's ultimate plan, even when it is not immediately visible.

Another powerful narrative is found in the life of Hannah, a woman deeply troubled by her inability to conceive. In her distress, she fervently prayed and committed her child to God if He would grant her the desire of her heart. Hannah's journey illustrates the significance of bringing our deepest struggles to God in prayer and the peace that can arise from surrendering our hopes and fears to Him. For those feeling the pressure of societal expectations regarding relationships and family, Hannah's story serves as a reminder that God hears our cries and can work wonders in our lives, often in unexpected ways.

The journey of the Israelites in the wilderness also exemplifies trusting God during times of uncertainty. Despite witnessing miraculous events, they often doubted God's provision and guidance. Yet, God remained faithful, providing manna and water, and leading them towards the Promised Land. This narrative reflects the reality that even in seasons of doubt, God is actively working behind the scenes for our good. For single Christians experiencing the wilderness of waiting for companionship or clarity in their life's direction, this story emphasizes the importance of relying on God's promises and recognizing His continuous presence in their lives.

Finally, the parable of the lost sheep illustrates God's unwavering commitment to each individual. In times of despair or feeling disconnected from faith, it is vital to remember that God cares deeply for every person, seeking them out in their struggles. This parable reinforces the idea of community support in faith crises, as it reminds us that we are part of a larger family of believers who can walk alongside us. For singles feeling isolated, connecting with a faith community can provide encouragement and support, fostering spiritual growth and emotional resilience during challenging times.

Building Trust in Unseen Moments

Building trust in unseen moments is a vital aspect of a Christian single's journey, especially during times when God's presence feels distant. It is in these moments of uncertainty that individuals often grapple with doubt and fear, questioning their faith and the path ahead. However, it is essential to remember that trust is not about having all the answers or seeing the complete picture; rather, it involves a deep-seated belief in God's character and His promises. By anchoring ourselves in the knowledge of who God is, we can find peace amidst the chaos and uncertainty that life frequently presents.

In seasons of doubt, it is common to feel isolated and disconnected from God. Engaging in prayer practices can help bridge this gap. When it feels like God is silent, speaking to Him through prayer can provide clarity and comfort. Journaling can also serve as a powerful tool, allowing individuals to articulate their feelings, reflect on their faith journey, and document instances of God's provision. Writing down prayers, questions, and even frustrations can illuminate the paths God has walked with us, helping to build a narrative of trust over time. This practice not only nurtures spiritual growth but also fosters emotional resilience as we acknowledge our struggles while simultaneously seeking God's presence.

Community support plays a crucial role in reinforcing trust during periods of doubt. Connecting with fellow believers can provide encouragement and shared experiences that remind us we are not alone in our struggles. Small groups, church activities, or online faith forums can create spaces where individuals feel safe to express their doubts and fears. Hearing stories of hope and restoration from others can be incredibly uplifting, affirming that God is actively working in the lives of His people, even when it is not immediately visible. Such connections can strengthen our faith, assuring us that God's heart is always towards us, even when His hand seems hidden.

Moreover, understanding that adversity is often a catalyst for spiritual growth can shift the perspective on difficult seasons. The Bible is replete with examples of individuals who faced trials and emerged with a deeper understanding of God's faithfulness. These narratives, such as Job's unwavering trust amidst suffering, remind us that struggles can refine our character and deepen our relationship with God. Embracing these challenges as opportunities for growth allows us to cultivate a more resilient faith, rooted in the assurance that God uses every moment, seen or unseen, for our good and His glory.

Ultimately, building trust in unseen moments is a journey that requires intentional effort and reflection. As Christian singles navigate the complexities of life, it is essential to anchor their trust in God's heart, knowing that He is with them in every season. By engaging in prayer, journaling, community support, and embracing adversity, they can foster a deeper sense of peace and confidence in their faith. In doing so, they not only navigate doubt more effectively but also cultivate a richer, more profound relationship with God that will sustain them through all of life's uncertainties.

Finding Peace in Uncertainty

The Role of Prayer in Uncertainty

The role of prayer in times of uncertainty serves as a vital lifeline for Christian singles navigating the tumultuous waters of doubt and fear. In moments when the path ahead seems obscured, prayer becomes a powerful tool for reconnecting with God. It allows individuals to voice their struggles and uncertainties, transforming feelings of isolation into opportunities for communion with the divine. Through prayer, single believers can lay bare their hearts, seeking comfort and clarity from a God who promises to walk alongside them, even when His presence feels distant.

Prayer is not just a means of expressing our challenges; it also fosters spiritual growth. By engaging in regular conversation with God, individuals cultivate a deeper understanding of His character and His faithfulness. This practice encourages introspection and invites singles to reflect on their experiences, leading to greater emotional resilience. As they navigate their doubts, the act of praying can reveal insights that might otherwise remain hidden, illuminating the ways God has been working in their lives, even when they cannot see His hands at work.

In the face of uncertainty, prayer can provide a profound sense of peace. When circumstances feel overwhelming, turning to prayer often brings a calming reassurance that transcends understanding. This sacred dialogue allows singles to surrender their fears, replacing anxiety with trust. The act of entrusting worries to God not only alleviates burdens but also reinforces the belief that He is in control. As believers practice this surrender, they cultivate a mindset anchored in faith, which can lead to a more profound peace during difficult times.

Additionally, communal prayer plays a significant role in strengthening faith during crises. When singles gather with others to pray, they create a support network that fosters shared experiences and encouragement. This collective approach to prayer can help individuals feel less isolated in their challenges and more connected to the larger body of Christ. Sharing stories of hope and restoration within a community can ignite faith and inspire resilience, reminding each member that they are not alone in their struggles.

Lastly, journaling as a form of prayer can also enhance spiritual clarity during seasons of doubt. Writing down prayers, thoughts, and reflections allows singles to track their spiritual journeys and recognize patterns in their relationship with God. This practice can illuminate moments of answered prayers and growth, reinforcing the assurance that God is present in every season. Through journaling, individuals can articulate their uncertainties while simultaneously documenting the ways in which their faith is restored, encouraging them to trust God's heart even when His hands seem hidden.

Cultivating Inner Peace

Cultivating inner peace is essential for Christian singles navigating the complexities of life, especially during seasons when God's presence may feel obscured. Embracing the promise that God is always working for our good can provide a foundation for tranquility amidst uncertainty. When doubt arises, it is crucial to remember that our feelings do not dictate the reality of God's faithfulness. By focusing on His heart, we can develop a deeper sense of peace that transcends our circumstances.

One effective way to cultivate inner peace is through dedicated prayer practices. Establishing a routine of prayer can help bridge the gap when you feel disconnected from God. This may involve setting aside specific times for prayer, using guided prayers, or simply speaking from the heart. Journaling can also play a significant role in this process, as writing down thoughts, feelings, and prayers can clarify emotions and reveal God's hand in our lives. Through journaling, individuals can reflect on past experiences of faith restoration, reminding themselves of God's promises and how He has provided peace in previous storms.

Community support is another vital aspect of cultivating inner peace. Engaging with fellow believers can provide encouragement and accountability during times of doubt. Finding a community that shares similar values and experiences allows for open discussions about faith, struggles, and the journey toward peace. Whether through church groups, online forums, or friendships, surrounding oneself with supportive individuals can help reinforce the belief that one is not alone in their struggles, fostering emotional resilience and a sense of belonging.

Additionally, spiritual growth often occurs through adversity. Embracing challenges as opportunities for growth can shift perspectives and lead to profound inner peace. It is essential to acknowledge the difficulties while also seeking the lessons they impart. Reflecting on how past challenges have shaped your faith can illuminate the path forward, helping you to trust in God's plan even when it feels unclear. Remembering that God uses trials to refine us can bring comfort and assurance that He is with us in every season of life.

Ultimately, cultivating inner peace is a continuous journey that requires intentionality and faith. By focusing on prayer, community, and personal growth, Christian singles can navigate their doubts and uncertainties with grace. Trusting in God's heart when His hand is not visible can transform moments of anxiety into opportunities for deeper connection and spiritual clarity. As you embark on this journey, remember that peace is not the absence of turmoil but the presence of God in your life, guiding you through every wave of doubt and uncertainty.

Mindfulness and Spirituality

Mindfulness, often associated with being present in the moment, has roots in various spiritual traditions, including Christianity. For Christian singles navigating the complexities of life, especially during seasons of doubt or uncertainty, mindfulness can serve as a powerful tool for deepening one's spiritual journey. By cultivating awareness of thoughts, feelings, and the divine presence, individuals can foster a greater sense of peace, even when external circumstances seem chaotic. This practice encourages believers to pause and reflect, allowing them to reconnect with God's promises amid life's challenges.

In difficult times, the practice of mindfulness can be transformative. It invites individuals to acknowledge their feelings without judgment, creating space for prayer and reflection. When faced with uncertainty about future relationships or personal goals, mindfulness can help singles recognize these emotions and surrender them to God. This surrender is an act of faith, trusting that God is active, even when His hands seem invisible. By focusing on the present and engaging in prayerful meditation, individuals can discover a profound sense of calm, reinforcing their trust in God's plan.

Spiritual growth often occurs through adversity, and mindfulness can facilitate this process. By encouraging individuals to sit with their discomfort, it allows for introspection and deeper understanding of one's faith journey. For many Christian singles, moments of doubt can lead to significant breakthroughs in their relationship with God. Journaling becomes a valuable practice during these times, as it provides a means to articulate thoughts and feelings. Through writing, individuals can track their spiritual progress, document prayers, and reflect on how God has worked in their lives, fostering a deeper sense of trust and resilience.

Community support is essential when navigating faith crises, and mindfulness can enhance these connections. Engaging in conversations about shared experiences and feelings can create a safe environment for healing and growth. Faith communities can incorporate mindfulness practices, such as group prayers or meditative scripture readings, that encourage members to explore their doubts collectively. This shared journey not only reinforces individual faith but also cultivates a sense of belonging, reminding singles that they are not alone in their struggles.

Ultimately, the intersection of mindfulness and spirituality offers a pathway to emotional resilience. By learning to trust God's heart during times of uncertainty, Christian singles can embrace a life anchored in faith. Prayer practices that incorporate mindfulness, such as breath prayers or contemplative reading, can help individuals feel more connected to the divine, even when they struggle to see His hand at work. As they navigate their unique journeys, these practices can illuminate the way toward hope and restoration, providing the strength needed to face life's challenges with confidence and grace.

Spiritual Growth Through Adversity

The Purpose of Trials

Trials serve a vital role in the Christian journey, especially for those navigating the complexities of being single. They are not merely obstacles but opportunities for spiritual growth and deepening one's faith. In moments of hardship, when it feels as if God's hands are hidden from view, trusting in His heart becomes essential. The purpose of these trials is multifaceted; they test our faith, refine our character, and ultimately draw us closer to God. Understanding this can help Christian singles find purpose even in their most challenging moments.

When faced with difficulties, it can be easy to question God's intentions. However, trials often serve as a refining fire, helping us to shed our reliance on worldly comforts and distractions. Just as gold is purified through fire, our faith is strengthened through adversity. This process encourages emotional resilience and deepens our trust in God. By recognizing that trials are intended for our growth, singles can cultivate a sense of peace amidst uncertainty, knowing that their struggles are not in vain but part of a divine plan.

The journey through trials also presents an opportunity for introspection and prayer. Engaging in journaling can provide clarity during these turbulent times, allowing individuals to express their thoughts and feelings, seek understanding, and document their spiritual journey. Writing can serve as a therapeutic outlet and a means to reflect on God's promises. In addition, establishing prayer practices can help reconnect with God when feelings of disconnection arise. These spiritual disciplines can transform the experience of trials from one of despair into a period of profound personal and spiritual development.

Community support is another critical aspect of enduring trials. As Christian singles, it is vital to surround oneself with a supportive network that can provide encouragement and accountability. Sharing struggles with trusted friends or engaging in group discussions can illuminate the path forward and foster a sense of belonging. This communal approach not only alleviates feelings of isolation but also reinforces the understanding that trials are a common part of the Christian experience. Through shared stories of hope and faith restoration, individuals can witness the transformative power of God's presence in times of difficulty.

Ultimately, the purpose of trials is to lead us to a deeper faith and a more profound understanding of God's character. In the midst of uncertainty, when hope seems distant, trusting in God's heart can provide the comfort and assurance needed to navigate life's challenges. By embracing trials as divine opportunities for growth, singles can emerge on the other side with a stronger faith, greater emotional resilience, and a clearer sense of purpose. This journey not only enriches their own spiritual lives but also equips them to support others in their struggles, creating a ripple effect of hope and encouragement within the Christian community.

Lessons Learned from Hardship

Hardship often serves as a powerful teacher, revealing lessons that can only be learned through experience. For Christian singles navigating their faith journey, periods of struggle can feel particularly isolating. However, these trials often forge a deeper connection with God, encouraging reliance on His promises even when circumstances seem bleak. By recognizing that hardships can lead to spiritual growth, individuals can cultivate emotional resilience and find a renewed sense of purpose in their faith.

One of the most profound lessons learned from hardship is the importance of trusting God's heart when His hands seem hidden. During difficult times, it may be challenging to see how God is actively working in our lives. Yet, trusting His nature—His goodness, faithfulness, and love— becomes essential. This trust allows individuals to maintain their faith even in the face of uncertainty, fostering a deeper relationship with God that can lead to transformative growth. When Christians embrace the belief that God is always present, even in silence, they can find peace amid chaos.

Moreover, facing adversity often leads to significant emotional resilience. Each challenge can build a stronger foundation for faith, teaching individuals how to rely on God's strength rather than their own. In times of doubt, remembering past experiences of divine intervention can serve as a powerful reminder of God's unwavering support. Journaling during these periods can provide clarity, allowing singles to process their emotions and recognize the ways in which God has been faithful in their lives. This practice can help illuminate the path forward, fostering hope and encouragement.

Community support becomes crucial during times of hardship, particularly for those who may feel alone in their struggles. Engaging with a faith community provides opportunities to share experiences, receive encouragement, and foster connections with others who share similar struggles. This communal aspect of faith not only alleviates feelings of isolation but also reinforces the idea that God often works through others to provide comfort and guidance. By leaning on the support of friends, mentors, and church members, individuals can experience a sense of belonging that bolsters their faith during challenging seasons.

Finally, the practice of prayer can be a lifeline during moments of disconnection from God. When hardship clouds perception, establishing a consistent prayer routine can help refocus the heart and mind on God's promises. Simple, honest conversations with God about doubts and fears can pave the way for spiritual clarity and renewed hope. In these moments of vulnerability, singles may discover a deeper understanding of God's character and His unwavering commitment to their well-being. Ultimately, the lessons learned from hardship can lead to a richer, more vibrant faith that anchors individuals in trust, even when the future seems uncertain.

Transforming Pain into Purpose

Transforming pain into purpose is a profound journey that many Christian singles navigate, especially during seasons of doubt and uncertainty. Life often presents challenges that leave us feeling isolated and questioning the very essence of our faith. However, it is crucial to recognize that pain can serve as a catalyst for spiritual growth and emotional resilience. Instead of allowing difficulties to define us, we can choose to see them as opportunities for transformation, leaning into God's promises and trusting His heart when His hands seem hidden.

Throughout scripture, we find numerous examples of individuals who faced immense pain yet emerged stronger and more purpose-driven. Consider the story of Joseph, who endured betrayal and imprisonment yet ultimately became a powerful leader in Egypt. His journey illustrates how suffering can lead to divine purpose. For Christian singles, this narrative encourages the understanding that the trials we face can refine our character and equip us for future roles in God's plan. Embracing this mindset allows us to transform our struggles into a foundation for resilience and faith.

In practical terms, transforming pain into purpose can be achieved through several spiritual practices. Journaling, for instance, serves as a therapeutic outlet for processing emotions and seeking clarity in moments of doubt. By documenting our feelings and reflections, we open ourselves to God's guidance and can identify patterns of growth in our spiritual journeys. This practice not only fosters self-awareness but also reinforces the belief that God is actively working in our lives, even when circumstances feel bleak.

Community support plays a vital role in navigating pain and purpose. Engaging with fellow believers during times of crisis can provide the encouragement and accountability needed to press on in faith. Sharing our stories and struggles within a supportive church or fellowship group can create an environment where healing takes place, and hope is restored. Together, we can remind each other of God's faithfulness and the transformative power of trusting His heart during difficult seasons.

Ultimately, prayer is a powerful tool for connecting with God and finding peace amid uncertainty. When feeling disconnected, dedicating time to prayer can shift our perspective and renew our faith. Seeking God's presence through prayer not only helps us process our pain but also opens the door for divine purpose to emerge. As we navigate our journeys as Christian singles, let us remember that every struggle has the potential to shape us into vessels of hope, demonstrating how God can turn our pain into a purpose that glorifies Him.

Emotional Resilience in Faith

Understanding Emotional Resilience

Understanding emotional resilience is essential for Christian singles navigating the often-tumultuous landscape of faith and personal growth. Emotional resilience refers to the ability to adapt to stress and adversity while maintaining a sense of hope and purpose. For those in a season of uncertainty, it is vital to recognize that resilience is not the absence of difficulty but rather the capacity to rise above challenging circumstances with a steadfast heart anchored in faith. When you find yourself questioning God's presence in your life, understanding emotional resilience can help you trust His heart even when you cannot see His hands at work.

In these times of doubt, cultivating emotional resilience begins with acknowledging your feelings. It is natural to experience sadness, confusion, or fear when faced with life's challenges. Rather than shying away from these emotions, allow yourself to process them through prayer and reflection. Journaling can be a powerful tool in this regard, providing a space to articulate your thoughts and feelings while inviting God into your struggles. Documenting your journey not only offers clarity but also allows you to recognize patterns of growth and the ways God has been faithful, even in moments of uncertainty.

Building emotional resilience also involves leaning into community support. Engaging with fellow believers can provide encouragement and wisdom during difficult times. Sharing your experiences and hearing others' testimonies can foster a sense of belonging and remind you that you are not alone in your struggles. Community can act as a lifeline, providing both practical support and spiritual nourishment, which are essential for fostering resilience. Whether through small groups, church events, or online forums, connecting with like-minded individuals can reinforce your faith and help you navigate seasons of doubt with greater confidence.

Another crucial aspect of developing emotional resilience is cultivating a consistent prayer life. Prayer serves as a direct line of communication with God, allowing you to express your fears, doubts, and desires. When feelings of disconnection arise, it is important to persist in prayer, even when words fail you. Engaging in prayer practices such as meditation, scripture reading, or guided prayers can help restore a sense of peace and connection to God. Trusting in His promises during these times not only strengthens your faith but also enhances your ability to bounce back from setbacks, fostering a deeper emotional resilience rooted in spiritual truth.

Ultimately, understanding emotional resilience through the lens of faith requires a commitment to personal growth and a willingness to embrace the lessons that adversity brings. Trusting God in seasons of uncertainty requires courage, but it also offers profound opportunities for transformation. As you confront challenges, remember that each experience equips you with the strength to face future difficulties with increased resilience. By anchoring yourself in God's promises and allowing your faith to guide you through life's storms, you can cultivate a spirit of resilience that empowers you to thrive, even when the path ahead is unclear.

Strategies for Building Resilience

Building resilience as a Christian single involves a combination of spiritual practices, emotional awareness, and community engagement. One key strategy is to deepen your relationship with God through consistent prayer and Bible study. When faced with uncertainty, turning to scripture can provide comfort and direction. Verses that speak of God's faithfulness, such as Jeremiah 29:11, remind us that He has plans for our lives, even when we can't see the path ahead. Engaging in regular journaling can also help clarify your thoughts and feelings, allowing you to articulate your doubts and seek God's guidance in a structured manner.

Another vital aspect of resilience is the practice of self-compassion. Acknowledge that it's normal to experience doubt and fear, especially during challenging times. By treating yourself with kindness and understanding, you can create a safe space for personal growth. Reflecting on past experiences where God has provided can reinforce your faith and help you recognize that He is present, even if His hand is not visible. This process encourages emotional resilience, allowing you to navigate life's uncertainties with a sense of hope and trust in God's plan.

Building a supportive community is essential for fostering resilience. Engage with fellow believers who can share their experiences and insights, providing encouragement when your faith feels weak. This may involve participating in small groups, attending church events, or seeking out mentorship relationships. Sharing your doubts and struggles in a safe environment can strengthen your faith and remind you that you are not alone in your journey. Community support serves as a reminder of God's love through others, reinforcing the idea that He often works through the people around us.

In times of crisis, incorporating structured prayer practices can help bridge the gap when you feel disconnected from God. Consider using guided prayers or prayer prompts that focus on trust and surrender. This intentional approach can help you articulate your feelings and allow God to speak into your situation. Additionally, exploring different forms of prayer, such as meditation or contemplative prayer, can deepen your spiritual experience and foster a greater sense of peace amidst uncertainty.

Lastly, embrace adversity as a pathway to spiritual growth. Each challenge presents an opportunity to rely more fully on God and to develop a deeper understanding of His character. Reflect on your experiences and look for lessons that can be gleaned from them. Sharing your stories of hope and faith restoration with others not only strengthens your own belief but can also inspire those around you. In doing so, you build a narrative of resilience that highlights God's unwavering presence and love, helping you to anchor your trust in Him through every season of life.

The Connection Between Faith and Emotional Health

The connection between faith and emotional health is profound and multifaceted, particularly for Christian singles navigating the complexities of life. In times of uncertainty, when it feels as though God's hands are hidden from view, trusting in His heart becomes essential. This trust fosters emotional resilience, enabling individuals to confront challenges with a sense of purpose and hope. By anchoring oneself in faith, singles can cultivate a deeper understanding of their emotional landscape, allowing them to respond to life's difficulties with grace and strength.

Faith serves as a foundation for emotional health, providing a framework through which individuals can interpret their experiences. During difficult times, the promises found in scripture act as a balm for the soul, instilling a sense of peace that transcends understanding. For Christian singles, embracing these promises can transform moments of doubt into opportunities for spiritual growth. Each challenge faced becomes a chance to deepen one's relationship with God, ultimately leading to greater emotional stability. Journaling about these experiences can further clarify thoughts and feelings, providing insight into how faith intersects with emotional well-being.

In seasons of doubt, community support becomes invaluable. Engaging with fellow believers allows individuals to share their struggles and receive encouragement. This connection reinforces the idea that no one is alone in their journey, fostering a sense of belonging and acceptance. As singles gather to discuss their faith, they often find shared experiences that highlight the importance of trusting God even when circumstances seem bleak. These relationships can serve as a reminder that faith is not solely an individual endeavor but one that flourishes in fellowship.

Prayer practices play a crucial role in bridging the gap between feeling disconnected and experiencing divine presence. For those grappling with emotional challenges, turning to prayer can facilitate a deeper connection with God. Through prayer, individuals can express their fears, uncertainties, and hopes, allowing their burdens to be lifted. This practice can transform feelings of isolation into a profound awareness of God's love and support. In the midst of turbulence, prayer becomes a lifeline, reinforcing the belief that God is attentive and responsive to our needs.

Ultimately, the journey of faith during times of uncertainty is one of hope and restoration. Stories of individuals who have navigated crises of faith often serve as powerful testimonies of God's faithfulness. These narratives remind Christian singles that even in the darkest moments, light can emerge through trust in God's promises. By embracing faith as a tool for emotional health, individuals can cultivate resilience, finding peace amid life's storms. As they anchor themselves in trust, they discover that their emotional well-being is intrinsically linked to their spiritual journey, leading to a richer, more fulfilling life.

Journaling for Spiritual Clarity

The Benefits of Journaling

Journaling serves as a powerful tool for Christian singles navigating the complexities of faith, doubt, and uncertainty. In moments when God's presence feels distant, writing can create a space for reflection and dialogue with Him. By putting pen to paper, individuals can articulate their thoughts, feelings, and struggles, allowing them to process emotions that might otherwise remain unaddressed. This practice not only fosters spiritual clarity but also helps in identifying the ways God may be working in their lives, even when His hand seems hidden.

One significant benefit of journaling is the opportunity for emotional resilience. When faced with challenges, such as loneliness or uncertainty about the future, expressing these feelings in a journal can be cathartic. It allows for a release of pent-up emotions, transforming pain into a pathway for healing. As Christian singles document their experiences and reflect on Scripture, they can gain a deeper understanding of their circumstances in light of God's promises. This self-exploration can cultivate a stronger sense of trust in God, reinforcing the belief that He is present and active, even in the trials of life.

Additionally, journaling can enhance one's prayer life. By writing down prayers, singles can articulate their desires, fears, and hopes more clearly. This practice helps in maintaining focus during prayer and creates a tangible record of communication with God. Over time, revisiting past entries can illuminate how prayers have been answered or how God has provided comfort during difficult times. This reflection serves as a reminder of God's faithfulness and encourages individuals to keep trusting Him, even when the path ahead is uncertain.

Moreover, journaling fosters spiritual growth through adversity. As singles document their journeys, they can trace their development and recognize patterns in their spiritual lives. This awareness can lead to profound insights about their faith and relationship with God. By confronting doubts and challenges on the page, they can explore how these experiences have shaped their character and resilience. This journey can be transformative, leading to a deeper reliance on God and a renewed commitment to their faith.

Finally, journaling can cultivate a sense of community and support. While it is a personal practice, sharing journal entries or reflections with trusted friends or within a faith group can create opportunities for connection and encouragement. As singles open up about their struggles, they may find solace in knowing they are not alone. This communal aspect of journaling can strengthen bonds within the Christian community and foster an environment where individuals feel safe to express their doubts and seek support. By combining personal reflection with shared experiences, journaling can play a vital role in navigating the complexities of faith during uncertain times.

Prompts for Exploring Your Faith

Prompts for exploring your faith can serve as vital tools for Christian singles navigating the complexities of life, especially during challenging times. When you encounter seasons of doubt or uncertainty, reflecting on your faith through journaling can help you articulate your feelings and seek clarity. Begin with questions such as, "What specific challenges am I facing right now?" or "In what ways have I seen God's faithfulness in my life?" These prompts encourage you to engage deeply with your experiences, fostering a sense of spiritual resilience as you identify patterns of God's presence, even when it feels hidden.

As you explore your faith, consider prompts that invite you to examine your emotional responses during difficult moments. For instance, ask yourself, "How do I typically respond to feelings of anxiety or fear regarding my future?" or "What biblical promises resonate with me in times of uncertainty?" This reflective practice can lead to greater self-awareness and a deeper understanding of how trust in God's heart can provide peace amidst turmoil. Journaling in this manner allows you to confront your emotions and align them with the truth of Scripture, reinforcing your spiritual foundation.

Community support plays a crucial role in faith exploration, so consider prompts that encourage you to reach out to others. Questions like, "Who are the people in my life that I can lean on during difficult times?" or "How can I share my struggles with my faith community?" can initiate meaningful conversations. Engaging with trusted friends or mentors can provide perspectives that enrich your understanding of faith and foster a sense of belonging. This communal aspect of faith not only helps you process your feelings but also reminds you that you are not alone in your journey.

Incorporating prayer practices into your exploration can enhance your connection with God, especially when you feel disconnected. Reflect on prompts such as, "What specific prayers can I offer regarding my doubts?" or "How can I create a space for God's presence in my daily routine?" Establishing a structured prayer time, whether through written prayers, meditation, or spontaneous conversations with God, can ground you in His promises. By intentionally seeking Him through prayer, you cultivate an atmosphere of trust, allowing His peace to fill the void of uncertainty.

Lastly, consider prompts that focus on stories of hope and faith restoration. Ask yourself, "What testimonies of faith have inspired me during tough times?" or "How can I share my own story of overcoming doubt with others?" Reflecting on personal and shared narratives of divine intervention can reignite your passion for faith and encourage others in their struggles. Remembering the faithfulness of God in the lives of others serves as a powerful reminder that hope is always present, even in the darkest seasons. Through these prompts, you not only explore your own faith but also contribute to a collective narrative of resilience and trust in God's unwavering heart.

Reflecting on God's Faithfulness

Reflecting on God's faithfulness is a vital exercise for Christian singles navigating the complexities of life, especially during seasons of uncertainty. When the path ahead seems unclear, and the noise of doubt surrounds us, it becomes essential to anchor ourselves in the truth of who God is. His faithfulness is not dependent on our circumstances or our feelings; it is an immutable aspect of His character. By intentionally reflecting on His past faithfulness in our lives, we can cultivate a deeper trust in His plans for our future, even when we cannot perceive His hands at work.

During difficult times, it is natural to question God's presence and purpose. However, reflecting on scripture can provide clarity and reassurance. The Bible is replete with examples of individuals who faced insurmountable challenges yet experienced God's unwavering support. From the Israelites in the wilderness to Job in his suffering, these narratives remind us that God is not distant in our struggles; He walks alongside us. By journaling our thoughts and prayers, we can document these moments of faith that serve as reminders of God's faithfulness, helping us to process our emotions and find peace amid turmoil.

Trusting God during seasons of doubt requires an active engagement with our faith. This might involve seeking out community support, as sharing our struggles with others can illuminate the faithfulness of God through their testimonies. Engaging in prayer practices, even when we feel disconnected, can also foster a renewed sense of intimacy with God. When we bring our doubts and fears to Him, we create space for His peace to infiltrate our hearts. This process not only strengthens our faith but also encourages emotional resilience, allowing us to face adversity with a renewed perspective.

As we reflect on God's faithfulness, we can also recognize that spiritual growth often occurs in the midst of adversity. Painful experiences can drive us closer to God, revealing aspects of His character that we might not have understood otherwise. The journey through doubt can lead to profound insights about our identity in Christ and our purpose in His kingdom. By embracing these challenges, we position ourselves to emerge stronger in our faith, equipped with the tools to support others who may be walking similar paths.

Ultimately, reflecting on God's faithfulness is an invitation to experience hope and restoration. Each story of faith, whether our own or that of others, serves as a testament to God's enduring promises. As Christian singles, it is crucial to remain anchored in this truth, allowing our reflections to transform doubt into a deeper reliance on God. By fostering a habit of gratitude for His faithfulness, we can cultivate a spirit of resilience that not only sustains us but also inspires those around us to trust in God's unchanging heart, even in the most uncertain seasons of life.

Community Support in Faith Crises

The Importance of Fellowship

The importance of fellowship cannot be overstated, especially for Christian singles navigating the complexities of faith and life. In a world that often feels isolating, connecting with others who share similar beliefs provides a vital support system. Fellowship fosters an environment where individuals can come together to share experiences, struggles, and triumphs in their faith journeys. This communal aspect of Christianity is essential for personal growth and emotional resilience, particularly during seasons of doubt or uncertainty. Being part of a faith community encourages individuals to lean on one another, reminding them that they are not alone in their struggles.

When facing difficult times, fellowship serves as a lifeline, offering encouragement and understanding. It is during these moments of hardship that the bonds of community can provide clarity and strength. Engaging with fellow believers allows individuals to witness firsthand how others navigate their own challenges, offering hope and practical insights. Sharing stories of faith restoration and the miraculous ways God has worked in the lives of others can reignite one's own trust in God's promises. In these shared experiences, one finds not just solace but also inspiration to press forward in faith, even when the path seems unclear.

The role of prayer within a fellowship is equally important, creating a sacred space for individuals to express their concerns and seek divine guidance. Group prayers can be a powerful way to connect with God and each other, reinforcing the idea that collective faith can move mountains. When participants share their personal struggles, they invite others to pray specifically for their needs, fostering deeper connections and a sense of belonging. This practice not only strengthens individual faith but also cultivates a culture of support and accountability, where members can hold each other up during moments of weakness.

Journaling emerges as a personal tool within the context of fellowship, allowing individuals to reflect on their thoughts and feelings while processing their faith journey. By documenting their experiences, Christian singles can gain greater clarity and insight into their spiritual growth. Sharing these reflections with trusted friends in the community can lead to deeper discussions and revelations. This exchange fosters a sense of vulnerability and authenticity, encouraging others to open up about their own doubts and fears. Ultimately, such interactions can lead to profound spiritual growth and emotional healing.

In conclusion, the importance of fellowship for Christian singles is multifaceted, offering emotional, spiritual, and practical support through the trials of life. It reinforces the understanding that, in times of uncertainty, one can lean on the strength of community to navigate doubt and build faith. As individuals actively participate in communal practices such as prayer, sharing stories, and journaling, they create a rich tapestry of support that nurtures personal and collective faith journeys. Through fellowship, individuals learn to trust in God's heart, even when they cannot see His hands, and find peace amid the storms of life.

Finding Your Faith Community

Finding your faith community is a vital step in navigating the complexities of faith, especially during times of doubt and uncertainty. For Christian singles, the search for a supportive community can feel daunting, but it is essential for spiritual growth and emotional resilience. A faith community can provide encouragement, accountability, and a sense of belonging, helping individuals to anchor themselves in God's promises. The right community not only fosters spiritual connections but also offers a safe space to explore doubts and questions about faith, allowing for deeper conversations and understanding.

When seeking a faith community, it's important to reflect on what you desire from the experience. Consider what aspects of faith are most important to you—whether it's a strong emphasis on prayer, a commitment to service, or opportunities for personal storytelling and sharing testimonies. Exploring different churches, small groups, or faith-based organizations can help you identify where you feel most comfortable and accepted. As you engage with various groups, pay attention to how they respond to challenges and uncertainties, as this will give you insight into their approach to faith during difficult times.

Establishing connections within a faith community can also enhance your journey of trusting God in seasons of doubt. Forming relationships with others who share similar experiences and struggles can provide a sense of camaraderie and support. Participating in group activities, attending Bible studies, or volunteering for community service projects can facilitate these connections. Through shared experiences and mutual encouragement, you can nurture emotional resilience and find peace amidst uncertainty, knowing that you are not alone in your struggles.

Incorporating practices such as journaling can further deepen your sense of clarity and connection within your faith community. Writing down your thoughts, prayers, and reflections can help you process your feelings of doubt and uncertainty. Sharing these insights with trusted friends in your community can lead to meaningful discussions and insights, reinforcing the understanding that faith is often a journey filled with ups and downs. This practice not only promotes personal spiritual growth but also opens pathways for others to share their stories, creating a richer, more supportive community environment.

Lastly, remember that finding your faith community is a journey that may take time and patience. It is perfectly normal to experience feelings of disconnect, especially during challenging seasons. Embrace the process of searching for a community that resonates with you, and remain open to the relationships and connections that God brings into your life. As you navigate this journey, keep in mind that your faith community can be a powerful source of hope and restoration, providing support and encouragement as you trust in God's heart, even when you cannot see His hands.

Sharing Stories and Building Trust

Sharing stories is a powerful way to build trust, particularly within the Christian single community. When individuals come together to share personal experiences of faith, hope, and resilience, they create a tapestry of narratives that reflect God's unwavering presence, even in seasons of doubt. Each story serves as a testament to God's promises, demonstrating that while we may not always see His hand at work in our lives, we can trust His heart through every challenge. This sharing fosters a sense of belonging and connection, reminding us that we are not alone in our struggles.

In times of adversity, stories of triumph and faith restoration can be incredibly uplifting. They remind us that others have walked similar paths and emerged with renewed strength and deeper faith. For Christian singles navigating the uncertainties of life, hearing how others have leaned on God during difficult times can provide a roadmap to emotional resilience. These narratives encourage individuals to hold fast to their faith, viewing challenges not as insurmountable obstacles but as opportunities for spiritual growth. When we listen to how God has worked in the lives of others, we gain insight into His character and His faithfulness.

Community support plays a crucial role in this process. Sharing stories within a trusted group can create a safe space for vulnerability, allowing individuals to express their doubts and fears without judgment. This sense of community can be particularly vital during faith crises, where feelings of isolation often surface. By opening up about personal experiences, singles can foster deeper relationships that are anchored in mutual understanding and support. As trust is built within these communities, members are more likely to seek guidance, share prayer requests, and hold each other accountable in their spiritual journeys.

Journaling can also be a meaningful practice for those seeking spiritual clarity amid uncertainty. Recording personal stories, reflections, and prayers allows individuals to process their emotions and track their spiritual growth over time. This practice not only provides an outlet for feelings but also serves as a reminder of God's faithfulness during challenging seasons. By revisiting past entries, one can see how God has worked through adversity, reinforcing the truth that even when circumstances seem bleak, there is hope for restoration and joy on the horizon.

Ultimately, the act of sharing stories and building trust is an invitation to experience the profound love of God in community. For Christian singles, it is a reminder that faith does not exist in isolation; it flourishes through connection with others. By coming together to share experiences, offer encouragement, and pray for one another, individuals can navigate their journeys with renewed strength and hope. In doing so, they affirm the truth that while we may not always understand what God is doing, we can always trust who He is and the promises He has made to us.

Prayer Practices for Feeling Disconnected

Types of Prayer for Different Seasons

In the journey of faith, the practice of prayer can take on different forms depending on the season of life one is experiencing. For Christian singles navigating their unique paths, understanding the types of prayer that resonate with various seasons can deepen their spiritual connection and foster resilience. In times of joy, thanksgiving prayers become a natural expression of gratitude, celebrating the blessings and milestones achieved. These prayers are not only a way to acknowledge God's goodness but also to reinforce a sense of community, as sharing joys with others can create bonds of support and encouragement.

During periods of uncertainty or doubt, supplication prayers play a crucial role. These prayers involve humbly presenting requests to God, seeking His guidance and strength in times of struggle. For singles facing the challenges of loneliness or indecision, turning to God in earnest prayer can provide clarity and comfort. It is essential to be honest in these moments, voicing fears and concerns while also opening the heart to receive God's responses, which may come in unexpected ways. This type of prayer can lead to profound insights and a renewed sense of purpose.

Lamentation prayers are particularly significant during tough seasons of life. When circumstances feel overwhelming, expressing sorrow or grief through prayer can be cathartic. For singles who may feel isolated or disconnected, lamenting can foster a sense of solidarity with others who have experienced similar struggles. This form of prayer acknowledges pain while simultaneously inviting God into the midst of it, fostering hope and healing. By articulating feelings of despair, individuals can begin to process their emotions and find solace in God's presence.

Intercessory prayer, which involves praying on behalf of others, allows singles to build community and demonstrate love. In seasons of doubt, reaching out to pray for friends, family, or even those in need can shift focus from personal struggles to collective upliftment. This practice not only cultivates emotional resilience but also reinforces the understanding that faith is not a solitary endeavor. When singles engage in intercessory prayer, they become part of a larger narrative of hope and restoration, reminding themselves that they are never truly alone.

Finally, contemplative prayer is an essential practice for those seeking peace amidst uncertainty. This form of prayer invites individuals to sit in silence, listen, and be present with God without the distractions of the world. For Christian singles, this quiet time can lead to profound moments of clarity and reassurance, especially when navigating life's complexities. Journaling during or after contemplative prayer can further enhance spiritual clarity, allowing reflections and revelations to be documented and revisited. Embracing these diverse types of prayer can significantly aid in the journey of trusting God through all seasons, reinforcing faith, and fostering spiritual growth.

Developing a Consistent Prayer Life

Developing a consistent prayer life is essential for Christian singles navigating the complexities of faith, especially during seasons of doubt and uncertainty. Establishing a regular prayer routine not only deepens your relationship with God but also provides a vital source of strength and clarity when life's challenges arise. A consistent prayer practice helps you stay anchored in trust, reminding you to lean on God's promises even when you cannot perceive His hand at work in your life. By integrating prayer into your daily routine, you create a safe space to express your thoughts, fears, and hopes, fostering emotional resilience and spiritual growth.

Creating a structured prayer life begins with setting aside specific times each day dedicated to prayer. This could be in the morning, during lunch breaks, or before bed— whenever you can be most focused and present. Consistency is key; committing to regular prayer helps establish a rhythm that can carry you through difficult times. As you develop this habit, consider using a journal to document your prayers, thoughts, and any insights you receive. Journaling not only allows for reflection but also helps clarify your feelings and experiences, making it easier to recognize God's presence in your life.

Incorporating different prayer practices can enrich your spiritual journey. For instance, you might explore contemplative prayer, which encourages silence and listening, allowing you to attune your heart to God's voice. Alternatively, praying through Scripture can provide context and direction, reminding you of God's promises during difficult seasons. You can also engage in group prayer with fellow believers, which fosters community support and accountability. Sharing prayer requests and experiences with others can provide encouragement and help you feel less isolated in your faith journey.

When you feel disconnected from God, it's crucial to remember that prayer is not always about eloquent words or clear answers. Sometimes, it involves simply being present with God, expressing your doubts, and inviting Him into your struggles. It's in these honest conversations that you may find peace and reassurance. Even when you do not feel His presence, trust that your prayers are heard. Developing a consistent prayer life means showing up, even when you feel distant, and believing that God is working behind the scenes for your good.

Ultimately, a consistent prayer life is about building trust—a trust that allows you to navigate the uncertainties of life with confidence. As a Christian single, you may face unique challenges, but through prayer, you can cultivate a deeper relationship with God that provides hope and restoration. Each prayer becomes an anchor in your faith, reminding you that even in stormy seas, you are not alone. Embrace this journey, and allow your consistent prayer life to transform your doubts into a stronger, more resilient faith.

Finding God in Silence

In the stillness of life, when the world seems to drown out our thoughts and prayers, many Christians find themselves grappling with feelings of doubt and disconnection. For singles navigating their faith journey, this silence can be particularly poignant. It is in these quiet moments that we often yearn for reassurance of God's presence. However, it's essential to recognize that silence can be a divine invitation to deepen our trust in God. Instead of viewing silence as abandonment, we can choose to see it as an opportunity for spiritual growth, a moment to cultivate resilience, and a chance to strengthen our relationship with God.

During challenging seasons, it may feel as though God's hand is hidden, leaving us to navigate our struggles alone. This is where the heart of faith comes into play. Trusting God's heart means believing in His goodness and love, even when we cannot perceive His actions. In times of uncertainty, journaling can serve as a powerful tool for reflection and clarity. Writing down our thoughts, fears, and prayers helps us to articulate our feelings and recognize patterns in our spiritual journey. This practice not only fosters emotional resilience but also allows us to witness how God has worked in our lives in the past, reminding us of His faithfulness.

The silence we experience can often lead to feelings of isolation, particularly for singles who may lack the immediate support of a partner. In these moments, seeking community support is crucial. Connecting with fellow believers provides a safe space to share our struggles and doubts. Engaging in group prayer, attending church services, or participating in faith-based activities can help break the silence and create bonds of encouragement. These connections remind us that we are not alone in our experiences and that God often speaks through the voices of others who share our faith.

Prayer practices can also play a significant role in finding God in silence. When feeling disconnected, it might be tempting to abandon prayer altogether. However, approaching God in prayer during these times can be transformative. Simple prayers of surrender, gratitude, or even lament can open our hearts to God's presence. Incorporating meditative practices or silent prayer can help us attune our spirits to hear God's whispers amidst the noise of our doubts. Learning to embrace silence in prayer can lead to profound moments of revelation and peace.

Ultimately, finding God in silence is about trusting His promises during times of uncertainty. Each moment of doubt can be a stepping stone toward deeper faith, as we learn to anchor ourselves in His love. By embracing the silence, engaging in community, practicing prayer, and reflecting through journaling, we can transform our periods of waiting into opportunities for spiritual renewal. God is always present, guiding us through our seasons of doubt, reminding us that even in silence, His heart remains steadfast and true.

Stories of Hope and Faith Restoration

Testimonies of Overcoming Doubt

In the journey of faith, doubt often emerges as a shadow that can cloud our vision and hinder our spiritual growth. For many Christian singles, this experience can feel particularly isolating, especially when navigating the complexities of relationships, career aspirations, and personal growth. However, testimonies of overcoming doubt can serve as powerful reminders that others have traversed similar paths, finding strength and clarity in their faith. These stories not only highlight the challenges faced but also illuminate the transformative power of trusting in God's promises, even when His presence seems hidden.

One compelling testimony comes from a single woman named Sarah, who felt overwhelmed by uncertainty regarding her future. As she approached her thirties, societal pressures and personal insecurities began to weigh heavily on her spirit. In her moments of doubt, Sarah found solace in journaling, pouring her heart out on paper and reflecting on God's faithfulness throughout her life. This practice allowed her to gain spiritual clarity, moving her from a place of despair to one of hope. She learned to articulate her fears and anxieties, ultimately discovering that her doubts could coexist with her faith, each leading her to a deeper understanding of God's heart.

Another inspiring story is that of James, a single man who faced a significant career setback. At a time when he felt lost and uncertain about his professional path, James turned to prayer, seeking guidance and comfort in God's Word. During this season of doubt, he found a community of fellow believers who provided support and encouragement. Their collective prayers and shared experiences fostered an environment where James could openly discuss his struggles. Through this connection, he realized that faith is often bolstered by community, and that isolation can exacerbate feelings of doubt. With their encouragement, he was able to embrace his circumstances and trust that God was leading him toward a greater purpose.

In the midst of adversity, testimonies reveal the importance of emotional resilience in faith. Take the story of Maria, who navigated the painful journey of a broken engagement. Initially consumed by feelings of betrayal and confusion, Maria sought refuge in her relationship with God. Through prayer and reflection, she learned to trust in God's plan despite her heartache. Her experience taught her that healing does not come from understanding every detail of our struggles but rather from surrendering to God's loving guidance. As she leaned into her faith, she discovered a renewed sense of purpose and a deeper relationship with God, ultimately transforming her pain into a testimony of resilience and strength.

Finally, the power of hope and restoration shines through the stories of those who have experienced the profound impact of trusting God in seasons of doubt. Each testimony serves as a beacon of light, illuminating the path for others who may feel lost or overwhelmed. By sharing these experiences, we cultivate a space where vulnerability is embraced and faith is nurtured. For Christian singles, understanding that doubt is a shared experience can foster community and encourage personal growth. As we continue to anchor ourselves in trust, we can hold onto the promise that God's heart remains steadfast, even when His hands are not visibly guiding us. Through this journey, we can find peace in uncertainty and hope in the midst of challenging seasons.

Miracles of Faith in Adversity

In times of adversity, the concept of miracles often feels distant or elusive, especially for Christian singles navigating the complexities of life. When faced with challenges, it can be difficult to see God's hand at work. However, trusting in His heart can bring a profound sense of peace. This trust is not blind; it is rooted in the understanding that God's promises are unwavering, even when circumstances seem bleak. Faith during difficult times becomes a lifeline, providing clarity and direction amidst chaos. This subchapter explores how miracles of faith can emerge in our lives when we choose to remain anchored in trust.

Adversity has a unique way of fostering spiritual growth. When confronted with trials, individuals often discover strengths they never knew they possessed. This process is not merely about enduring hardship but about transformation. For Christian singles, who may feel isolated during these times, the experience of overcoming challenges can lead to deeper faith and emotional resilience. As they reflect on their struggles, they can find comfort in the knowledge that each trial has the potential to refine their character and deepen their relationship with God.

Finding peace in moments of uncertainty can be challenging, yet it is in these very moments that miracles can occur. By practicing intentional journaling, individuals can articulate their fears, frustrations, and hopes. Writing serves as a therapeutic outlet, allowing for reflection on God's faithfulness throughout their journeys. As they document their thoughts and prayers, they may begin to recognize patterns of divine intervention and support that they had previously overlooked. This practice not only fosters clarity but also serves as a reminder that God is always present, even when His presence feels hidden.

Community support plays a crucial role during faith crises. Engaging with fellow believers provides a sense of belonging and encouragement. Sharing experiences of doubt and uncertainty can lead to collective healing and strengthened faith. Christian singles can find solace in knowing they are not alone in their struggles. Building a supportive network can create an environment where miracles of faith are more readily recognized, as individuals uplift one another through prayer, shared stories, and encouragement.

Finally, cultivating a vibrant prayer life is essential for those feeling disconnected from God. Prayer practices, especially during adversity, can be transformative. Simple yet profound conversations with God can lead to revelations and renewed hope. In moments of desperation, turning to prayer enables individuals to express their burdens and seek divine guidance. As they navigate their challenges, they may witness small miracles manifest in their lives, reinforcing the truth that trusting God's heart during uncertain times can yield extraordinary results. Through these practices, Christian singles can discover that even in adversity, faith can flourish and miracles can happen.

Encouragement from the Community

Encouragement from the community can serve as a vital lifeline for Christian singles navigating seasons of doubt and uncertainty. In times when it feels challenging to see God's hand at work, the presence and support of like-minded individuals can remind us of His unfailing heart. This communal encouragement fosters a sense of belonging and solidarity, illustrating that we are not alone in our struggles. Sharing experiences with others who understand the unique challenges of being single can provide reassurance and help us recognize that our faith journey is a collective one.

When facing difficult times, the impact of community support cannot be understated. Engaging with a group that shares your values can offer insights and perspectives that might otherwise be overlooked. In moments of doubt, hearing testimonies of others who have weathered similar storms can inspire hope and strengthen resolve. These stories serve as powerful reminders of God's faithfulness, encouraging us to trust in His promises even when circumstances are overwhelming.

The encouragement we receive from others can help us cultivate emotional resilience, enabling us to face our challenges with renewed strength.

Incorporating practices such as journaling into our community interactions can further enhance our spiritual clarity. When we share our thoughts and feelings with trusted friends or mentors, we can better articulate our doubts and fears. This collaborative process of reflection not only brings clarity but also invites others to join us in prayer and support. Journaling becomes a tool for spiritual growth, allowing us to document our journey and witness how God has moved in our lives and those of our community. Writing together can create a safe space for vulnerability and healing, reinforcing the idea that we are not navigating these waters in isolation.

Prayer practices within the community can also significantly bridge the gap during times of disconnection from God. Engaging in corporate prayer or small group prayer sessions can reignite our relationship with Him and provide a sense of spiritual connection that might feel absent in solitary moments. When we pray with others, we are reminded of God's presence and the power of collective faith. This shared experience cultivates an atmosphere of support that can encourage us to maintain our trust in God's heart, even when His hand seems hidden.

Ultimately, the encouragement from the community acts as a beacon of hope and restoration. By surrounding ourselves with fellow believers who uplift and inspire us, we can navigate our faith crises with greater confidence. The bonds formed in these supportive environments not only foster spiritual growth but also create lasting relationships that can carry us through life's uncertainties. As we lean on one another and share our journeys, we become living testimonies of God's unwavering love and faithfulness, demonstrating the power of community in the pursuit of trust and hope.

Chapter 7 Strengthening Faith: Scriptures for the Journey to Your Kingdom Spouse

Understanding the Journey

The Importance of Seeking a Kingdom Spouse

The journey toward finding a Kingdom spouse is not merely a personal quest but a profound spiritual pursuit that aligns with God's divine purpose for our lives. Seeking a partner who shares your faith and values is crucial, as it lays the groundwork for a relationship rooted in mutual respect, love, and commitment to God's principles. In a world filled with distractions and differing ideologies, prioritizing a Kingdom spouse helps ensure that your relationship reflects the teachings of Christ and supports your spiritual growth. This pursuit requires prayerful consideration and a focus on aligning your desires with God's will.

Understanding the significance of seeking a Kingdom spouse begins with recognizing that marriage is a covenant established by God. Scripture emphasizes the importance of this covenant, as seen in Genesis 2:24, which states that a man shall leave his parents and be united to his wife, becoming one flesh. This divine union is intended to mirror the relationship between Christ and the Church, illustrating the depth of commitment required in a Kingdom marriage. By actively seeking a spouse who shares your faith, you are honoring this divine intention and creating a foundation that can withstand life's challenges.

As you navigate the waiting period before meeting your Kingdom spouse, patience becomes a vital aspect of your journey. Scriptures such as Psalm 27:14 remind us to wait for the Lord and be strong. During this time, it is essential to cultivate a heart of patience and trust in God's timing. Engaging in prayer, journaling, and daily affirmations can help reinforce your faith and keep you grounded. These practices encourage reflection on God's promises and allow you to remain hopeful while you await the fulfillment of His plan for your life.

Another key element in seeking a Kingdom spouse is understanding the importance of community support. Building a prayer group with other singles can provide encouragement and accountability as you all navigate similar journeys. This communal approach fosters an environment where you can share your experiences, pray for one another, and celebrate milestones together. Such support is vital in overcoming feelings of loneliness and isolation during the waiting period, reminding you that you are not alone in your desires and struggles.

Ultimately, seeking a Kingdom spouse is about fostering a Christ-centered foundation before marriage. This includes focusing on personal spiritual growth, building a strong relationship with God, and understanding the qualities that reflect His love and grace. By prioritizing these elements in your life, you set the stage for a relationship that honors God and exemplifies His love in your partnership. Embracing this journey with faith and commitment aligns your heart with God's purpose, paving the way for a fruitful and fulfilling union with your future spouse.

Biblical Foundations for Relationships

The Bible provides a robust framework for understanding and nurturing relationships, particularly for those who are single and seeking a kingdom spouse. The foundation laid in Scripture emphasizes the importance of love, respect, and commitment. In Genesis, the creation of Adam and Eve illustrates that companionship is a divine design, highlighting the significance of relationships in God's plan. This foundational truth encourages Christian singles to recognize that their longing for a partner is valid and aligned with God's intent for human connection.

Scripture encourages singles to prepare their hearts and minds for the blessings of a kingdom spouse. Proverbs 3:5-6 teaches the importance of trusting in the Lord and seeking His guidance in all aspects of life, including relationships. This trust is essential during times of waiting, as it allows individuals to remain patient and faithful. By embracing this wisdom, singles can cultivate a posture of prayer, seeking God's will and timing rather than succumbing to the pressures of societal expectations regarding relationships.

Daily affirmations rooted in biblical promises can empower singles as they navigate their journey toward a kingdom spouse. Philippians 4:19 assures believers that God will meet their needs according to His riches in glory. By reflecting on this promise, singles can affirm their worth and the assurance that God has a plan for them. Journaling can also provide a valuable tool for reflection, allowing individuals to document their prayers, thoughts, and any revelations they receive regarding their future spouse and relationship goals.

The Bible is rich with stories of singles who found their kingdom spouses, providing inspiration and hope. For instance, the story of Ruth exemplifies loyalty, faithfulness, and divine provision. Ruth's journey from widowhood to becoming part of the lineage of Christ illustrates how God orchestrates relationships in His perfect timing. Such narratives serve as reminders that waiting does not equate to inactivity; rather, it is a time for personal growth and deepening one's relationship with God.

Lastly, community support plays a pivotal role in the journey toward finding a kingdom spouse. Building a prayer group for singles fosters an environment of encouragement and accountability. Hebrews 10:24-25 calls believers to spur one another on toward love and good deeds, emphasizing the necessity of community in the waiting period. As singles gather to pray, share their experiences, and support one another, they create a strong foundation for future relationships rooted in Christ, enhancing their readiness for the blessings God has in store.

Praying for Your Kingdom Spouse

Scriptures for Prayer

Scriptures for prayer serve as a powerful resource for Christian singles who are seeking their kingdom spouse. These verses not only provide comfort and encouragement but also guide individuals in their conversations with God. When praying for a partner, it is essential to anchor those prayers in biblical truths that reflect the desires of the heart and align with God's will. Verses such as Psalm 37:4 remind us to delight in the Lord, and He will give us the desires of our hearts. This scripture highlights the importance of cultivating a close relationship with God, allowing Him to shape our desires in accordance with His plan.

While waiting for a kingdom spouse, patience becomes a critical virtue. Scriptures like Isaiah 40:31 encourage believers to wait upon the Lord and renew their strength. This verse serves as a reminder that the waiting period is not a time of inactivity but an opportunity for spiritual growth and reliance on God's timing. Praying these verses can help singles cultivate a spirit of patience, trusting that God's timing is perfect. Incorporating these scriptures into daily prayers fosters a mindset that embraces waiting as part of God's divine plan.

Affirmations based on biblical promises can be a powerful part of prayer for singles. Romans 8:28 reassures us that all things work together for good for those who love God. By affirming this truth, singles can approach their prayers with confidence, believing that their journey toward finding a kingdom spouse is under God's sovereign care. Regularly speaking these affirmations can help reinforce faith and combat feelings of doubt and loneliness. Creating a list of personal affirmations based on scripture can enhance this practice, allowing individuals to declare God's promises over their lives.

Journaling can also be a transformative practice in understanding God's will for relationships. Reflecting on scriptures such as Proverbs 3:5-6 encourages singles to trust in the Lord with all their hearts and lean not on their own understanding. By writing down thoughts, prayers, and insights, individuals can track their spiritual journey and recognize how God is working in their lives. Journaling not only aids in clarifying thoughts but also serves as a record of God's faithfulness and guidance, providing encouragement during times of waiting.

Finally, building a community of support through prayer groups can significantly enhance the journey of seeking a kingdom spouse. Ecclesiastes 4:9-10 emphasizes the strength found in companionship, reminding us that two are better than one. Engaging with fellow singles encourages shared prayers and collective support, creating an environment where individuals can grow together in faith. Establishing a prayer group focused on seeking kingdom spouses can foster accountability and encouragement, reinforcing the belief that God is at work in their lives, even amidst the waiting.

How to Pray Effectively

Prayer is a powerful tool for Christians, especially for those who are single and seeking their kingdom spouse. To pray effectively, one must first cultivate a deep and personal relationship with God. This involves setting aside dedicated time for prayer, free from distractions, where one can communicate openly with God. Begin by expressing gratitude for the journey thus far and for the promises He has for your future. As you pray, be specific about your desires for a kingdom spouse, including qualities you seek and the kind of relationship you envision. This specificity not only helps clarify your thoughts but also aligns your heart with God's will.

Incorporating biblical scriptures into your prayers can enhance their effectiveness. Scripture serves as a foundation for faith, providing the assurances and promises of God. For instance, praying with verses like Jeremiah 29:11, which speaks of God's plans for hope and a future, can instill confidence in His timing. Additionally, verses such as Philippians 4:6-7 remind us to present our requests to God, assuring us that peace will follow. By weaving these scriptures into your prayers, you reinforce your petitions with God's word, which is a source of strength and encouragement.

Patience is often a challenging aspect of waiting for a kingdom spouse. Scriptural prayers focused on patience can be transformative. Consider praying through James 1:2-4, which encourages us to view trials as opportunities for growth. As you wait, ask God to cultivate patience within you, helping you to trust in His perfect timing. Journaling your prayers can also aid in this process, allowing you to reflect on your feelings and insights as you navigate the waiting period. Writing down your prayers and any revelations can create a tangible record of your spiritual journey.

In addition to personal prayer, building community support is vital. Forming a prayer group with fellow singles can foster encouragement and accountability. Sharing your prayer requests and lifting each other up in prayer can create a sense of belonging and reduce feelings of loneliness. Together, you can explore scriptures related to relationships and discuss how to apply them in your lives. This communal approach not only strengthens your faith but also allows for shared experiences and insights that can deepen your understanding of God's will.

Lastly, fasting and prayer can be powerful strategies for gaining clarity in relationship decisions. By dedicating time to fast, you create space to hear God's voice more clearly regarding your future spouse. This practice, combined with prayer, can help you discern His will and strengthen your resolve to wait for His best. Remember that building a Christ-centered relationship foundation before marriage is essential. Focus on developing your relationship with God, understanding His character, and embodying His love. This not only prepares you for your kingdom spouse but also nurtures a relationship built on faith and trust in God's perfect plan.

Scriptural Prayers for Patience

Embracing the Waiting Period

Embracing the waiting period is a transformative phase in the journey of a Christian single seeking a kingdom spouse. It is essential to recognize that waiting is not synonymous with inactivity; rather, it is a time for spiritual growth, self-reflection, and deepening one's relationship with God. Scripture provides numerous examples of individuals who waited faithfully for God's promises to unfold. By embracing this waiting period, you open yourself up to the profound work God is doing in your life, preparing you for the future He has in store.

In the waiting, prayer becomes a powerful tool for cultivating patience and aligning your heart with God's will. Philippians 4:6-7 encourages believers to bring their requests to God in prayer, assuring them of His peace. Developing a habit of daily prayer can help you articulate your desires for a kingdom spouse while also fostering a spirit of trust in God's timing. Scriptural prayers for patience can serve as a guide, reminding you that delays often come with divine purpose. As you pray, consider journaling your thoughts and feelings, allowing God to reveal His plans through your reflections.

Affirmations based on biblical promises can also provide encouragement during this waiting period. Verses like Jeremiah 29:11 remind us that God has plans for our future, filled with hope and purpose. Daily affirmations rooted in Scripture can help reinforce your faith and combat feelings of doubt and loneliness. By speaking these truths over your life, you strengthen your mental and spiritual resilience, creating a positive mindset that is essential for navigating the challenges of waiting.

Engaging with the stories of biblical singles who found their kingdom spouses can inspire hope and perseverance. Figures such as Ruth and Isaac exemplify patience and trust in God's timing. Their journeys reveal that God often orchestrates circumstances in unexpected ways, leading to beautiful unions. Reflecting on these narratives can provide reassurance that your waiting period is a valuable part of your journey, one that can ultimately lead to a fulfilling relationship grounded in faith.

Building community support is vital during this season of waiting. Connecting with other singles who share similar aspirations can foster encouragement and accountability. Establishing a prayer group focused on seeking kingdom spouses can create a nurturing environment where you can share your experiences, pray for one another, and celebrate each step of your journey. As you wait, remember that God is not only preparing your future spouse but also molding you into the partner He desires you to be, reinforcing the importance of embracing this waiting period with faith and hope.

Key Scriptures for Patience

Patience is a vital virtue for Christian singles who are praying for their kingdom spouse. The journey toward finding a loving and God-centered relationship often requires waiting, which can be challenging. However, the Bible offers numerous scriptures that emphasize the importance of patience and the blessings that come from it. One foundational verse is James 1:4, which states, "Let perseverance finish its work so that you may be mature and complete, not lacking anything." This scripture encourages singles to view their waiting period as an opportunity for personal growth and spiritual maturity, reinforcing the idea that God is actively working in their lives even when they cannot see it.

Another powerful scripture is Psalm 27:14, which advises, "Wait for the Lord; be strong and take heart and wait for the Lord." This verse serves as a reminder that patience is not just about inactivity but involves strength and courage. In the context of waiting for a kingdom spouse, it encourages singles to remain steadfast in their faith and trust in God's timing. The act of waiting can be transformed into a period of preparation where individuals can strengthen their relationship with God, ensuring they are spiritually and emotionally ready for their future partner.

Isaiah 40:31 offers additional insight into the rewards of patience: "But those who hope in the Lord will renew their strength. They will soar on wings like eagles; they will run and not grow weary; they will walk and not be faint." This scripture emphasizes that patience is intertwined with hope and reliance on God. Singles can find comfort in knowing that their hope in God will renew their strength, helping them to endure the waiting period. This promise can be claimed in daily affirmations, reinforcing the belief that waiting on God leads to renewed energy and purpose.

The story of Abraham and Sarah in Genesis illustrates the challenges of waiting for God's promises. Despite their long wait for a child, God remained faithful to His word. Genesis 15:5 highlights God telling Abraham, "Look up at the sky and count the stars—if indeed you can count them. So shall your offspring be." This narrative serves as a testament to the importance of trusting God's timing and His ability to fulfill promises, even when circumstances appear impossible. Christian singles can draw inspiration from this story, learning to trust in God's plan for their lives and their future relationships.

Finally, Romans 12:12 encourages believers to "Be joyful in hope, patient in affliction, faithful in prayer." This verse encapsulates the essence of the Christian journey while waiting for a kingdom spouse. It calls for a joyful hope, a steadfast patience in difficult times, and a commitment to prayer. By embracing these principles, singles can cultivate a deeper relationship with God and prepare themselves for the blessings He has in store. Reflecting on these key scriptures for patience not only strengthens faith but also equips individuals with the spiritual tools necessary to navigate their waiting period with grace and confidence.

Daily Affirmations for Singles

Affirmations Based on Biblical Promises

Affirmations based on biblical promises can serve as powerful tools for Christian singles seeking encouragement and strength during their journey to find a kingdom spouse. By aligning their thoughts and beliefs with Scripture, individuals can cultivate a mindset that reflects faith in God's promises. These affirmations can help to combat feelings of doubt, loneliness, or impatience that often arise during the waiting period. They remind believers that God has a plan for their lives, including their romantic relationships, and that His timing is perfect.

One effective way to incorporate biblical affirmations into daily life is by selecting specific verses that resonate with one's current situation. For example, affirmations based on Jeremiah 29:11 can remind singles that God has a purpose and a future for them. Phrases like "God has a wonderful plan for my life" or "I trust that my future spouse is being prepared for me" can be repeated throughout the day, reinforcing the belief that God is actively working in their lives. This practice not only strengthens faith but also fosters a sense of peace as individuals wait for God's timing.

Journaling can enhance the impact of these affirmations. By writing down both affirmations and personal reflections on relevant Scripture, singles can deepen their understanding of God's will for their relationships. Journaling allows for a personal dialogue with God, where individuals can express their hopes, fears, and gratitude. As they reflect on biblical stories of singles who found their kingdom spouse, they can see God's faithfulness in action, inspiring them to hold onto their own promises with confidence.

Community support is an essential aspect of maintaining a positive mindset while waiting for a kingdom spouse. Building a prayer group for singles can provide a platform for sharing affirmations and testimonies of faith. By uplifting one another and praying collectively, individuals can experience the power of community in their journey. Regular gatherings can serve as a reminder that they are not alone, and they can encourage each other to remain steadfast in their affirmations and prayers.

Ultimately, embracing affirmations based on biblical promises allows Christian singles to maintain hope and trust in God's perfect timing. By focusing on Scripture, reflecting through journaling, and engaging with a supportive community, individuals can navigate the waiting period with assurance that their desires for a kingdom spouse align with God's greater plan. As they affirm their faith daily, they cultivate a heart that is prepared for the love that God has in store for them.

Incorporating Affirmations into Daily Life

Incorporating affirmations into daily life can serve as a powerful tool for Christian singles who are on the journey of waiting for their kingdom spouse. Affirmations are positive statements that align with biblical truths and can help reinforce faith, build confidence, and foster a hopeful mindset. By regularly declaring these affirmations, individuals can remind themselves of God's promises, counter negative thoughts, and maintain a focus on their purpose and worth in God's eyes.

To effectively incorporate affirmations, it is essential to start each day with a clear intention. Begin by selecting specific biblical verses that resonate with your current situation, such as Jeremiah 29:11, which assures that God has plans for you that are good. Craft affirmations based on these scriptures, such as "I trust that God has a perfect plan for my love life" or "I am patiently waiting for the spouse God has chosen for me." Reciting these statements each morning can set a positive tone for the day and help reinforce your faith in God's timing.

Another effective method is to write down affirmations in a journal. This practice not only allows for reflection but also creates a tangible record of your faith journey. As you write, consider including personal insights and experiences that relate to your affirmations. For instance, you might write, "I am worthy of a loving and supportive relationship" alongside examples of how God has shown love in your life. Journaling can deepen your understanding of God's will and help you track your spiritual growth as you await your kingdom spouse.

In addition to personal affirmations, it can be beneficial to share affirmations with a community of like-minded individuals. Forming or joining a prayer group can provide support and encouragement as you collectively affirm God's promises. In these gatherings, take turns sharing affirmations based on scripture, which can strengthen group bonds and foster an environment of faith and hope. This communal practice not only uplifts individual spirits but also transforms the group dynamic into a powerful force for personal and collective growth.

Lastly, integrating affirmations into daily routines can enhance their impact. Consider setting reminders on your phone or placing affirmation cards in visible locations around your home. Whenever you encounter these reminders, take a moment to pause and declare the truth of these statements aloud. This consistent reinforcement helps build resilience and a positive mindset, allowing you to navigate the waiting period with confidence and a heart full of hope. By weaving affirmations into the fabric of daily life, Christian singles can cultivate a spirit of trust and anticipation as they await their kingdom spouse, grounded in the assurance of God's unfailing love and perfect timing.

Journaling Ideas for Reflection

Reflecting on God's Will

Reflecting on God's will is an essential practice for Christian singles who are navigating the journey of waiting for their kingdom spouse. This reflection involves seeking to understand how God's purpose intersects with their personal desires for companionship and love. Scripture serves as a guiding light during this period of singleness, providing insights into how God's plans unfold in our lives. For instance, Jeremiah 29:11 reminds us that God has plans for us, plans that are intended for our welfare and not for harm, giving us hope for a future that aligns with His will. Engaging with these scriptures helps singles build a foundation of faith and trust in God's timing for their relationships.

Incorporating prayer into daily life is a powerful strategy for reflecting on God's will. Scriptural prayers can help singles express their desires while also yielding to God's timing. For example, praying Psalms such as Psalm 37:4, which encourages us to delight in the Lord, can align our hearts with His purpose. This prayer not only articulates a longing for a spouse but also invites God to shape our desires according to His will. Journaling can complement this practice, allowing individuals to record their thoughts and feelings while also noting how God responds over time. Through this process, singles can discern patterns and guidance in their lives, further confirming God's involvement in their relationship journey.

Patience is a virtue frequently mentioned in the Bible, especially in the context of waiting for God's promises. Scriptures like Isaiah 40:31 teach us about the strength that comes from waiting on the Lord. This principle is crucial for singles as they navigate the often-challenging emotions of loneliness and impatience. Affirmations based on biblical promises can reinforce this patience, reminding individuals of their worth and God's faithful provision. Daily declarations such as "I am fearfully and wonderfully made" from Psalm 139:14 can uplift spirits and foster a sense of peace during the waiting period.

Biblical stories of singles who found their kingdom spouse serve as powerful testimonies of faith and divine timing. The narratives of Ruth and Boaz or Isaac and Rebekah illustrate how God orchestrates relationships in unexpected ways. These stories encourage singles to remain hopeful and trust in God's plan. Learning from these biblical figures can inspire practical steps in their own lives, such as engaging in community and service, which often leads to meeting like-minded individuals. Understanding that God's timing is perfect reassures singles that their wait is not in vain.

Finally, building a supportive community can significantly enhance the journey of reflecting on God's will. Establishing a prayer group for singles allows individuals to share their experiences, pray together, and encourage one another in their respective journeys. Shared prayer for clarity and guidance can foster a deeper understanding of God's will and create a sense of belonging among participants. As singles engage in fasting and prayer, they can seek clarity in relationship decisions, further aligning their desires with God's purpose. Ultimately, as they reflect on God's will, they will find strength in their faith and a renewed sense of hope as they wait for their kingdom spouse.

Prompts for Relationship Insights

Prompts for relationship insights can be a valuable tool for Christian singles seeking guidance and clarity as they navigate their journey toward finding a kingdom spouse. These prompts encourage deep reflection and prayer, aligning one's desires with God's will. By engaging with these prompts, individuals can foster a more profound understanding of their own hearts and the intentions God has for their relationships. The insights gained can serve as both a compass and a source of encouragement during the often-challenging wait for a kingdom spouse.

One effective prompt may involve journaling about personal desires and expectations in a future partner. Singles can reflect on qualities that are not only attractive but also align with biblical values. This exercise can help clarify what is truly important in a relationship, shifting the focus from superficial traits to qualities that foster a Christ- centered life. Scriptures such as Proverbs 31:30 remind us that "charm is deceitful, and beauty is vain, but a woman who fears the Lord is to be praised," emphasizing the significance of character over outward appearance.

Another insightful prompt could involve creating a list of prayers that specifically address patience and trust during the waiting period. Reflecting on scriptures like Isaiah 40:31, which speaks about renewing strength through hope in the Lord, can inspire powerful prayers for endurance and faith. By writing these prayers down and revisiting them regularly, singles can strengthen their resolve and deepen their relationship with God, reinforcing the understanding that waiting is part of His divine plan.

Exploring biblical stories of singles who eventually found their kingdom spouses can provide both inspiration and practical insights. For instance, the story of Ruth illustrates loyalty and faithfulness, qualities that are essential in any relationship. By reflecting on such narratives, individuals can glean lessons about God's timing and the blessings that come from remaining steadfast in faith while waiting for His promises to manifest.

Lastly, community support plays a crucial role in this journey. Singles are encouraged to form prayer groups where they can share their experiences, pray for one another, and encourage each other in their pursuits. This shared experience can create a sense of belonging and accountability, reminding individuals that they are not alone in their desires. Connecting with others who share similar goals can provide strength and encouragement, reinforcing the belief that God is at work in their lives. Through these prompts and collective support, Christian singles will find themselves growing closer to God while preparing for the kingdom spouse He has in store for them.

Biblical Stories of Singles

Examples of Faithful Waiting

In the journey of seeking a kingdom spouse, faithful waiting is an essential aspect that can be illustrated through various biblical examples. One of the most profound stories is that of Hannah, the mother of Samuel. For years, Hannah faced the deep sorrow of infertility, which caused her immense distress. Yet, instead of succumbing to despair, she turned her anguish into fervent prayer. Hannah's faithfulness in waiting is marked by her commitment to God, as she promised to dedicate her child to the Lord if He granted her request. This narrative teaches singles the importance of persistent prayer and the expectation that God hears their cries, reinforcing the scriptural promises that God will fulfill His purpose in His timing.

Another notable example is that of Ruth. After losing her husband, Ruth chose to stay with her mother-in-law, Naomi, demonstrating loyalty and faithfulness during a time of grief and uncertainty. Ruth's decision to embrace Naomi's God and people highlights a profound trust in God's plan. Her patience and dedication ultimately led her to Boaz, who became her kingdom spouse. This story encourages singles to remain steadfast in their commitment to God and to seek relationships that align with His will, reminding them that their loyalty and faith can lead to divine connections.

Joseph's journey from the pit to the palace also serves as a compelling illustration of faithful waiting. Betrayed by his brothers and sold into slavery, Joseph maintained his integrity and faith in God, even in the face of adversity. His waiting was not passive; he actively served and excelled in his circumstances, which eventually led to his rise in Egypt and a pivotal role in God's plan. This example emphasizes that while waiting for a kingdom spouse, singles should focus on personal growth, serving others, and aligning their lives with God's purpose, trusting that their faithfulness will be rewarded.

The account of Esther further exemplifies the theme of waiting with purpose. Esther, a Jewish woman who became queen, found herself in a position to save her people from destruction. Her journey involved waiting, praying, and preparing for the right moment to act. Esther's story illustrates that waiting can be a time of preparation, where individuals can deepen their relationship with God and cultivate the qualities necessary for a healthy marriage. This encourages singles to use their waiting period for spiritual growth, aligning themselves with God's will while preparing for future relationships.

Finally, the parable of the ten virgins emphasizes the importance of being prepared while waiting. In the story, five virgins were wise and brought extra oil for their lamps, while the others were not. When the bridegroom arrived, only those who were prepared could enter the wedding feast. This parable serves as a sobering reminder for singles to remain vigilant and prepared in their faith journey, actively seeking God's guidance and nurturing their spiritual lives as they await their kingdom spouse. Through these biblical examples, singles are encouraged to embrace their waiting period as an opportunity for growth, prayer, and unwavering faith in God's perfect timing.

Lessons Learned from Their Journeys

The journeys of biblical figures provide profound insights for Christian singles who are praying for a kingdom spouse. Many individuals in scripture faced challenges and uncertainties similar to those experienced today. For instance, the story of Ruth highlights the importance of faithfulness and obedience during times of waiting. Ruth's commitment to Naomi and her willingness to glean in the fields illustrate a heart ready to serve and trust in God's provision. This narrative serves as a reminder that while waiting for a kingdom spouse, cultivating a spirit of service and reliance on God can lead to unexpected blessings.

Patience is a recurring theme in the lives of many biblical characters. Abraham and Sarah's story teaches us about the significance of trusting God's timing. Despite their long wait for a child, they eventually received the promise God made to them. This journey reminds singles to practice patience and to understand that God's plans unfold in His perfect timing. Scripture encourages believers to trust in the Lord and lean not on their understanding, emphasizing that waiting can be a transformative experience that deepens faith and character.

Another important lesson comes from the life of Esther, who exemplified courage and purpose. Her journey from an ordinary life to becoming queen illustrates that God can elevate anyone for His divine purpose. For singles, this story emphasizes that God often prepares individuals for their future roles, both in relationships and in life. Building a strong relationship with God during the waiting period can lead to personal growth and readiness for a kingdom spouse. Engaging in prayer and seeking God's will through journaling can help singles discern their path and purpose.

Community support is vital, as demonstrated by the friendships seen in the life of David and Jonathan. Their bond illustrates the power of strong, supportive relationships. Singles should consider building a prayer group or engaging with fellow believers who are also waiting for their kingdom spouse. Sharing experiences, seeking prayer support, and encouraging one another can create a nurturing environment that fosters hope and strength. This community can serve as a reminder that they are not alone in their journey.

Lastly, the story of Mary and Joseph teaches the importance of faithfulness in the midst of uncertainty. Their willingness to embrace God's plan, despite the challenges they faced, underscores the significance of obedience and trust. For singles, this serves as an encouragement to remain faithful to God's calling while waiting for their kingdom spouse. Embracing a mindset of faith, combined with prayer strategies for overcoming loneliness, can help maintain a hopeful perspective. Through these lessons from scripture, Christian singles can find strength and guidance as they navigate their own journeys toward a kingdom spouse.

Prayer Strategies Against Loneliness

Scriptural Support for Loneliness

Scripture provides profound insights into the experience of loneliness, which many Christian singles encounter while waiting for their kingdom spouse. The Bible acknowledges that loneliness is a universal human condition, with verses that reflect both the emotional and spiritual struggles associated with it. For instance, Psalm 25:16- 17 expresses a heartfelt plea for God's presence in times of distress, illustrating how loneliness can lead one to seek divine companionship and guidance. This scriptural foundation reassures singles that they are not alone in their feelings and that turning to God can provide solace and strength.

Moreover, the Bible offers powerful narratives that reveal God's understanding of our loneliness. In Genesis 2:18, God states that it is not good for man to be alone, highlighting His intention for companionship. This verse not only affirms the desire for relationships but also emphasizes that God is aware of our needs for connection. Understanding this divine perspective can encourage singles to embrace their current season while remaining hopeful for future relationships. It reinforces the notion that God sees their struggles and desires to be a partner in their journey.

The book of Isaiah also offers comfort to those feeling isolated. Isaiah 41:10 assures us that God is with us, providing strength and support during lonely times. This promise serves as a reminder to singles that they can rely on God's presence and power as they navigate the waiting period. Engaging with this scripture through prayer can empower individuals to confront their loneliness with faith, transforming their perspective from one of despair to one of hope and expectancy.

In addition to individual reflection, community support is crucial during times of loneliness. Hebrews 10:24-25 encourages believers to gather, stimulate one another toward love and good deeds, and not to neglect meeting together. This scriptural directive can inspire singles to form prayer groups or support networks, fostering a sense of belonging and mutual encouragement. By sharing experiences and praying together, individuals can combat feelings of isolation while collectively seeking God's guidance for their futures.

Ultimately, embracing the scriptural support for loneliness can lead to a deeper understanding of God's timing and purpose in relationships. Ecclesiastes 3:1 reminds us that there is a time for everything, including a time to wait. By meditating on this scripture, singles can cultivate patience and trust in God's plan. As they continue to pray and affirm their faith, they can confidently move forward, knowing that their season of waiting is a vital part of their journey toward discovering their kingdom spouse.

Building a Personal Prayer Routine

Building a personal prayer routine is an essential step for Christian singles seeking a kingdom spouse. Establishing a consistent prayer life can help deepen your connection with God, provide clarity in your desires, and strengthen your faith as you wait patiently for the partner, He has planned for you. Begin by setting aside a specific time each day dedicated to prayer. This could be in the morning as you start your day, during lunch, or in the evening before bed. Choose a quiet space where you can focus without distractions, allowing your heart to open and your mind to settle into God's presence.

Incorporate biblical scriptures into your prayer routine to guide your thoughts and intentions. Scriptures such as Psalm 37:4, which encourages you to delight in the Lord, and Proverbs 3:5-6, which reminds you to trust in Him, can serve as powerful affirmations during your prayers. You might also consider creating a prayer list that includes specific requests related to your future spouse, attributes you desire in a partner, and personal growth areas you wish to address. This intentional focus allows you to align your prayers with God's will and promises, cultivating a hopeful mindset as you wait.

Daily affirmations based on biblical promises can enhance your prayer routine by reinforcing your faith and encouraging a positive outlook. Speak affirmations such as, "I trust that God has a perfect plan for my life," or "I am worthy of love and partnership in God's timing." Write these affirmations in a journal, along with your prayers, to reflect on how God is working in your life.

Journaling not only provides a record of your spiritual journey but also acts as a tool for reflecting on God's will for your relationships, helping you to discern His guidance.

As you build your personal prayer routine, consider developing prayer strategies to combat loneliness and anxiety during your waiting period. Engage in prayers that specifically address feelings of loneliness, asking God for comfort and companionship. You can also seek community support by forming or joining a prayer group with other singles. Sharing your experiences, praying together, and lifting each other up can provide encouragement and foster a sense of belonging during this season of waiting.

Finally, remember that understanding God's timing is crucial in your journey. Scripture teaches us that there is a time for everything (Ecclesiastes 3:1). By incorporating fasting into your prayer routine, you can seek clarity in your relationship decisions and deepen your reliance on God. Use this time to focus on His voice and direction, trusting that He is preparing you for the relationship He has in store. Building a Christ-centered foundation now will not only strengthen your faith but also equip you to enter into a healthy, God-honoring relationship when the time is right.

Understanding God's Timing

Scriptures on Timing in Relationships

In the journey of seeking a kingdom spouse, understanding the concept of timing is crucial. The Bible offers profound insights into how God's timing influences our relationships. Ecclesiastes 3:1 reminds us, "To everything, there is a season, and a time for every matter under heaven." This verse emphasizes that God has a divine schedule for every aspect of our lives, including our romantic relationships. As Christian singles, it is vital to recognize that waiting for the right person is not a sign of inactivity but an opportunity for spiritual growth and preparation for the future.

Patience is a key theme woven throughout the scriptures, especially in relation to waiting for a spouse. James 1:4 states, "Let perseverance finish its work so that you may be mature and complete, not lacking anything." This scripture encourages singles to view the waiting period as a time to develop character and faith. Engaging in prayerful reflection during this season can help individuals cultivate a deeper relationship with God, which is essential for strengthening their foundation for a future partnership. By praying for patience, singles can align their hearts with God's timing and purpose.

Daily affirmations based on biblical promises can serve as a powerful tool for those waiting for their kingdom spouse. Philippians 4:6-7 assures us not to be anxious about anything, but in every situation, by prayer and petition, with thanksgiving, present our requests to God. Affirmations rooted in this promise can help reinforce trust in God's plan. Additionally, journaling can be an effective practice for singles to reflect on their desires and God's will for their relationships. Writing down prayers, thoughts, and scriptural insights can provide clarity and insight as they navigate their journey.

The Bible is rich with stories of singles who waited for God's perfect timing before entering into significant relationships. The account of Ruth is particularly relevant, as she exemplified loyalty and faithfulness while waiting for God's provision in her life. Her story illustrates that even in seasons of waiting, God is actively working behind the scenes to fulfill His promises. Such narratives serve as encouragement for singles, reminding them that their patience is not in vain and that God has a beautiful plan instore.

Finally, community support can play an integral role in understanding God's timing in relationships. Building a prayer group for singles can create a space for shared experiences, prayers, and insights. Proverbs 27:17 states, "As iron sharpens iron, so one person sharpens another." Being surrounded by fellow believers who share similar desires can foster encouragement and accountability. Through prayer, fasting, and shared testimonies, singles can grow together, deepening their faith and understanding of God's perfect timing for their future spouses.

Trusting God's Plan

Trusting in God's plan for your life, particularly when it comes to relationships, is essential for Christian singles navigating the path to finding their kingdom spouse. The Bible is filled with verses that remind us of God's sovereign will and His perfect timing. Proverbs 3:5-6 encourages believers to "trust in the Lord with all your heart and lean not on your own understanding." This verse underscores the importance of surrendering our desires and expectations to God, knowing that He has a purpose for every season of our lives. As you pray for guidance and a future partner, remember that trusting God means acknowledging that His ways are higher than ours.

During the waiting period, patience is often tested. It's crucial to incorporate scriptural prayers into your daily routine, asking God to cultivate patience within you. James 1:4 states, "Let perseverance finish its work so that you may be mature and complete, not lacking anything." This verse can serve as a powerful affirmation during moments of doubt. As you affirm God's promises, reflect on the truth that your waiting is not in vain; it is an opportunity for growth and preparation for the relationship He has in store for you.

Journaling can be a helpful tool for reflecting on God's will for your relationships. Consider writing down your thoughts, prayers, and any insights you receive about your future spouse. This practice not only allows you to articulate your desires but also helps you track how God is working in your life. As you look back on your entries, you may notice patterns or specific prayers that He has answered, reinforcing your trust in His plan. Use this time to express gratitude for the lessons learned during your single season, as they will shape your future relationship.

Biblical stories of singles who found their kingdom spouse offer encouragement and hope. Characters like Ruth and Esther exemplify faithfulness and trust in God's timing. Ruth's journey to Boaz was not immediate; it involved waiting and trusting that God would provide. Her story emphasizes that even when circumstances seem uncertain, God is orchestrating events for His glory and your good. This assurance can help you remain steadfast as you await God's perfect match for your life.

Building a supportive community around you can also bolster your faith and trust in God's plan. Consider forming a prayer group with fellow singles who share similar desires for kingdom relationships. Acts 2:42 highlights the importance of fellowship and prayer among believers.

Sharing your journey, praying for one another, and celebrating milestones together can create a strong support system. As you collectively seek God's guidance, your faith will deepen, and you will find strength in knowing that you are not alone in your journey toward finding a kingdom spouse.

Community Support for Singles

Building a Prayer Group

Building a prayer group is a powerful way for Christian singles to unite in faith and purpose as they seek their kingdom spouses. Establishing a supportive community allows individuals to share their journeys, pray for one another, and encourage each other in their walk with God. To begin, it is essential to identify like-minded individuals who share the same desire for prayer and growth in their faith. This could be done through local churches, social media platforms, or community events. Once a group is formed, it is crucial to set a regular meeting time and create a welcoming atmosphere where everyone feels comfortable sharing their thoughts and concerns.

Incorporating scripture into the group's activities can deepen the experience and provide a solid foundation for the prayers offered. Each meeting can start with a designated scripture reading, focusing on verses that speak to the joys and challenges of waiting for a kingdom spouse. This could include passages such as Proverbs 3:5-6, which encourages trust in the Lord, or Psalm 37:4, which reminds participants to delight in the Lord as He grants the desires of their hearts. By centering conversations around the Word of God, members can be reminded of His promises and the importance of patience and faith during their waiting period.

Creating specific prayer strategies can enhance the effectiveness of the group's time together. Setting aside moments for individual prayer requests allows members to share their personal struggles and victories, fostering a sense of accountability and support. Additionally, incorporating themes into each meeting—such as praying for patience, clarity in relationship decisions, or community support—can keep the focus on relevant topics. Members can also be encouraged to journal their thoughts and prayers, reflecting on God's will for their relationships and documenting their growth over time.

Affirmations grounded in biblical promises can be a transformative aspect of the prayer group. Encouraging members to declare positive statements about their identities as children of God and their future spouses can help reinforce their faith. Scriptures like Jeremiah 29:11, which speaks of God's plans for hope and a future, can serve as the basis for these affirmations. By repeating these truths, members can combat feelings of loneliness and doubt, fostering a mindset of anticipation and joy in God's timing.

Finally, celebrating milestones and victories together is essential for maintaining a positive and encouraging environment. Whether it's a member receiving clarity on their relationship or a testimony of finding peace during the waiting period, sharing these moments can uplift the entire group. Building a prayer group not only strengthens each individual's faith but also cultivates a community rooted in love, support, and shared aspirations. As members grow in their relationship with God and one another, they are better equipped to wait patiently for their kingdom spouses, trusting in God's perfect plan for their lives.

The Power of Community in Waiting

The journey of waiting for a kingdom spouse can often feel isolating, but the power of community can transform this experience into one of growth and support. Building connections with fellow believers who share the same hopes and dreams can provide encouragement and a sense of belonging. In the Bible, we see numerous examples of community playing a pivotal role in the lives of individuals awaiting God's promises. Establishing a prayer group with other singles can foster a space where members uplift each other, share their struggles, and celebrate their victories in faith. This unity aligns with the scriptural principle found in Hebrews 10:24-25, which encourages believers to spur one another on toward love and good deeds, emphasizing the importance of coming together.

Incorporating communal prayer into your waiting period can be particularly powerful. When you gather with others to pray for clarity, patience, and the right timing in relationships, you create an atmosphere where God's presence can be felt. This collective approach not only strengthens your individual faith but also deepens your understanding of God's timing. As you pray together, you can reflect on biblical scriptures such as Isaiah 40:31, which promises that those who hope in the Lord will renew their strength. This shared hope can help alleviate feelings of loneliness and impatience, reminding everyone involved that they are not alone in their journey.

Furthermore, community support can enhance your spiritual growth during this waiting season. Engaging in group activities, whether it's a Bible study focused on relationships or a service project, can help shift your focus from waiting to actively participating in God's work. This engagement allows you to cultivate a Christ-centered foundation, which is essential before entering into any relationship. Biblical stories, such as that of Ruth and Naomi, illustrate how companionship and guidance can lead to divine outcomes. By reflecting on these narratives within a community, you can gain insights into God's design for relationships and the importance of support during transitional phases.

Daily affirmations grounded in biblical promises can also be a communal practice. Sharing affirmations that remind each participant of their worth and God's plan for their lives can uplift spirits and reinforce faith. For instance, affirmations drawn from scriptures like Jeremiah 29:11 can remind singles that God has a specific plan and purpose for them, even in their waiting. These affirmations can be shared in prayer groups or through journaling, allowing individuals to reflect on their identity in Christ and the significance of their waiting period. This practice not only builds confidence but also encourages a mindset focused on hope and divine timing.

In conclusion, the power of community in waiting for a kingdom spouse cannot be overstated. By surrounding yourself with like-minded individuals who are also seeking a deeper relationship with God, you can experience encouragement, shared wisdom, and collective strength. As you pray, affirm, and engage in community activities, you will find that your waiting period becomes a time of spiritual enrichment rather than mere inactivity. Trusting in God's perfect timing and allowing the support of your community to guide you can lead to a profound understanding of His plans for your life and relationships.

Strengthening Faith Through Scripture

Key Scriptures for Faith Building

As Christian singles embark on the journey of waiting for their kingdom spouse, certain scriptures can serve as powerful reminders of God's promises and faithfulness. These verses are essential for reinforcing faith, especially during moments of doubt or impatience. Philippians 4:6-7 encourages believers to present their requests to God with thanksgiving, assuring them that His peace will guard their hearts and minds. This scripture highlights the importance of prayer in cultivating a strong faith while waiting, reminding singles that their desires for companionship are known and understood by God.

Another vital passage is Jeremiah 29:11, which states, "For I know the plans I have for you," declares the Lord. This verse reassures singles that God has a divine plan for their lives, including their relationships. Understanding that God is actively working behind the scenes can provide comfort and hope. It invites singles to trust in God's timing, knowing that His plans are ultimately for their welfare and not for harm. Reflecting on this scripture can help individuals maintain a positive outlook while waiting for their kingdom spouse.

James 1:2-4 offers insights into the purpose of waiting and trials. This passage encourages believers to consider it pure joy when facing challenges, as these moments produce perseverance, character, and ultimately, maturity in faith. Singles can use this scripture to frame their waiting period as an opportunity for growth, developing qualities that will benefit future relationships. Journaling about personal experiences during this time can help articulate feelings and track spiritual growth, making the waiting process more meaningful.

In addition to these scriptures, Hebrews 10:23 serves as a reminder to hold unswervingly to the hope we profess, for He who promised is faithful. This verse underscores the importance of community support, as sharing struggles and testimonies with others can strengthen faith. Building a prayer group with fellow singles can create a supportive environment, fostering encouragement and accountability in the waiting process. Praying together not only reinforces faith but also nurtures a sense of belonging during what can sometimes feel like a lonely journey.

Lastly, Romans 8:28 assures believers that God works all things together for good for those who love Him. This scripture emphasizes that even in the wait, God is orchestrating circumstances for our benefit. It invites singles to trust that every experience, whether joyful or challenging, is part of a greater purpose. Engaging in fasting and prayer can enhance clarity in relationship decisions, allowing individuals to align their desires with God's will. By meditating on these key scriptures, Christian singles can build a robust foundation of faith as they await their kingdom spouse.

Practical Applications of Scripture

Practical applications of scripture provide invaluable guidance for Christian singles navigating the journey toward finding their kingdom spouse. By engaging with biblical texts, individuals can cultivate a deeper understanding of God's will in their relationships. This process begins with prayer, where scripture can serve as a foundation for petitions and intercessions. Incorporating verses such as Jeremiah 29:11, which assures believers of God's plans for their future, can bring comfort and clarity as they seek a partner aligned with their faith.

While waiting for a kingdom spouse, patience can often be a challenge. Scriptural prayers focusing on patience can help reinforce the importance of trusting in God's timing. Verses like Psalm 27:14 remind believers to "wait for the Lord; be strong and take heart," emphasizing that the waiting period is not a time of inactivity but an opportunity for spiritual growth. By meditating on these scriptures, singles can develop resilience and a hopeful outlook as they navigate their season of waiting.

Daily affirmations grounded in biblical promises can also empower singles on their journey. Affirmations rooted in scripture, such as "I am fearfully and wonderfully made" from Psalm 139:14, can foster a positive self-image and reinforce the belief that they are worthy of a loving relationship. These affirmations serve not only as reminders of personal worth but also as declarations of faith that God has a plan for their romantic future.

Journaling can be a powerful tool for reflecting on God's will regarding relationships. Singles can use journaling prompts inspired by scripture to explore their thoughts and feelings about love, commitment, and God's purpose. Reflections on stories of singles who found their kingdom spouses, such as Ruth and Boaz, can offer inspiration and practical insights into how faith and obedience play crucial roles in relationship dynamics. This practice helps individuals discern their desires and align them with biblical principles.

Finally, understanding God's timing through scripture is essential for building a solid foundation for future relationships. Verses like Ecclesiastes 3:1 remind believers that there is a time for everything, including love and partnership. Developing prayer strategies to overcome loneliness while waiting can strengthen community ties and provide support. Forming prayer groups can create an environment of accountability and encouragement, allowing singles to share their journeys, pray for one another, and collectively seek God's guidance in finding their kingdom spouses. Through these practical applications of scripture, Christian singles can navigate their path with faith and purpose.

Fasting and Prayer for Clarity

The Role of Fasting in Decision Making

Fasting serves as a powerful spiritual discipline that can significantly enhance decision- making, especially for Christian singles seeking their kingdom spouse. When individuals fast, they intentionally abstain from food or certain activities to focus more on prayer and spiritual growth. This practice allows for a clearer connection with God, enabling them to seek His guidance and wisdom regarding their relationships. By setting aside time to fast, singles can quiet the noise of daily life and create space for divine communication, which is crucial in understanding God's will for their future spouse.

In the context of seeking a kingdom spouse, fasting can help individuals discern their desires and motives. Often, the hustle and bustle of life can cloud one's judgment, leading to decisions based on societal pressures or personal insecurities. Through fasting, singles can reflect on their true intentions and align their hearts with God's purpose. This period of self-denial can highlight any unhealthy attachments or unrealistic expectations they may have regarding relationships, allowing for a more authentic approach to finding a partner who shares their faith and values.

Fasting also cultivates a spirit of humility and dependence on God. As singles surrender their physical needs, they are reminded of their reliance on Him for emotional and spiritual sustenance. This act of humility can open their hearts to receive the guidance of the Holy Spirit in making relationship decisions. By acknowledging their limitations and seeking God's wisdom, individuals can gain clarity and peace about the path they should take, whether that involves waiting, pursuing a relationship, or making necessary changes in their current approach to dating.

Moreover, fasting in community can amplify the effectiveness of this spiritual practice. Singles can come together to fast and pray, creating a supportive environment where they can share their insights, struggles, and revelations. This collective effort not only strengthens their faith but also fosters a sense of belonging, reducing feelings of loneliness during the waiting period. As they seek God's will together, they can encourage one another to stay patient and hopeful, reinforcing the belief that God's timing is perfect.

Ultimately, fasting provides a framework for making wise and informed decisions about relationships. By intertwining prayer and fasting, singles can approach their desire for a kingdom spouse with a renewed perspective. This discipline encourages trust in God's plan and timing, helping them to wait confidently and patiently for the person He has destined for them. Through this process, they can build a solid foundation for a future relationship, rooted in faith and guided by divine wisdom.

Scriptural Guidance for Fasting

Fasting is a spiritual discipline that has been practiced by believers throughout biblical history, serving as a means to deepen one's relationship with God. For Christian singles seeking a kingdom spouse, incorporating fasting into prayer can provide clarity, guidance, and strength during the waiting period. Scripture underscores the importance of fasting as a way to humble oneself before God, seek His will, and prepare one's heart for the blessings He has in store. By turning to scriptural guidance on fasting, individuals can align their desires with God's purpose and cultivate a spirit of readiness for their future spouse.

In Matthew 6:16-18, Jesus teaches about the attitude with which one should fast. He emphasizes the necessity of sincerity and humility, instructing believers to avoid outward displays of piety. This principle is crucial for singles who are fasting for a kingdom spouse; the focus should remain on seeking God's will rather than seeking validation or attention from others. By approaching fasting with a genuine heart, individuals can create a sacred space for God to reveal His plans, ensuring that their motives align with His divine purpose.

The book of Isaiah also provides profound insight into the purpose and benefits of fasting. Isaiah 58:6-7 reveals that true fasting is not simply about abstaining from food but is tied to acts of justice, mercy, and compassion. For singles, this means that while one is waiting for a kingdom spouse, fasting should also be accompanied by actions that reflect love and service to others. Engaging in community service or supporting fellow singles can create a positive impact, reinforcing the understanding that God's blessings are often intertwined with how we treat those around us.

In James 1:5, believers are encouraged to ask God for wisdom, promising that He will generously provide it without finding fault. This promise serves as a powerful reminder for those fasting while praying for their future spouse. During this time of seeking clarity, individuals can focus on asking God for discernment regarding their desires and relationships. Fasting can amplify this request, creating an environment in which God's voice can be heard more clearly, and His guidance can be more readily understood.

Lastly, the practice of fasting should lead to personal reflection and growth. Christian singles can use this time to journal about their experiences, thoughts, and the revelations they receive during their fast. By documenting prayers and insights, individuals can track their spiritual journey, helping to identify patterns in their waiting and understanding God's timing in their lives. This practice not only fosters a deeper connection with God but also prepares the heart for the future, ensuring that when the time comes to enter into a relationship, it is built on a solid foundation of faith and purpose.

Building a Christ-Centered Foundation

Principles for a Strong Relationship

A strong relationship is built on a foundation of mutual respect, love, and a shared commitment to faith. For Christian singles seeking their kingdom spouse, understanding these principles can be transformative. First and foremost, it is essential to prioritize a relationship with God. Scripture teaches that when you draw near to God, He draws near to you (James 4:8). This intimate connection not only strengthens your personal faith but also prepares your heart to love and be loved in return. By seeking God first, you align your desires with His will, ensuring that your future relationship is rooted in divine purpose.

Communication is another critical principle that undergirds strong relationships. In the context of a kingdom marriage, open and honest dialogue is vital. Proverbs 15:1 reminds us that a gentle answer turns away wrath, emphasizing the importance of kindness in communication. As you prepare for a future spouse, practice sharing your thoughts, feelings, and aspirations with God through prayer and journaling. This habit will help you articulate your needs and expectations clearly when the time comes to engage with your partner. Additionally, fostering a culture of respect and understanding can help navigate the complexities that arise in any relationship.

Trust is fundamental to any lasting partnership. It is essential to cultivate trust in your relationship with God as you wait for your spouse. Trusting God means believing that He knows your needs and timing better than you do. Jeremiah 29:11 assures us that God has plans for our future, filled with hope. As you pray for your kingdom spouse, ask God to help you develop trust in His divine timing. This trust not only alleviates anxiety during your waiting period but also prepares you to extend that same trust to your future partner, creating a safe space for love to grow.

Another principle to consider is the importance of supporting one another's spiritual growth. A kingdom marriage should be a partnership that encourages both individuals to deepen their faith and relationship with God. Ecclesiastes 4:9-10 highlights the strength found in companionship, stating that two are better than one. As you prepare for your future relationship, seek out opportunities for spiritual growth, such as joining a prayer group or participating in community events. These experiences will not only enrich your own faith journey but will also help you foster a supportive environment for your future spouse.

Lastly, patience is a virtue that cannot be overstated in the pursuit of a kingdom spouse. The journey may be filled with uncertainty, but Romans 12:12 encourages us to be joyful in hope, patient in affliction, and faithful in prayer. Embrace this time of waiting as an opportunity for personal growth and reflection. Engage in practices such as fasting and prayer to seek clarity and direction in your relationship decisions. By fostering patience and a hopeful spirit, you cultivate a heart that is ready to embrace the love and companionship that God has in store for you.

Preparing for Marriage Through Faith

Preparing for marriage through faith requires a purposeful approach grounded in biblical teachings and practices. For Christian singles, this journey begins with a deep commitment to seeking God's will. This involves immersing oneself in prayer, asking for guidance and clarity regarding the future spouse. Scriptures such as Proverbs 3:5-6 remind believers to trust in the Lord and lean not on their own understanding, emphasizing the importance of faith in the decision-making process. By committing time to pray specifically for a kingdom spouse, individuals align their desires with God's plans, fostering a heart open to divine direction.

Patience is a crucial virtue to cultivate while waiting for a kingdom spouse. Single individuals are encouraged to engage in scriptural prayers that focus on developing a patient spirit. James 1:4 underscores the value of perseverance, stating that testing of faith produces patience. Incorporating daily affirmations based on biblical promises can reinforce a positive mindset. For instance, affirming one's worth in Christ and the belief that God has a perfect plan can help mitigate feelings of doubt or impatience in the waiting period.

Journaling can serve as a powerful tool for reflection during this season of singleness. By documenting thoughts, prayers, and insights, individuals can gain a clearer understanding of God's will for their relationships. Journaling prompts might include questions like "What qualities do I desire in a future spouse?" or "How can I prepare myself spiritually for marriage?" Reflecting on these questions in light of Scripture can illuminate personal growth areas and help singles recognize God's hand in their journey toward marriage.

Biblical stories of singles who found their kingdom spouse provide inspiration and encouragement. Exploring narratives such as Ruth and Boaz or Isaac and Rebekah reveal how faith and divine timing played pivotal roles in their relationships. These stories illustrate that God often orchestrates connections in unexpected ways, reminding singles that they are not alone in their quest for companionship. By understanding these biblical accounts, individuals can cultivate hope and trust that their story will unfold according to God's perfect timing.

Building a Christ-centered foundation before marriage is essential for lasting relationships. Engaging in community support through prayer groups for singles fosters a sense of belonging and accountability. Such groups allow individuals to share their experiences, pray for one another, and encourage each other in their journeys. Additionally, incorporating fasting and prayer for clarity in relationship decisions can enhance one's spiritual discernment. Through these practices, singles are better equipped to navigate the complexities of relationships, ensuring they are grounded in faith as they prepare for the sacred covenant of marriage.

Chapter 8 Guarding Your Heart: Identifying Counterfeits and Embracing True Love

The Importance of Guarding Your Heart

Understanding the Value of Your Heart Understanding the value of your heart is crucial for Christian singles navigating the complex landscape of relationships. Your heart is not just an emotional center; it represents your hopes, dreams, and deepest desires. Recognizing its worth helps you avoid counterfeit relationships that can delay your journey to finding your kingdom spouse. When you understand the intrinsic value of your heart, you become more intentional about who you allow into your life, ensuring that you protect your emotional and spiritual well-being. This understanding serves as a foundation for building healthy, loving relationships rooted in respect and genuine intention.

In identifying red flags in relationships, it is essential to approach potential partners with discernment. A heart that knows it's worth can quickly spot behaviors that signal manipulation or insincerity. Red flags such as inconsistent communication, lack of accountability, or controlling tendencies should not be ignored. By being vigilant and educated about these warning signs, you can safeguard your heart from individuals who may not have your best interests at heart. Empowering yourself with knowledge enables you to make informed decisions and fosters resilience against deceitful behaviors.

Building trust with your future partner involves more than just time spent together; it requires open communication and shared experiences. When you value your heart, you understand the importance of establishing boundaries that protect your emotional space. These boundaries help both partners feel secure, allowing trust to flourish. Taking the time to discuss past experiences and challenges openly fosters a deeper connection and shows mutual respect for each other's journeys. This willingness to communicate creates a strong foundation for a relationship that honors both partners' hearts.

Understanding the psychology of manipulation is another key aspect of valuing your heart. Manipulative behaviors can take many forms, from guilt-tripping to subtle coercion. By educating yourself about these tactics, you can better recognize when someone is not being genuine in their intentions. This awareness not only protects your heart but also empowers you to assertively address any concerns in your relationship. Emotional resilience against such deceit enables you to maintain your sense of self- worth and to remain steadfast in your pursuit of a healthy partnership.

Lastly, the role of spiritual discernment in relationships cannot be overstated. As you engage with potential partners, seeking guidance through prayer and reflection can illuminate the true intentions behind their actions. Genuine intentions in courtship are often accompanied by a sense of peace and alignment with your values. By cultivating a deeper relationship with God, you strengthen your ability to discern His will for your life and future relationships. This spiritual grounding reinforces your commitment to protecting your heart and embracing the love that aligns with your divine purpose.

The Consequences of Entertaining Counterfeits

The consequences of entertaining counterfeits in romantic relationships can be profound and far-reaching, particularly for Christian singles seeking true love. Engaging with individuals who do not align with one's values or intentions can lead to a significant delay in discovering a kingdom spouse. When one invests time and emotional energy into a relationship built on false pretenses, it distracts from the pursuit of authentic love and may result in missed opportunities for genuine connections. This diversion can create a cycle of disappointment, making it crucial for singles to recognize and avoid such counterfeits.

Identifying red flags in relationships is essential for protecting one's heart and future. Counterfeit relationships often display patterns of manipulation, where an individual may attempt to control or influence their partner's feelings and decisions. This manipulation can manifest as gaslighting, inconsistent behavior, or emotional volatility, which can obscure the true nature of the relationship. By developing the ability to identify these warning signs early on, singles can make informed decisions about whom to invest their time and emotions in, ultimately leading to healthier and more fulfilling relationships.

Building trust with a future partner is foundational for any successful relationship, yet entertaining counterfeits can erode this essential element. When individuals find themselves in relationships marked by deceit or insincerity, it creates barriers to establishing genuine trust. Trust built on shaky ground is difficult to maintain and can lead to emotional scars that hinder future connections. Singles are encouraged to prioritize transparency and honesty in their interactions, fostering an environment where trust can flourish and genuine intentions can be recognized.

Understanding the psychology of manipulation is another critical factor in navigating romantic relationships. Those who engage in counterfeit behavior may employ tactics designed to exploit vulnerabilities, leading the unsuspecting partner to question their self-worth and judgment. This manipulation can create an emotional dependency that is difficult to break. By educating themselves on these psychological strategies, singles can become more empowered to resist manipulation, set healthy boundaries, and protect their hearts from deceitful influences.

Lastly, spiritual discernment plays a vital role in recognizing genuine intentions in courtship. For Christian singles, cultivating a strong spiritual foundation can enhance their ability to discern between authentic and counterfeit relationships. Engaging in prayer, seeking guidance from mentors, and immersing oneself in scripture can provide clarity and insight into the intentions of potential partners. Additionally, developing emotional resilience against deceit through self-discovery and growth allows individuals to approach future relationships with confidence and wisdom, ultimately leading them closer to the love they desire and deserve.

Identifying Counterfeits

Defining What a Counterfeit Relationship Looks Like

Counterfeit relationships often masquerade as genuine connections, making it crucial for Christian singles to recognize the signs that differentiate true love from deceit. A counterfeit relationship typically lacks a foundation of mutual respect and understanding, often prioritizing superficial attributes over spiritual compatibility. These relationships can thrive on manipulation, where one partner may use charm or emotional tactics to maintain control and gain affection, leaving the other feeling confused or unfulfilled. By understanding the characteristics of counterfeit relationships, singles can better navigate their courtship journey and avoid unnecessary heartache.

One of the primary indicators of a counterfeit relationship is the presence of red flags that signal manipulation or insincerity. These red flags can manifest as inconsistent communication, sudden changes in behavior, or an unwillingness to discuss important topics such as faith and values. When these signs appear, it is essential to take a step back and assess whether the relationship aligns with God's intentions for partnership. A genuine connection will foster open dialogue about past experiences and future aspirations, while a counterfeit dynamic often leads to silence or evasiveness when critical subjects arise.

Building trust with a future partner is fundamental to any relationship, yet counterfeit relationships often inhibit this process. Trust is cultivated through transparency, accountability, and shared experiences. In a counterfeit scenario, one partner may withhold information or create a façade that hinders true intimacy. Recognizing the importance of trust allows singles to set healthy boundaries that protect their hearts from deceit. Establishing these boundaries requires discernment and a willingness to prioritize one's emotional and spiritual well-being over the desire for companionship.

Understanding the psychology of manipulation is vital for singles seeking to defend themselves against counterfeit relationships. Manipulative behaviors can include gaslighting, guilt-tripping, or playing the victim to elicit sympathy. These tactics can disrupt a person's emotional resilience, making it challenging to recognize genuine intentions. By educating themselves on these psychological patterns, singles can develop a sharper sense of awareness and a more profound capacity for self-protection, leading them to healthier, more authentic connections.

Finally, spiritual discernment plays an essential role in identifying counterfeit relationships. Prayer, reflection, and seeking guidance from trusted mentors can help individuals navigate their feelings and the dynamics they encounter. Engaging in self- discovery and growth allows one to cultivate a deeper understanding of their values and desires, ultimately empowering them to recognize and embrace true love. By aligning their relationship goals with God's will, Christian singles can effectively guard their hearts against counterfeits and prepare for the kingdom spouse that God has in store for them.

Common Characteristics of Counterfeit Partners

Counterfeit partners often exhibit a range of common characteristics that can serve as red flags for Christian singles seeking genuine relationships. One of the most prominent traits is inconsistency in behavior and communication. These individuals may initially present themselves as charming and attentive, but over time, their actions may not align with their words. For example, they might profess deep affection and commitment but fail to follow through on promises or maintain regular communication. This inconsistency can create confusion and emotional turmoil, making it crucial for singles to remain vigilant and attentive to any discrepancies.

Another characteristic of counterfeit partners is their tendency to prioritize their needs over the needs of others. This self-serving behavior often manifests as manipulation, where the individual seeks to control or influence their partner's decisions and feelings for personal gain. They may employ tactics such as guilt-tripping or emotional blackmail to maintain dominance in the relationship. Recognizing this pattern is essential for singles, as it can help them establish healthy boundaries and protect their hearts from emotional harm.

Additionally, counterfeit partners often lack genuine interest in spiritual growth and mutual support. While they may outwardly express a desire for a God-centered relationship, their actions may not reflect this commitment. They might resist engaging in discussions about faith or spiritual matters, demonstrating a superficial understanding of what it means to build a relationship rooted in Christ. For Christian singles, it is important to seek partners who not only share their faith but also actively strive to grow spiritually together, fostering a foundation of trust and shared values.

Emotional resilience is another critical aspect to consider when identifying counterfeit partners. These individuals may exploit vulnerabilities and past traumas, using them as leverage to manipulate or control their partners. They often create an environment where the other person feels compelled to cater to their emotional needs, leaving little room for mutual support or healing. Christian singles should focus on developing their emotional resilience and self-awareness, equipping themselves to recognize when they are being drawn into unhealthy dynamics that could delay their journey toward a true kingdom spouse.

Lastly, understanding the role of spiritual discernment is vital in recognizing counterfeit partners. This involves seeking guidance through prayer, scripture, and counsel from trusted mentors or friends. Genuine partners will respect and encourage this process, while counterfeit partners may dismiss or ridicule the importance of spiritual insight. By cultivating a deeper relationship with God and relying on His wisdom, singles can enhance their ability to discern genuine intentions in courtship, ultimately leading them closer to the true love they seek.

Recognizing Red Flags in Relationships

Emotional Manipulation

Emotional manipulation is a subtle yet powerful tactic that can derail your journey toward finding genuine love. For Christian singles, it's essential to be aware of how manipulation can manifest in relationships, often disguised as affection or concern. This form of deceit can create confusion, leading you to question your feelings and intentions. Recognizing the signs of emotional manipulation allows you to protect your heart and delay the arrival of your kingdom spouse until the right person comes along.

Common tactics of emotional manipulators include guilt-tripping, gaslighting, and playing the victim. These behaviors can create an environment where you feel responsible for the manipulator's emotions and well-being. For instance, if someone uses your empathy against you by expressing feelings of loneliness or sadness when you prioritize your own needs, it may signal a red flag. Understanding these tactics is crucial for identifying counterfeits in the dating scene and ensuring that you are building relationships based on mutual respect and genuine intentions.

Building trust with a future partner involves open communication and a shared commitment to honesty. When confronted with emotional manipulation, it is vital to establish clear boundaries. This means being vocal about what behaviors are unacceptable and holding your partner accountable for their actions. By doing so, you foster a healthy dynamic where both individuals can grow without fear of emotional coercion. It also sets the tone for future interactions, ensuring that both partners feel safe and valued in the relationship.

Recognizing genuine intentions in courtship requires a keen understanding of the psychology behind manipulation. Emotional manipulators often prey on vulnerabilities, using charm and flattery to gain an advantage. Developing emotional resilience against deceit involves self-reflection and spiritual discernment, allowing you to differentiate between authentic affection and manipulative behavior. Engage in prayer and seek counsel from trusted mentors to sharpen your ability to discern motives, ensuring you are not swayed by superficial connections that lack depth.

Finally, empowering yourself through self-discovery and growth is an essential aspect of navigating relationships as a Christian single. By understanding your own emotional triggers and past experiences, you can communicate effectively with potential partners about your boundaries and expectations. This proactive approach not only safeguards your heart but also encourages healthy relationships built on trust and mutual respect. As you embark on this journey, remember that true love is rooted in authenticity, and protecting your heart from emotional manipulation is a vital step toward embracing it fully.

Lack of Transparency Lack of transparency in relationships can significantly hinder the development of trust and intimacy, which are essential components of a healthy partnership. For Christian singles, understanding the importance of openness is crucial, especially in the context of courtship. When individuals withhold information about their past, feelings, or intentions, it creates an environment ripe for misunderstanding and deceit. This lack of clarity can lead to emotional turmoil, as partners may find themselves questioning each other's motives and honesty. Therefore, recognizing the signs of opacity is vital in order to avoid entertaining counterfeits that could delay the arrival of a genuine kingdom spouse.

One of the key red flags associated with a lack of transparency is the consistent avoidance of deeper conversations. If a potential partner frequently sidesteps discussions about their past relationships or significant life experiences, it may indicate a reluctance to share important aspects of themselves. This behavior can serve as a defense mechanism to protect against vulnerability, but it ultimately undermines the foundation of trust necessary for a lasting relationship. As Christian singles navigate the complexities of courtship, it is essential to engage in open dialogues about past experiences, allowing both partners to build a deeper understanding of each other and fostering a sense of security.

In addition to recognizing red flags, developing emotional resilience against deceit is crucial. When faced with ambiguous communication or evasive answers, it can be easy to rationalize or ignore these warning signs, especially when desire for companionship is strong. However, cultivating emotional resilience allows individuals to maintain their self-worth and discernment in the face of manipulation. It is important to remember that true love is built on honesty and transparency, and any relationship that lacks these qualities may ultimately lead to heartache. Trusting one's instincts and prioritizing emotional health can empower Christian singles to make wiser choices in their pursuit of genuine connections.

Spiritual discernment plays a pivotal role in identifying the authenticity of intentions in courtship. When individuals rely on prayer and seek guidance from God, they can gain clarity on the motives of those around them. A lack of transparency often correlates with ulterior motives, and spiritual discernment can illuminate these hidden agendas. By fostering a close relationship with God and seeking His wisdom, singles can better navigate their interactions, ensuring that they are drawn toward partners who are genuine and committed to a relationship grounded in faith and honesty.

Setting boundaries is another vital aspect of protecting one's heart from the detrimental effects of a lack of transparency. Clear boundaries communicate expectations and foster an environment where both partners feel safe to express themselves openly. By establishing what is acceptable in terms of communication and emotional sharing, individuals can create a framework that encourages honesty and vulnerability. This approach not only safeguards one's heart but also promotes mutual respect and understanding. In the journey of self-discovery and growth, Christian singles must prioritize transparency, both in themselves and in their relationships, to cultivate lasting and meaningful connections.

Controlling Behaviors

Controlling behaviors in relationships can often masquerade as affection or concern, making it difficult for individuals to recognize them as red flags. For Christian singles seeking a genuine partnership, understanding these behaviors is crucial in order to guard their hearts against counterfeits. Controlling partners may use emotional manipulation, isolating tactics, or even guilt-tripping to maintain power over their significant other. It is essential to identify these behaviors early on to ensure a healthy foundation built on trust and mutual respect.

Recognizing the signs of controlling behavior can prevent unnecessary heartache and delay in finding your kingdom spouse. Common indicators include excessive jealousy, constant checking in, or dictating how one should act in social situations. These behaviors can stem from insecurity and fear of abandonment, but they can also signal a deeper issue of control that can be detrimental to a relationship. By being vigilant about these red flags, singles can empower themselves to walk away from relationships that do not align with their values.

Building trust with a future partner requires open communication and vulnerability. It is vital to discuss personal boundaries and expectations early in the relationship, ensuring that both individuals feel safe and respected. This dialogue can help dispel any controlling tendencies, as each partner should be encouraged to express their thoughts and feelings without fear of retribution. Establishing a safe space for these discussions fosters emotional resilience and helps both parties grow individually and together.

Understanding the psychology of manipulation can further equip singles to discern genuine intentions in courtship. Manipulators often exploit emotional vulnerabilities to gain control, which can lead to a toxic dynamic. It is important to reflect on past experiences and recognize patterns that may signal manipulative behavior. This self- awareness not only aids in identifying red flags but also empowers individuals to set firm boundaries that protect their hearts from deceitful intentions.

Spiritual discernment plays a significant role in navigating relationships. Inviting God into the process can provide clarity and wisdom in recognizing controlling behaviors. Prayer and reflection can guide individuals in making decisions that align with their faith and values. By developing a strong sense of self through self-discovery and growth, Christian singles can build a foundation of emotional resilience that allows them to engage in relationships with confidence, ensuring they remain vigilant against counterfeit love while waiting for their true kingdom spouse.

Building Trust with Your Future Partner

The Foundations of Trust

The concept of trust serves as a cornerstone in any relationship, particularly in the context of romantic engagements for Christian singles. Trust is built upon a foundation of honesty, reliability, and consistency. When you first meet someone, it is essential to observe their actions and words over time. Genuine intentions are often reflected in how a person treats others and handles challenging situations. By prioritizing trust, you establish a space where both partners can express their true selves without fear of judgment or betrayal. This foundation not only protects your heart but also fosters a deeper connection with your future partner.

Identifying red flags early on is crucial in maintaining this foundation of trust. Signs of manipulation, dishonesty, or inconsistency can jeopardize a relationship before it has the chance to flourish. It's important to remain vigilant and aware of behaviors that may indicate a lack of genuine intentions. This could include a partner who quickly shifts the conversation away from personal topics or one who frequently contradicts themselves. By developing a keen sense of awareness, you can protect yourself from potential counterfeit relationships that may delay the arrival of your kingdom spouse.

Building trust takes time and effort, but it can be greatly enhanced through effective communication. Sharing past experiences and being open about your feelings fosters an environment where both partners can feel safe. This vulnerability not only strengthens the bond but also allows both individuals to understand each other's perspectives and backgrounds, which is essential for spiritual discernment in relationships. Engaging in honest conversations can reveal a partner's character, helping you to recognize whether their intentions align with your values and beliefs.

Setting boundaries is another vital aspect of building trust. Boundaries protect your heart from being hurt while allowing your relationship to grow at a healthy pace. Establishing clear expectations regarding emotional and physical intimacy will help both partners understand where they stand and what is acceptable. This proactive approach empowers you to maintain your integrity and encourages your partner to respect your needs. When boundaries are communicated effectively, trust can flourish, creating a solid base for a lasting relationship.

Finally, developing emotional resilience against deceit is essential for maintaining trust. Life experiences can sometimes lead to skepticism, but it is important to approach new relationships with an open heart. Self-discovery and growth empower you to identify your own triggers and insecurities, allowing you to navigate relationships with a clearer mindset. By actively working on your emotional health, you position yourself to recognize and embrace true love, all while guarding your heart against counterfeits. In this way, trust becomes not just a foundation but a guiding principle in your journey toward finding a kingdom spouse.

Steps to Foster Trust in Relationships

To foster trust in relationships, particularly among Christian singles, it is essential to establish a foundation built on open communication and honesty. Begin by prioritizing transparency in interactions with potential partners. This means sharing your thoughts and feelings openly while also encouraging your partner to express themselves without fear of judgment. When both parties feel safe to communicate, it lays the groundwork for trust. Discussing past experiences, including both successes and failures, can further enhance understanding and empathy, allowing you to recognize and appreciate each other's journeys.

Another vital step in fostering trust is setting clear boundaries. Boundaries protect your emotional well-being and help define the nature of your relationship. It is crucial to articulate your expectations regarding communication, intimacy, and personal space. When boundaries are established and respected, both partners can feel secure and valued. This clarity not only strengthens trust but also signals to your partner that you are committed to maintaining a healthy dynamic, free from manipulation or deceit.

Understanding the psychology of manipulation is also crucial in identifying red flags that may arise during courtship. Be vigilant for behaviors that seem overly controlling or deceptive, as these can undermine the trust you are trying to build. A partner who respects your autonomy and supports your personal growth is more likely to have genuine intentions. By learning to recognize signs of manipulation, you can protect your heart and ensure that your relationship is rooted in mutual respect and trust.

Spiritual discernment plays a significant role in fostering trust as well. Engaging in prayer and seeking guidance from God can provide clarity in your relationship. Trust your instincts and listen to the Holy Spirit's nudges, especially when something feels off or when you encounter red flags. This spiritual insight can help you navigate the complexities of dating and courtship, allowing you to discern between genuine intentions and counterfeit behaviors. Trust is deeply intertwined with faith, and relying on spiritual wisdom can enhance your ability to build and maintain trustworthy relationships.

Lastly, developing emotional resilience is essential in the journey of building trust. Life experiences, including past disappointments and betrayals, can create barriers to trusting others. However, embracing self-discovery and growth allows you to heal and move forward. Engage in practices that nurture your emotional well-being, such as journaling, meditation, or counseling. By strengthening your emotional foundation, you will be better equipped to trust again, fostering deeper connections with future partners and ultimately preparing your heart for the love that God has in store for you.

Understanding the Psychology of Manipulation

Recognizing Manipulative Tactics

Recognizing manipulative tactics in relationships is crucial for Christian singles who desire to build a foundation of trust and genuine love with their future partners. Manipulation often manifests through subtle behaviors that can easily go unnoticed, especially when one is eager to find companionship. It is essential to remain vigilant and develop an acute awareness of these tactics to avoid compromising your values and delaying your journey toward meeting your kingdom spouse.

One common manipulative tactic is gaslighting, where the manipulator distorts facts or denies reality to make the victim feel confused or question their own judgment. This can create an unhealthy dynamic where the victim feels insecure and dependent on the manipulator for validation. Recognizing this behavior involves being attuned to how conversations make you feel. If you often feel unsettled or unsure about your perceptions after interacting with someone, it may indicate manipulative behavior. Maintaining a strong sense of self and relying on spiritual discernment can help you navigate these situations more effectively.

Another tactic to watch for is the use of guilt or emotional blackmail. A manipulative partner may employ guilt to control your actions or decisions, often framing their needs as more important than your own. This can lead to a cycle where you continuously prioritize their feelings over your own well-being. To counteract this, it is vital to establish clear boundaries that protect your heart and emotions. Communicating your needs openly and standing firm in your decisions can foster a healthier relational dynamic and discourage manipulative behaviors.

Additionally, some individuals may employ flattery and excessive charm to disarm you and gain your trust quickly. While compliments can be genuine, excessive praise may be a red flag indicating insincerity. It is important to evaluate the consistency of a person's actions with their words. Genuine intentions in courtship are often marked by authenticity and reliability over time. Take the time to observe how a potential partner behaves in various situations and whether their actions align with their professed beliefs.

Finally, emotional resilience is key in recognizing and responding to manipulation. Building this resilience involves understanding your own value and self-worth in Christ, which empowers you to resist deceitful tactics. When you are grounded in your identity and purpose, you become less susceptible to manipulation. Engage in self-discovery and growth through prayer, reflection, and community support. This holistic approach not only strengthens your ability to identify red flags but also equips you to build a loving relationship based on trust and mutual respect with your future partner.

The Impact of Manipulation on Relationships

Manipulation can profoundly affect relationships, particularly for Christian singles seeking genuine connections. When individuals enter relationships with ulterior motives or deceptive intentions, it creates an environment ripe for distrust and emotional turmoil. Recognizing manipulation is crucial, as it allows you to identify potential counterfeit partners who may delay your journey toward finding a true kingdom spouse. Being vigilant about manipulative behaviors can help safeguard your heart and ensure that you remain open to authentic love.

One of the primary red flags of manipulation is the consistent disregard for your feelings and boundaries. Manipulative individuals often employ tactics like gaslighting, guilt- tripping, or emotional blackmail to achieve their goals. They may present themselves as caring and attentive at first, only to gradually reveal their true colors once they have gained your trust. Understanding these psychological tactics can empower you to set firm boundaries, making it less likely for manipulators to infiltrate your life. By identifying these behaviors early on, you can better protect yourself from emotional harm and foster healthier relationships.

Building trust with a future partner requires transparency and the ability to communicate openly about past experiences. If you've encountered manipulation in previous relationships, discussing these experiences can be vital in establishing a foundation of honesty. Sharing your concerns and fears with a prospective partner allows for mutual understanding and growth. This open line of communication not only strengthens your bond but also serves as a deterrent against manipulative tactics. A partner who respects your past and is willing to engage in these discussions is more likely to have genuine intentions.

Spiritual discernment plays a vital role in recognizing manipulation within relationships. Praying for wisdom and guidance as you navigate dating can help you see beyond surface-level charm and identify individuals whose intentions may not align with your values. Trusting your instincts, combined with spiritual insight, can lead you to make wiser choices in whom to invest your heart. This discernment allows you to differentiate between genuine affection and manipulation, ensuring that you do not compromise your standards in your quest for love.

Emotional resilience is essential when facing the potential deceit of others. Cultivating a strong sense of self-worth and understanding your value in Christ can fortify your heart against manipulation. Engaging in self-discovery and personal growth will empower you to remain steadfast and confident in your decisions. When you are rooted in your identity and purpose, you are less likely to be swayed by those who seek to manipulate or control you. By prioritizing your emotional health and spiritual well-being, you can navigate relationships with clarity and strength, ultimately drawing closer to the true love intended for you.

Recognizing Genuine Intentions in Courtship

Signs of Authenticity

In the journey of finding true love, recognizing the signs of authenticity is crucial for Christian singles who seek to guard their hearts against counterfeits. Authenticity in relationships is characterized by honesty, transparency, and a genuine desire for connection. True partners will not only express their feelings but also demonstrate their intentions through their actions. It is essential to pay attention to how someone communicates and behaves, as these elements can reveal their true character and commitment. By understanding these signs, you can better navigate the complexities of dating while remaining focused on your goal of finding a kingdom spouse.

One significant sign of authenticity is consistency in actions and words. A genuine partner will align their statements with their behavior, showing that they are trustworthy and dependable. If someone frequently contradicts themselves or makes promises they do not keep, it may indicate a lack of sincerity. True love is built on a foundation of reliability, where both partners can count on each other to follow through on commitments. Observing how a potential partner behaves over time, especially in various situations, can provide valuable insights into their authenticity.

Another vital aspect to consider is the openness of communication. Authentic individuals are willing to share their thoughts, feelings, and experiences candidly. They will listen actively and encourage open dialogue about each other's pasts, beliefs, and aspirations. This willingness to communicate fosters trust and paves the way for deeper emotional connections. In contrast, if someone is evasive or avoids discussing meaningful topics, it may be a red flag indicating that they are not ready for a genuine relationship. Engaging in honest conversations can help you discern whether someone's intentions are true or if they are merely playing a role.

Emotional resilience is essential when evaluating potential partners. Authentic love requires vulnerability, and it is crucial to be equipped to handle the ups and downs that may arise in a relationship. Developing emotional resilience means understanding your own feelings and boundaries, which will empower you to recognize when someone is being manipulative or insincere. A genuine partner will respect your boundaries and support your emotional well-being, fostering a safe environment for love to grow. By setting clear boundaries and being attentive to your emotional health, you can protect your heart while remaining open to the right person.

Lastly, spiritual discernment plays a pivotal role in identifying authentic intentions in courtship. As Christian singles, relying on prayer and seeking guidance from God can illuminate the path toward true love. It is essential to cultivate a relationship with God, as this connection will enhance your ability to recognize the signs of authenticity in others. When you are grounded in your faith, you can more easily discern between genuine love and counterfeit affection, allowing you to make wise decisions in your pursuit of a kingdom spouse. Trusting in His guidance will not only protect your heart but also lead you to a love that is fulfilling and true.

The Role of Consistency and Accountability

The journey of identifying and embracing true love requires a strong foundation built on consistency and accountability. Consistency in one's actions, beliefs, and values not only reinforce personal integrity but also establishes a reliable framework for relationships. For Christian singles navigating the complexities of modern dating, showcasing consistent behavior can serve as a beacon of authenticity. This consistency allows potential partners to gain a clearer understanding of your intentions and values, creating an environment where trust can flourish.

Accountability plays a vital role in this process, acting as a safeguard against the allure of counterfeit relationships. When individuals hold themselves accountable, they are more likely to recognize and address red flags in their interactions. This self-awareness helps prevent the emotional pitfalls that can arise from manipulation and deceit. By fostering a culture of accountability, both partners can engage in open dialogues about their expectations and boundaries, ensuring that their relationship is built on mutual respect and understanding.

Moreover, transparency is key to building trust with a future partner. When both individuals commit to being consistent in their communication and actions, it nurtures a sense of safety within the relationship. Christian singles are encouraged to share their past experiences and lessons learned, allowing their partner to better comprehend their emotional landscape. This exchange not only strengthens the bond but also encourages growth and healing, paving the way for a more resilient partnership.

Developing emotional resilience against deceit is another significant aspect of consistency and accountability. By remaining steadfast in their values, individuals can better navigate the challenges of dating without compromising their integrity. It is essential to recognize that genuine love is characterized by stability and reliability. By embodying these traits, Christian singles can effectively guard their hearts against counterfeit relationships that may threaten their journey toward finding a kingdom spouse.

Lastly, spiritual discernment is crucial in identifying true intentions during courtship. Consistency in spiritual practices, such as prayer and seeking guidance through scripture, can enhance one's ability to discern the motives of potential partners. When individuals are accountable to their faith and values, they can more readily recognize the signs of genuine love versus manipulation. This discernment, coupled with the commitment to maintain healthy boundaries, empowers singles to protect their hearts while remaining open to the possibilities of true love.

Setting Boundaries to Protect Your Heart

Defining Personal Boundaries

Defining personal boundaries is a crucial step for Christian singles seeking to navigate the complex landscape of relationships while avoiding counterfeit connections. Personal boundaries are the limits we set to protect our emotional and physical well-being. They serve as guidelines that help us understand what is acceptable and unacceptable in our interactions with others. Establishing these boundaries is not only essential for maintaining self-respect but also crucial for fostering healthy, trusting relationships that align with God's purpose for our lives.

When it comes to relationships, many singles may struggle with identifying their own boundaries. Understanding your values, needs, and limits is the first step toward defining what you will and will not accept in a romantic partnership. This involves self- reflection and honest assessment of your past experiences, which can illuminate patterns that may have led to unhealthy dynamics. By recognizing these aspects, you can establish clear boundaries that help you navigate potential relationships with discernment, ensuring that you are not easily swayed by counterfeit intentions.

Effective communication is key to upholding personal boundaries. Once you have identified your limits, it is vital to articulate them clearly to potential partners. This can involve discussing your expectations regarding emotional intimacy, physical affection, and even the pace of the relationship. Open dialogue fosters trust and understanding, allowing both parties to feel safe and respected. Moreover, communicating about boundaries can help you identify red flags early on, as a partner who disregards your limits may not have genuine intentions.

In addition to communication, developing emotional resilience is essential for maintaining your boundaries. This resilience allows you to stand firm in your convictions, even when faced with pressure or manipulation. Understanding the psychology of manipulation can empower you to recognize when someone is attempting to overstep your limits. By being aware of common tactics used to undermine personal boundaries, you can protect your heart and remain steadfast in your pursuit of true love that aligns with God's will.

Finally, personal boundaries should be viewed as a dynamic aspect of your relationship journey. As you grow and evolve, your boundaries may need to be reassessed and adjusted. Engaging in self-discovery and spiritual discernment will help you stay attuned to your needs and desires in a relationship. By continually evaluating your boundaries and communicating them effectively, you can cultivate a healthy environment that nurtures genuine connections, ultimately guiding you closer to your kingdom spouse.

Communicating Boundaries Effectively

Communicating boundaries effectively is essential for Christian singles seeking to navigate the complex waters of relationships while guarding their hearts. Establishing clear boundaries is not just a protective measure; it is a vital component of mutual respect and understanding in any courtship. To communicate these boundaries effectively, one must first understand their own values and limitations. This self- awareness allows individuals to articulate what is acceptable and what is not, thereby creating a healthy framework for interactions. By grounding discussions in biblical principles, singles can reinforce the importance of boundaries in relationships, emphasizing the need for respect, patience, and love.

It is crucial to approach boundary-setting conversations with clarity and confidence. When discussing personal limits, individuals should strive to be direct yet compassionate. This means using "I" statements to express feelings and needs without placing blame on the other person. For example, saying "I feel uncomfortable when..." rather than "You make me uncomfortable..." can foster a more open dialogue. This approach not only helps in conveying personal boundaries but also encourages the other party to engage in the conversation without feeling attacked. Establishing a safe space for discussion allows both individuals to share their thoughts and feelings candidly, paving the way for deeper trust and understanding.

Recognizing red flags during the communication of boundaries is vital. If a potential partner reacts defensively or dismissively, it may indicate a lack of respect for your limits or an unwillingness to engage in healthy dialogue. Such reactions can be warning signs of manipulative behavior, which is essential to identify early on. By remaining vigilant and discerning, singles can protect themselves from counterfeit relationships that may delay their journey to finding a kingdom spouse. Understanding these dynamics encourages individuals to prioritize their emotional well-being and recognize when a relationship may not align with their values.

Moreover, effective communication about boundaries should include discussions of past experiences. Sharing personal history can offer insights into why certain boundaries are important. However, this should be approached with a spirit of vulnerability balanced with wisdom. It is essential to gauge the other person's readiness to hear about past experiences without becoming overwhelmed. This sharing can build empathy and foster deeper connections, allowing both parties to understand each other's journeys and the lessons learned along the way. Thus, it creates an environment where both individuals can grow together and support each other in their healing processes.

Ultimately, empowering oneself through self-discovery and growth enhances the ability to communicate boundaries effectively. Christian singles should take the time to reflect on their experiences, identify their needs, and develop a strong sense of self-worth. This journey of self-discovery fosters emotional resilience, enabling individuals to stand firm in their boundaries without fear of manipulation or deceit. By incorporating spiritual discernment into their relationships, singles can better assess the intentions of potential partners. When boundaries are clearly communicated and respected, it lays the foundation for a relationship built on trust, genuine intentions, and a shared commitment to honoring each other's hearts.

Developing Emotional Resilience Against Deceit

The Importance of Emotional Resilience

Emotional resilience is a vital aspect of navigating the complexities of modern relationships, especially for Christian singles who are keen on guarding their hearts against counterfeits. This resilience allows individuals to recover from setbacks, learn from experiences, and maintain a positive outlook despite challenges. In the context of dating and courtship, emotional resilience equips singles with the ability to discern genuine intentions from manipulative behaviors, thereby fostering a healthier approach to potential relationships. By cultivating this resilience, individuals can more effectively avoid the pitfalls of counterfeit love that may hinder their journey toward finding a true kingdom spouse.

Developing emotional resilience begins with self-awareness and understanding one's emotional triggers. Recognizing how past experiences shape current reactions is crucial in building a strong foundation. For many, past heartbreaks or manipulative relationships can create barriers to trusting future partners. By addressing these emotional wounds, singles can create a mindset that views relationships as opportunities for growth rather than sources of fear. This proactive approach not only empowers individuals but also enhances their ability to set healthy boundaries, ensuring they protect their hearts while remaining open to the possibility of true love.

In relationships, recognizing red flags becomes easier with emotional resilience. When individuals are equipped to manage their emotions, they can assess potential partners more clearly and objectively. This clarity helps in identifying behaviors that may indicate manipulation or insincerity. For instance, if a partner consistently disregards boundaries or attempts to control situations, emotionally resilient singles are better positioned to address these issues directly or to walk away if necessary. By trusting their instincts and promoting open communication, they can foster relationships grounded in mutual respect and understanding.

Moreover, emotional resilience plays a critical role in building trust with future partners. When individuals approach relationships with a sense of stability and self-assurance, they create an environment conducive to vulnerability and honesty. This foundation of trust encourages partners to share their past experiences and challenges without fear of judgment. As communication deepens, so does the understanding of each other's backgrounds, allowing for a more profound connection. In this way, emotional resilience not only fortifies individual hearts but also strengthens the bond between partners, paving the way for a more authentic relationship.

Lastly, emotional resilience is intricately linked to spiritual discernment, an essential element for Christian singles seeking true love. By fostering a strong relationship with God, individuals can nurture their emotional health and gain insights that guide their decisions in dating. This spiritual grounding allows for clearer discernment of intentions and encourages reliance on divine wisdom when faced with uncertainty. Ultimately, emotional resilience enables singles to navigate the dating landscape with confidence, ensuring that they remain true to themselves and their values while waiting for the right partner to enter their lives.

Strategies for Building Resilience

Building resilience is essential for Christian singles navigating the complexities of relationships, especially when striving to identify and avoid counterfeit connections. One fundamental strategy is to cultivate a strong sense of self-awareness. This involves understanding your own values, beliefs, and emotional triggers. When you know yourself well, you are better equipped to recognize red flags in potential partners. This self-awareness creates a solid foundation upon which you can build trust with your future spouse. By engaging in regular self-reflection and seeking feedback from trusted friends or mentors, you can enhance your ability to discern genuine intentions and avoid relationships that do not align with your spiritual and emotional well-being.

Another vital strategy for building resilience is establishing clear boundaries. Setting boundaries is not only about protecting your heart but also about communicating your needs and expectations to potential partners. This may involve discussing your values regarding faith, family, and relationship goals early in the courtship process. When boundaries are clearly defined, it helps both you and your partner understand what is acceptable and what is not. This clarity fosters an environment of mutual respect, where both individuals feel safe to express themselves without fear of manipulation or deceit. Learning to say no and advocating for your own needs is a crucial component of emotional resilience.

Developing emotional resilience also requires a commitment to spiritual discernment. This involves praying for guidance and wisdom as you navigate relationships. Engaging in regular prayer and meditation can help you attune your heart to God's voice, allowing you to recognize when something feels off in a relationship. Spiritual discernment can illuminate the differences between genuine love and counterfeit affection, helping you to see beyond surface-level charm to the true character of a potential partner. Trusting in God's timing and plan for your life provides reassurance and strength, enabling you to withstand the pressures of societal expectations and the desire for companionship.

Effective communication is another key strategy. It is essential to express your past experiences and how they shape your current expectations in relationships. Open dialogue about previous heartbreaks or disappointments not only fosters intimacy but also builds trust. When both partners are willing to share their vulnerabilities, it creates a safe space for growth and understanding. This level of communication can also serve as a warning system for potential manipulation, allowing you to spot red flags before they escalate. Remember that transparency is a two-way street; encourage your partner to share their own stories and listen actively.

Lastly, empowering yourself through self-discovery and growth is crucial for building resilience. Engage in activities that develop your interests and talents, and seek opportunities for personal development, whether through education, hobbies, or ministry. This not only enhances your self-esteem but also prepares you for a healthy relationship where both partners can grow together. As you invest in your personal growth, you become more attractive to a potential partner who values a similar journey of self-improvement. Ultimately, embracing resilience equips you to guard your heart against counterfeit relationships, ensuring that when your kingdom spouse arrives, you are ready to build a relationship founded on trust, respect, and genuine love.

The Role of Spiritual Discernment in Relationships

Understanding Spiritual Discernment

Spiritual discernment is the ability to perceive and understand the deeper truths within ourselves and our relationships, particularly in the context of seeking a future partner. For Christian singles, this skill is essential for navigating the complexities of modern dating, especially when it comes to identifying counterfeit relationships that can delay the arrival of a kingdom spouse. Discernment involves more than just intuition; it requires a grounded understanding of scripture, prayerful reflection, and an awareness of how God's voice speaks to our hearts. By cultivating spiritual discernment, individuals can better differentiate between genuine connections and those that may lead to emotional harm.

One of the key components of spiritual discernment is recognizing red flags in relationships. These warning signs often manifest as inconsistencies in behavior, communication breakdowns, or a lack of respect for personal boundaries. When singles take the time to pray and reflect on their experiences, they can develop a sharper eye for these red flags, allowing them to step back and evaluate whether a potential partner's intentions align with their own values and beliefs. This process not only protects the heart from potential deceit but also fosters a deeper understanding of what a healthy relationship should look like.

Building trust with a future partner is another critical aspect of spiritual discernment. Trust must be earned and nurtured, and it flourishes in an environment of open communication and vulnerability. When singles actively engage in conversations about their past experiences and how they've grown from them, they lay a strong foundation for mutual trust. Discernment plays a pivotal role here, as it enables individuals to gauge their partner's reactions and attitudes toward shared experiences, further informing their decision about the relationship's viability.

Understanding the psychology of manipulation is essential for anyone entering the dating scene. Manipulative behaviors can often disguise themselves as charm or affection, making it challenging to identify genuine intentions. By exercising spiritual discernment, singles can discern when they are being influenced or coerced into compromising their values or desires. This awareness not only empowers them to set necessary boundaries but also enables them to engage in self-discovery, recognizing their worth and the standards they deserve in a relationship.

Ultimately, developing emotional resilience against deceit is a vital aspect of spiritual discernment. It requires a commitment to personal growth and an understanding of one's own emotional triggers. As singles become more aware of their vulnerabilities and the tactics that manipulators may employ, they strengthen their ability to guard their hearts. By prioritizing spiritual discernment in their relationships, individuals not only protect themselves from counterfeits but also position themselves to embrace true love, grounded in faith and mutual respect, as they await the arrival of their kingdom spouse.

Practical Ways to Cultivate Discernment

To cultivate discernment, it's essential first to engage in self-reflection and prayer. As Christian singles navigate the complexities of relationships, understanding oneself is foundational. Take time to assess your values, desires, and past experiences. This process not only aids in recognizing personal patterns but also prepares your heart for a future relationship. Prayer is a powerful tool that connects you with God, enabling you to seek wisdom and clarity regarding your relationship choices. As you deepen your spiritual life, you become more attuned to the signs that indicate a genuine connection versus a counterfeit one.

Next, familiarize yourself with common red flags in relationships. These can range from controlling behaviors to a lack of respect for your boundaries. By educating yourself on what constitutes unhealthy dynamics, you empower yourself to identify these issues early on. Keep an eye out for inconsistencies in a potential partner's words and actions. Often, genuine intentions will align with consistent behavior, while manipulative tactics may reveal themselves through subtle contradictions. Discussing these red flags with trusted friends or mentors can also provide additional perspectives and insights.

Setting clear boundaries is another practical way to enhance discernment. Boundaries are not merely rules; they are vital to protecting your emotional well-being. Communicate your limits openly and assertively, ensuring your partner understands what is acceptable and what is not. This practice not only fosters respect but also helps in identifying how well a potential partner responds to your needs. A healthy relationship should honor and reinforce your boundaries, allowing you both to feel safe and valued.

Developing emotional resilience is crucial in recognizing deceitful behaviors. Engage in activities that strengthen your emotional health, such as journaling, therapy, or support groups. These practices help you process your feelings and experiences, making it easier to spot manipulation or insincerity in others. Building resilience empowers you to remain grounded, even when faced with challenging situations. By understanding your emotions, you can better navigate the complexities of courtship and discern genuine intentions more effectively.

Lastly, prioritize effective communication about past experiences. Being open about your relationship history can foster deeper understanding and trust between you and your future partner. Share your lessons learned, fears, and hopes, allowing for a more authentic connection. This transparency not only clears the air but also serves as a litmus test for your partner's character. Genuine intentions will be met with empathy and understanding, while a lack of concern may reveal red flags. Through these practices, you will cultivate discernment, guiding you toward a healthy, loving relationship aligned with God's purpose for your life.

Communicating Effectively About Past Experiences

The Importance of Open Communication Open communication stands as a cornerstone in any relationship, particularly for Christian singles navigating the complexities of courtship. Establishing an environment where both partners feel safe to express their thoughts and feelings is essential in identifying genuine intentions. When both individuals are open about their past experiences, aspirations, and boundaries, it not only fosters trust but also helps to unveil any red flags that may indicate a counterfeit relationship. This proactive approach ensures that both partners are working from a place of honesty, which is vital in building a foundation for a lasting relationship.

In the realm of identifying red flags, effective communication allows for the revelation of behaviors and patterns that might otherwise go unnoticed. For instance, if one partner is evasive or inconsistent in their responses, this may signal deeper issues such as manipulation or a lack of genuine commitment. By openly discussing these concerns, singles can protect their hearts from potential deceit and emotional turmoil. Engaging in candid conversations about expectations and relationship dynamics not only aids in recognizing warning signs but also empowers individuals to make informed decisions about their future partners.

Building trust with a future partner hinge on the ability to communicate effectively. When partners share their thoughts, feelings, and concerns without fear of judgment, they create an atmosphere of vulnerability that strengthens their bond. This trust is particularly important in a Christian context, where the values of honesty and integrity are emphasized. As individuals learn to communicate their needs and boundaries, they also cultivate emotional resilience, enabling them to better withstand any attempts at manipulation or deceit. Trust becomes a protective barrier, ensuring that both partners can navigate challenges with a united front.

Furthermore, understanding the psychology of manipulation and recognizing genuine intentions are critical in the process of courtship. Open communication serves as a tool for discernment, allowing individuals to engage in meaningful discussions about their relationship goals and values. By asking the right questions and being attentive to their partner's responses, singles can gauge the sincerity of their intentions. This level of awareness is crucial in avoiding counterfeit relationships, as it empowers individuals to discern whether they are genuinely connecting with someone who shares their faith and values or if they are being led astray by superficial charm.

Lastly, setting boundaries is an integral aspect of guarding one's heart, and open communication is vital in establishing these parameters. When both partners are clear about their limits and values, they can create a respectful environment that honors each individual's journey. This clarity not only protects the heart but also enhances the overall health of the relationship. As Christian singles engage in self-discovery and growth, they must prioritize open communication as a means of fostering relationships that reflect their commitment to faith and love, ultimately leading them closer to their kingdom spouse.

Sharing Your Past Without Fear

Sharing your past without fear is a vital step for Christian singles who seek to build authentic relationships rooted in trust and mutual understanding. Many individuals carry the weight of their past experiences, which can include mistakes, heartaches, and lessons learned. When approaching potential kingdom spouses, it is crucial to communicate openly about these experiences, as this honesty lays the groundwork for a healthier relationship. By confronting the fears associated with sharing your story, you can foster an environment of trust and support, essential for any meaningful connection.

Understanding the psychology of manipulation is key to recognizing genuine intentions in courtship. When individuals hide their pasts or present a facade, they may inadvertently invite deception into their relationships. By sharing your past, you not only demonstrate vulnerability but also encourage your partner to do the same. This mutual openness can help expose any red flags that may otherwise go unnoticed, allowing both partners to assess their compatibility based on honesty and integrity rather than illusions.

Setting boundaries is another crucial aspect of protecting your heart while sharing your past. It is essential to establish what you feel comfortable discussing and what remains private. These boundaries ensure that your sharing is constructive rather than overwhelming. By clearly communicating these limits, you empower yourself and your partner to engage in a dialogue that respects both individuals' emotional safety. This approach not only builds trust but also cultivates emotional resilience against potential deceit.

Spiritual discernment plays a significant role in navigating the complexities of relationships. As you share your past, seeking guidance through prayer and reflection can help you understand the intentions behind your disclosures and your partner's reactions. When both partners are grounded in their faith, they can better discern whether the relationship aligns with their spiritual values. This discernment can serve as a protective measure, helping to identify those who may not have genuine intentions.

Ultimately, sharing your past is an empowering act of self-discovery and growth. It allows you to acknowledge your journey and the lessons learned, transforming past pain into a source of strength. By embracing your story, you not only heal but also position yourself to attract a partner who appreciates your authenticity. In doing so, you create a relationship built on a solid foundation of trust, understanding, and genuine love, paving the way for a future that honors both your heart and your faith.

Empowering Yourself Through Self- Discovery and Growth

The Journey of Self-Discovery

The journey of self-discovery is a vital aspect of preparing for a healthy and fulfilling relationship, especially for Christian singles seeking to guard their hearts against counterfeits. This journey involves understanding who you are, your values, and what you desire in a future partner. By reflecting on your past experiences, you can identify patterns and behaviors that may have led to unhealthy relationships. This introspection not only strengthens your resolve to wait for God's best but also equips you with the tools to recognize genuine intentions in potential courtships.

As you embark on this journey, it is essential to develop emotional resilience against deceit. This resilience begins with acknowledging your past and understanding how it has shaped you. Embracing your experiences—both positive and negative—can lead to greater self-awareness. By learning to set healthy boundaries, you protect your heart from those who may not have your best interests at heart. Establishing these boundaries is not about building walls but rather creating a safe space where you can engage with others while maintaining your emotional integrity.

Another critical element of self-discovery is honing your spiritual discernment. This involves seeking God's guidance through prayer and scripture to better understand His will for your life and relationships. When you cultivate a strong spiritual foundation, you become more adept at identifying red flags and manipulative behaviors that may arise in courtship. This discernment allows you to differentiate between genuine love and counterfeit affection, ensuring that you do not compromise your values or rush into relationships that are not aligned with your faith.

Effective communication about your past experiences is also crucial in the journey of self-discovery. Being open and honest with yourself and potential partners fosters trust and vulnerability. Sharing your journey not only helps you articulate your needs and boundaries but also encourages your future partner to do the same. This exchange builds a foundation of mutual understanding, which is essential for a healthy and lasting relationship.

Ultimately, empowering yourself through self-discovery and growth is about embracing your identity in Christ. Recognizing your worth and understanding that you are fearfully and wonderfully made enables you to approach relationships from a place of confidence rather than desperation. As you navigate the complexities of courtship, remember that your journey is not just about finding a partner but also about becoming the person God has called you to be. This commitment to self-discovery enriches your life and prepares you for the love that God has in store for you.

Tools for Personal Growth and Empowerment

Personal growth and empowerment are essential tools for Christian singles navigating the complexities of relationships and courtship. Developing a strong sense of self not only equips individuals to recognize and avoid counterfeit connections but also positions them to embrace the authentic love that God intends for them. This journey begins with self-discovery, which involves understanding one's values, desires, and spiritual calling. Engaging in prayer, reflection, and journaling can facilitate this process, allowing individuals to clarify their intentions and recognize what they truly seek in a future partner.

Identifying red flags in relationships is another critical aspect of personal growth. By fostering awareness of one's own emotional triggers and past experiences, singles can better discern warning signs in potential partners. This heightened awareness requires a commitment to honesty and self-examination. By understanding their own patterns of behavior and emotional responses, individuals can learn to spot manipulative tactics and recognize when they are being drawn into unhealthy dynamics. This proactive approach helps to build a foundation of trust and respect, both for oneself and for future relationships.

Effective communication is also a vital tool for empowerment. Being able to articulate one's needs, boundaries, and past experiences fosters deeper connections with future partners. It is important for singles to practice sharing their stories in a way that is open yet protective of their hearts. This includes discussing past relationships and the lessons learned, which can demonstrate emotional maturity and resilience. By communicating effectively, individuals can set the stage for honest dialogue that encourages vulnerability and trust within a relationship.

Setting boundaries is essential for protecting one's heart and maintaining emotional resilience against deceit. Empowering oneself to establish clear boundaries helps to create a safe space within which love can flourish. This involves knowing when to say no and recognizing that one's worth is not contingent upon pleasing others. Establishing boundaries is not an act of selfishness; rather, it is a demonstration of self-respect and an understanding of personal values. When singles are clear about their limits, they are better equipped to navigate courtship with clarity and confidence.

Lastly, spiritual discernment plays a crucial role in the journey of personal growth and empowerment. Engaging in prayer, seeking guidance from scripture, and surrounding oneself with a supportive community can strengthen one's ability to recognize genuine intentions in relationships. This spiritual foundation not only aids in identifying counterfeit connections but also fosters a deeper understanding of true love as defined by faith. By cultivating a relationship with God and seeking His wisdom, Christian singles can approach courtship with a discerning heart, leading to healthier, more fulfilling relationships that align with their divine purpose.

Embracing True Love

Characteristics of True Love

True love is characterized by several key attributes that set it apart from counterfeit relationships. First and foremost, true love is rooted in mutual respect and understanding. In a genuine relationship, both partners honor each other's individuality and personal beliefs. This respect creates a safe space for open communication, where both individuals can express their thoughts and feelings without fear of judgment. As Christian singles navigate the dating landscape, it becomes essential to identify whether a potential partner demonstrates a genuine appreciation for their values and boundaries.

Another hallmark of true love is the presence of unconditional support. In a healthy relationship, partners uplift each other through challenges and celebrate successes together. This support transcends mere emotional comfort; it involves a commitment to each other's growth and well-being. When dating, it is crucial for singles to assess whether their partner shows a willingness to invest in their development and encourage their aspirations. Recognizing this trait can help distinguish between a true partner and someone who may only be interested in superficial connections.

True love is also characterized by honesty and transparency. Authentic relationships thrive on trust, which is built through open dialogue and shared experiences. It is important for singles to engage in conversations that delve into past experiences, aspirations, and fears. By doing so, they can gauge the level of sincerity in their partner's intentions. Being forthright about one's past, including any relationship struggles, not only fosters trust but also lays the groundwork for a deeper emotional connection.

Emotional resilience is another significant aspect of true love. A healthy relationship encourages both partners to grow individually and collectively, allowing them to navigate difficult situations together. True love involves recognizing and addressing red flags while maintaining a strong sense of self. It is vital for Christian singles to develop their emotional resilience, which enables them to discern manipulation and deceit. This resilience will empower them to stand firm in their convictions and prioritize their well- being, ultimately leading to stronger, healthier relationships.

Finally, spiritual discernment plays a crucial role in identifying true love. For Christian singles, aligning their relationship with their faith can provide clarity on their partner's intentions. Prayer, reflection, and seeking guidance from trusted mentors or spiritual leaders can help singles remain grounded in their values. By fostering a strong connection with God, individuals can better navigate their relationships and recognize genuine intentions, ensuring they are not swayed by counterfeits that may delay their journey to finding their kingdom spouse.

The Blessings of a God-Centered Relationship

A God-centered relationship serves as a foundation for singles seeking a meaningful and fulfilling partnership. In such relationships, the focus is not only on the romantic connection but also on the spiritual growth of both individuals involved. By prioritizing faith, couples can cultivate an environment where love flourishes, guided by shared values and a commitment to serve one another and God. This alignment lays the groundwork for a healthy relationship, making it easier to identify counterfeits and avoid distractions that may delay the arrival of a kingdom spouse.

When both partners center their relationship around God, it fosters trust and safety, essential elements for any successful partnership. This trust is built on the understanding that both individuals are seeking to honor God in their interactions, which reduces the likelihood of manipulation or deceit. In a God-centered relationship, open communication about past experiences becomes a valuable tool for building that trust. Sharing personal journeys can help clarify intentions, establish common goals, and encourage vulnerability, allowing each person to feel secure in the relationship.

Recognizing red flags in relationships is crucial for singles, and a God-centered focus can enhance this discernment. When individuals are rooted in their faith, they can better identify behaviors that contradict their values or indicate potential manipulation. Spiritual discernment plays a vital role in this process, enabling one to seek divine guidance in assessing a partner's character. This awareness allows singles to make informed decisions, protecting their hearts from counterfeit relationships that may lead to emotional distress or spiritual disconnection.

Setting boundaries is another blessing of a God-centered relationship. When both partners are committed to honoring their faith, they are more likely to respect each other's limits and needs. These boundaries create a protective space that fosters emotional resilience, enabling individuals to navigate challenges while maintaining their integrity. By establishing clear guidelines, couples can cultivate a relationship that nurtures personal growth and mutual respect, further solidifying their bond.

Ultimately, a God-centered relationship empowers singles to embrace self-discovery and growth. By aligning their hearts with God's purpose, individuals learn to prioritize their spiritual health, which in turn enriches their romantic connections. This journey of self-awareness encourages emotional maturity and resilience, equipping singles to recognize genuine intentions in courtship. As they cultivate a deeper relationship with God, they become better prepared to engage in healthy partnerships that reflect His love and grace.

Grace D. Mamigo is a Full Time Missionary in Cambodia and a dedicated professional with a diverse educational background encompassing mass communication, ministry, education, nursing, and leadership counseling. With a passion for service and a commitment to lifelong learning, she integrates her knowledge and skills to make a positive impact in her community

Educational Background:

Bachelor of Arts in Mass Communication
Southern Mindanao Institute of Technology, General Santos City, 2010
 Developed strong communication skills and a deep understanding of media and its societal impact.

Bachelor of Ministry
Jubilee Theological Seminary, Cebu, 2012
 Equipped with theological knowledge and pastoral skills, focusing on community service and spiritual leadership.

Diploma in Professional Education
Mandaue City College, Cebu, 2012
 Gained foundational teaching methodologies, enhancing her ability to educate and inspire others.

Bachelor of Nursing (Undergraduate)
 Cebu Doctors University, Cebu.
 Pursuing a career in nursing to blend healthcare and compassion in service to others.

Masters of Ministry in Leadership and Counseling
Asia Pacific Institute of International Studies, Singapore, 2023
Focused on developing leadership skills and counseling techniques to support individuals and communities in their spiritual and personal growth.

Areas of Expertise:

Communication and Media: Proficient in crafting messages that resonate with diverse audiences, utilizing various media platforms for effective outreach.

Spiritual Leadership: Experienced in guiding individuals and groups through spiritual counseling and community engagement.

Education: Committed to fostering a positive learning environment and mentoring students in their educational journeys.

Healthcare: Knowledgeable in nursing practices, providing compassionate care and support to patients and their families.

Counseling: Skilled in offering guidance and support, promoting mental and emotional well-being

Professional Philosophy:

She believes in the power of education, community service, and compassionate care. She is dedicated to continuous personal and professional growth, aiming to empower others through her work in communication, ministry, education, and healthcare.